Barnes & Noble Shakespeare

David Scott Kastan
Series Editor

BARNES & NOBLE SHAKESPEARE features newly edited texts of the plays prepared by the world's premiere Shakespeare scholars. Each edition provides new scholarship with an introduction, commentary, unusually full and informative notes, an account of the play as it would have been performed in Shakespeare's theaters, and an essay on how to read Shakespeare's language.

DAVID SCOTT KASTAN is the Old Dominion Foundation Professor in the Humanities at Columbia University and one of the world's leading authorities on Shakespeare.

Barnes & Noble Shakespeare
Published by Barnes & Noble
122 Fifth Avenue
New York, NY 10011
www.barnesandnoble.com/shakespeare

Image on p. 396:
Shakespeare, William. *Hamlet*. 1604 [B1r]. This item is reproduced by permission of *The Huntington Library, San Marino, California*, RB 69305.

ISBN: 978-1-4114-0034-4

Library of Congress Cataloging-in-Publication Data

Shakespeare, William, 1564–1616
Hamlet / [William Shakespeare].
p. cm. — (Barnes and Noble Shakespeare)
Includes bibliographical references.
ISBN-13: 978-1-4114-0034-4 (alk. paper)
ISBN-10: 1-4114-0034-8 (alk. paper)
1. Hamlet (Legendary character)—Drama. 2. Kings and rulers—Succession—Drama. 3. Murder victims' families—Drama. 4. Fathers—Death—Drama. 5. Revenge—Drama. 6. Denmark—Drama. 7. Princes—Drama. I. Title. II. Series: Shakespeare, William, 1564–1616. Works. 2006.

PR2807.A1 2006
822.3'3—dc22 2006009004

Printed and bound in the United States.
40 39 38 37 36 35 34

HAMLET

William SHAKESPEARE

JEFF DOLVEN
EDITOR

Barnes & Noble Shakespeare

Contents

Introduction to *Hamlet*

by Jeff Dolven

Hamlet's "To be, or not to be? That is the question" is the most famous line ever spoken on the English stage; it may be the most famous line of verse in the language. How familiar it is—and how strange that it should be so familiar. Why, of all lines, that one? It is such an odd string of words for history to have picked out to stand for Shakespeare, who himself can stand for so much with us: for drama, for poetry, for high culture generally. To begin with, it is neither particularly dramatic nor poetical. The same soliloquy offers up such impassioned metaphors as "The slings and arrows of outrageous fortune" (3.1.57) just a moment later: why don't we remember them the same way? By contrast, "To be, or not to be" is so much starker and plainer, so much more, one might say, philosophical. It does little more than state the principle of logic that Aristotle called the law of the excluded middle: either α or not α, being or not being, but nothing in between. It is hard to imagine a barer thought, one more perfectly abstracted from the conditions of our ordinary lives.

Perhaps that abstraction has something to do with why the line is so often abstracted from the play. It has proven to travel exceptionally well, pried out of its context and passed freely around the larger culture (indeed around so many cultures: *sein oder nicht sein*, *ser o no ser*). In this, it is like the character who delivers it. Hamlet is abstracted, preoccupied with thoughts he will not speak at the expense of the forms and rituals of daily life. He thinks a lot, and spends a lot of time alone. He is also chronically abstracted from his play: over four centuries of reading and staging, his character has become iconic, the melancholy, black-clad Prince in conversation with somebody's skull, recognizable anywhere. It scarcely matters that he speaks less than a third of the play's lines. Hamlet is *Hamlet*; the man is the play.

Over the last two centuries, this elevation of the Prince has gone hand in hand with claims that he is somehow ahead of his time, in his complexity and depth and "inwardness" (a word that seems as if it could have been coined for him). With the character of Hamlet, this story goes, we witness nothing less than the birth—perhaps the premature birth—of modern consciousness, a phenomenon larger and more contradictory than any fiction could contain. The history of Hamlet criticism could be cast as an argument between the partisans of this outsized and overintricate Prince and those who prefer to consider him as part of the play and of the world where it was written and performed. On one side (more or less) are the Romantics, from Goethe to Coleridge to Bloom, and a line of psychoanalytic critics that begins with Freud himself; on the other, students of the arts of drama, aesthetic formalists, and historicists.

Something about Shakespeare's play keeps renewing this dispute: Hamlet or *Hamlet*? Nor is it fought out solely among the critics, for it might be said to puzzle Hamlet himself. This introduction will follow the development of the problem—should we call it a choice?—through the play, and in so doing it will propose one way of getting to know the text, by tracking a couple of small, apparently innocuous words up and down the winding stairs of Elsinore. Everything Shakespeare wrote has its linguistic signatures, terms or tricks of rhetoric that gather meaning as the action proceeds, the particular music (as one critic has put it) of his thinking. Here the words will be *part* and *like*. Many others would serve as well, but around these two—which recur with obsessive frequency—gather a set of traditional problems about solitude and company, autonomy and belonging, in the play's three spheres of family, state, and theater. They will lead us back again, at the end, to Hamlet's ultimate question.

The first scene sows these words in the audience's ear. The night watch is changing on the bitter cold battlements of the castle Elsinore, and Marcellus has brought Hamlet's friend Horatio to see the "dreaded sight" (1.1.27) that has twice surprised the soldiers there. As he speaks, the ghost appears again, "In the same figure like the King that's dead," as Barnardo says. "Looks 'a not like the King?" he asks, and Horatio responds, "Most like" (1.1.43, 46). A few lines later Marcellus puts the same question, "Is it not like the King?" and Horatio has a still stranger answer: "As thou art to thyself" (1.1.61). The refrain is taken up in the next scene: Hamlet says of his father, "I shall not look upon his like again," only to have Horatio describe "a figure like your father. . . . I knew your father; / These hands are not more like" (1.2.188, 1.2.200–213). It is the likeness of this specter to the dead King that amazes these men, but Horatio's odd phrases—"As thou art to thyself," "These hands are not more like"—are more deeply disquieting. *Are you really like yourself?* they ask in a whisper. What a strange question: for what would it mean *not* to be? These intimations of fracture can be heard, too, in the first soundings of *part* and its cognates. The Ghost has a story to "im*part*"; Horatio does not know "In what *part*icular thought to work," and believes only "in part" (1.1.69, 167); when Bernardo first asks, "What, is Horatio there?" Horatio answers, "A piece of him" (1.1.21). All this talk is like the overture to an opera, or even the orchestra warming up, practicing in bits and scraps the themes that will hold the play together (if anything can).

We are well embarked on *Hamlet* if we can catch the confusion, even paranoia of this first scene. The old King is dead; the kingdom is full of hurried, ominous preparations; the soldiers barely know each other in the dark. But Denmark was not ever thus. There was a time, Horatio explains, when the elder Hamlet held the throne as a great warrior-king. When he was challenged by the elder Fortinbras of Norway—"Thereto pricked on by a most emulate pride" (1.1.85)—he slew his would-be imitator in single combat. By rights this should be young Hamlet's destiny, to rule Denmark and do battle in his own time with his own proper likeness. But "The time is out of joint" (1.5.188): if the Ghost is to be believed—and it bears remembering that we go some ways into the play before we can be sure—then young Hamlet's uncle Claudius, new King of Denmark and new husband to the widowed Gertrude, poisoned the old King as he slept in his garden. Claudius's unfitness and *unlikeness* to the old King preoccupy Hamlet: "My father's brother, but no more like my father / Than I to Hercules" (1.2.152–153), he says in his first soliloquy; he tells Gertrude that her new husband is a goat-footed satyr to the old King's sun god (1.2.140), a "moor" that lies in the shadow of a "fair mountain" (3.4.66–67).

Claudius is no old Hamlet: the ancient code of "emulate pride" (1.1.85), the open combat of equals, has been broken. But the same might be said of old Hamlet's son. The ghost that Horatio describes is armed "cap-à-pie" (1.2.201), head to foot, an image of his former warlike glory. By contrast, Hamlet is dressed in mourning clothes, the "inky cloak" (1.2.77) that suggests both his sorrow and a scholar's ink-stained fingers. Not only is he unlike his father, but he does not much resemble the promising young Prince the other characters remember. What has happened, asks Ophelia, to a man who was once "Th' expectation and rose of the fair state, / The glass of fashion and the mold of form" (3.1.151–152)? Hamlet in his suits of woe cannot live up to these descriptions, and Horatio's peculiar phrase "as thou art to thyself" comes back to haunt him. The demand implicit in this phrase *to be like yourself* has a Stoic ring to it: do not pattern yourself on others or attach yourself to them; cultivate detachment from the world as a defense against fortune's slings and arrows; and as Hamlet says to the actors, "Suit the action to the word, the word to the action" (3.2.17–18), and both to the inner man. Hamlet the scholar would have been brought up reading such wisdom in the books of Stoic philosophers like Seneca and Marcus Aurelius, but he is hard pressed to keep their counsel. He hates seeming, hates the vain displays of emotion that the Stoics hate, and yet when he declares, "But I have that within which passes show" (1.2.85), he admits that he cannot fit his appearance to the turbulent excess of his thoughts. His madness—whether it is an act, or real, or some alchemy of the two—is the ultimate symptom of this self-difference. "If Hamlet from himself be ta'en away," he says before his combat with Laertes, "Then Hamlet does it not, Hamlet denies it" (5.2.204, 206).

That drumbeat of *like* is a clue to this complex of ideas: both the dream of being like yourself, and all the bonds (to others) and fractures (of the self) that keep spoiling that dream. Psychoanalytically minded readers have been especially attentive to the trouble this little word makes. If Hamlet rails against Claudius's unlikeness to his father, and despairs of his own shortcomings (again, at 1.2.152–153, "no more like my father / Than I to Hercules"), does this make him all too like the man he loathes? It may be bad logic (if old Hamlet ≠ Claudius, and old Hamlet ≠ young Hamlet, then young Hamlet = Claudius), but it is powerful psychology. Such speculations form the basis of Freud's Oedipal interpretation of the play, where what Hamlet sees in Claudius is a mirror of his own primitive, unacknowledgeable desires to kill his father and marry his mother. Such readings take strength from the peculiar sexual intensity of the language in the so-called "closet scene" with Gertrude, when Hamlet so vividly imagines the King giving her "reechy kisses / Or paddling in your neck with his damned fingers" (3.4.184–185). Here the very likeness of sons to fathers—which seemed as though it might guarantee the regularity of succession—becomes instead a source of contamination.

The other word, *part*, is equally important to the music of these considerations. "Why seems it so particular with thee?" (1.2.75), asks Gertrude of Hamlet in his first scene. He has returned home from the university at Wittenberg to attend his father's funeral, only to find himself celebrating his mother's marriage. Now he wants nothing more than to return to his studies. Scholarship was an unusual ambition for a Renaissance prince: Hamlet sets himself deliberately apart not only from his family but from the obligations of the King's son and heir. To those obligations the story of his father's murder returns him with a vengeance. "Let us im*part* what we have seen tonight / Unto young Hamlet" (1.1.171–172), says Horatio after he sees the Ghost; when they encounter it together, he says, "It beckons you to go away with it, / As if it some im*part*ment did desire / To you alone" (1.4.58–60). The *part* in "impart"—a word Shakespeare uses five times in Hamlet, only six in all the other plays combined—hints at how this story compels Hamlet to become *part of* court and of family again, how it folds him back into a world he had sought to escape. Even as it entangles, however, it also exiles him, for he is now the keeper of a dangerous secret. The same word captures the pathos of this new estrangement: "I hold it fit that we shake hands and part," he says to the others on the battlement, "and for my own poor part, / I will go pray" (1.5.130–134).

This serious play with words explores wide territories of feeling, as Hamlet veers between the equally painful predicaments of being *part of* and *apart*. It also revolves around a conceptual problem that is peculiarly close to the heart of the play. A part, considered in the most abstracted terms, is something separate, distinct: we can single it out because it stands alone and because it is unlike what is around it. At the same time, if it is a part, it must be part *of* something else, entailed to some whole—a whole that it might even be, in some sense, like. Shakespeare could have encountered formal versions of this problem in the study of grammar or logic, of which he likely had a taste in Stratford's grammar school. What counts most in the play is how he, or any of us, might slip into thinking of the word as a paradox, a problem that puzzles the mind the way "To be, or not to be" puzzles the will. A part is dependent *and* independent, like *and* unlike. In that paradox the very word becomes an image of the mind's helplessness.

To follow *part* into such high abstraction is not only to track a tendency in Hamlet's mind, but also in Shakespeare's: many of his plays are deeply structured by the thinking through of an intellectual problem (for example, twinning in *The Comedy of Errors*, motion and stasis in *Antony and Cleopatra*). One can follow the paradox back down again into almost any of the play's more concrete preoccupations. Politics, for instance: as when Laertes cautions Ophelia that Hamlet the Prince is not free to love whom he will. His choice is "circumscribed / Unto the voice and yielding of that body / Whereof he is the head" (1.3.21–23). Behind this passing analogy is an important idea in the political theory of the time, that the king has two bodies, his physical body and the metaphorical body of the state. Rosencrantz and Guildenstern play on the same notion when they flatter Claudius, "Never alone / Did the king sigh, but with a general groan" (3.3.22–23). Here are the lineaments of the same partial predicament: Hamlet is (or stands someday to be) the body's head, its governor, its legislator; yet as part of that body, he is never private, never alone, never free.

Then, of course, there is the echo in all of these parts—*part, particular, impart*—of a part in a play. We use the word now as a casual synonym for an actor's role, and Hamlet uses it that way himself when he is joshing with Polonius (3.2.99). But in the overdetermining echo chamber of Elsinore the sense of a *single* or a *mere* part, a part of something bigger, becomes inescapable. Any actor, after all, is only one element of a complex production, and for Hamlet—who is so peculiarly self-conscious about being onstage—that simultaneous dependence and independence is yet another register of his existential crisis. What part is there to play, mad or sane, that does not by its nature insist on his unwanted implication in the whole? (An actor on Shakespeare's stage might have felt his partiality just a bit more acutely: the price of paper and the demands of manuscript copying meant that he worked from a script that gave only his own lines and his cues, a part indeed.)

With these two little words and the concepts they unfold, *Hamlet* gives us a language for thinking about a character who is inescapably central to the world of the play—"Th' observed of all observers," as Ophelia puts it (3.1.153)—and yet who longs to abstract himself from its designs. His alienation has always been obvious to audiences. Not quite as easy to recognize is the extent of Elsinore's hospitality: the standing offer for the Prince to accept his part in the court and the royal family, to be like everyone else. After all, Hamlet still stands to become king; when Claudius calls him "my son" (1.2.64), the offer of love and protection might well be perfectly genuine, so long as Hamlet will accept the new order. The Prince is surrounded by advice to be reasonable, to give over his grieving, to accept things as they are. Even the Player King in the play-within-a-play that Hamlet himself chooses, *The Murder of Gonzago*, counsels, "Most necessary 'tis that we forget" (3.2.180).

But, of course, Hamlet cannot forget. Not only does he burn with the revenge he is so slow to take, but he has a kind of contempt for the society he has grown up in, where men of state lose themselves in the "heavy-headed revel" (1.4.17) of Claudius's banquets. He is tenaciously skeptical of "fashion and ceremony" (2.2.305–306), of false friendship and empty ritual, even of the cosmetics with which we gild our corruptible bodies. He rails against "That monster, custom, who all sense doth eat, / Of habits devil" (3.4.161–162). Customs (such as weddings and funerals) are the ways we ordinarily feel a part of a culture and assert our likeness to one another; for Hamlet, they are a way the world has of not knowing its crimes, sinking itself in oblivious courtesies. It is when the Prince's alienation rises to the pitch of social critique that readers have been most inclined to insist on his modernity. His outsideness to his society, even to the drama itself, and his constant advertisement of impulses and desires too large for full expression capture a modern sense that the old forms of life, and of art, no longer hold us.

That double sense of alienation from one's culture and one's self has one more crucial dimension, expressed in the unfolding of the play's plot. It is clear enough what is supposed to happen: as in any revenge tragedy, the crime revealed at the beginning will be revenged at the end, after a suitable interval for planning and fulminating. *Hamlet*'s first audiences knew the script, for such plays had been all the rage in the public theaters a decade before. They would therefore also have recognized that Hamlet refuses to play his part: among the customs and conventions he defies is the single-minded vehemence of the revenger. By Act Four it seems possible that this famous delay could continue indefinitely, or at least until Claudius figures out a way to dispatch the so-far not-so-dangerous young man. And yet, Hamlet does finally act (another knowing pun), after a fashion. That word *like* can once more point toward an explanation, if we stretch it now to compass Fortinbras's sense when he speaks of Hamlet as "likely . . . To have proved most royal" (5.2.373–374)—*likely*, that is, meaning "probable." (As the word like itself could mean in the period: "Very like," muses Hamlet at 1.2.234, after Horatio says that the Ghost would have amazed him.) This probable *like* touches the play's obsession with futurity, an obsession that is everywhere: the Ghost is full of portent and omen; there is the peculiar dumb show before the play, to tell us what is coming; Gertrude worries that "Each toy seems prologue to some great amiss" (4.5.17); Hamlet's first reaction to the Ghost's news is to cry out, "O my prophetic soul!" (1.5.40).

The problem that these and so many other references to prologue, prophecy, and likeliness define is that time itself in *Hamlet* has come apart, or as Hamlet says, "The time is out of joint" (1.5.188). The river that flows from thoughts and words to acts is dammed up with thinking, and the Prince is trapped in prologue, trapped in prediction, what is merely *likely*. It may be the exhilarating opportunism of stabbing Polonius behind the arras that changes everything, a deed complete almost before the intention is formed. Or perhaps it is the strange events of his sea voyage, which left no time for contemplation: "Or I could make a prologue to my brains, / They had begun the play" (5.2.30–31). However it happens, the luxury of prologue is gone by Act Five, and, somehow, the need for it, too. Now Hamlet's relation to time is different. "We defy augury," he famously tells Horatio: "There is special providence in the fall of a sparrow. If it be now, 'tis not to come. If it be not to come, it will be now. If it be not now, yet it will come. The readiness is all" (5.2.191–194). Hamlet claims to care no more for predictions and prophecies, or for that bank or shoal or part of time (as Macbeth might put it) from which one looks down on the river of events before plunging in. His insouciantly acrobatic juggling of tenses suggests that they are all one to him now.

As, indeed, he tells us in the Folio text of the play: "man's life's no more than to say 'one.'" Hamlet has given himself over to readiness, and in a peculiar way, he has given himself over to death as well. Death has been the play's ultimate partition: "The undiscovered country from whose bourn / No traveler returns" (3.1.78–79). Nightmares of the body's corruption haunt Hamlet's imagination from the start, flesh melting into dew, "kissing carrion" (2.2.179), the "convocation of politic worms" (4.3.19–20) that he imagines feasting on the dead Polonius. But Act Five finds him in a graveyard, bantering with the gravedigger and handling, if queasily, the skull that has become his signature prop. He allows himself to wonder aloud, with new equanimity, what has become of the body of the ancient emperor Alexander, whose dust may even now be used to "stop a beer barrel" (5.1.194). "'Twere to consider too curiously to consider so" (5.1.188), advises the philosophic Horatio, who is discomfited by this train of thought. But Hamlet clearly finds a kind of peace in the idea.

For four acts Hamlet has tried to keep himself apart and has cherished his singularity. Even the verse from Genesis, "man and wife is one flesh" (4.3.49–50), has given him pain, for it recalls him to his part in the play's tangled family romance. But now it is as though he has overleaped all the broken relations that so dismayed him. On the other side of family, state, and custom—mere custom—is our true commonality, our deepest bond, the fact that all of us will die and that our bodies will be food for worms. Such tortuous compounds as "uncle-father and aunt-mother" (2.2.309–310) lose their sting if fathers, brothers, mothers, and sisters resolve themselves into the same dust. When Hamlet stands by the grave of Ophelia, and then in the grave of Ophelia, all of the agonies anatomized by those tenacious words *part* and *like* are passing away. There are no parts; everything is like, because we are all the same stuff. The poison pearl that will seal his revenge in the next scene is called a "union."

Like, part: these two words haunt the play more surely even than the Ghost. Others might have been enlisted to define the same problems, say *joint*, or *common*. The play is rich enough, moreover, that they cannot begin to touch on all its complexities; every time you hear a word you think you have heard before, then hear it again, you have found another way in. Elsinore is a house with many mansions. We can exit with one more glance back at the problem of its modernity, or its hero's. That modernity may now look like a problem of the first four acts, a problem of the Hamlet who is tortured by his part in a culture, a family, and a play. If his alienation signals the birth of modern consciousness—or, better, if we moderns recognize ourselves in Hamlet as in no literary character before him—we must also confront the fact that that consciousness is born already struggling to be free of itself. Hamlet is desperate to escape Hamlet, perhaps even to escape *Hamlet*. When he finally does so in Act Five, and he sheds that unease and out-of-placeness, he leaves us moderns behind, too.

That does not necessarily mean that Hamlet wants to die—not the way we might fear, at least. It is true that in Act Three he longs to make his "quietus," stayed only by a dread of that undiscovered country. A certain kind of philosophy—the philosophy of Horatio,perhaps, who is so baffled by the Ghost—insists on this partitioning, the hard logic of "to be, or not to be." But by the end of the play, this logic has broken down, or at any rate it hardly matters to Hamlet anymore. Alexander the King and Alexander the plug of earth both are; that loam both *is and is not* Alexander. Aristotle's logic cannot compass this idea. Shakespeare's language, however, can do it easily enough. The journey to this recognition is one way of thinking about the strange progress we go with Hamlet through the guts of the play that bears his name. He has by the end an uncanny power to stand astride those two worlds, an achieved indifference that we can only wonder at—we who cling with such a singular intensity to the absoluteness of a question that Hamlet, for his part, has outgrown.

Shakespeare and His England

by David Scott Kastan

Shakespeare is a household name, one of those few that don't need a first name to be instantly recognized. His first name was, of course, William, and he (and it, in its Latin form, *Gulielmus*) first came to public notice on April 26, 1564, when his baptism was recorded in the parish church of Stratford-upon-Avon, a small market town about ninety miles northwest of London. It isn't known exactly when he was born, although traditionally his birthday is taken to be April 23rd. It is a convenient date (perhaps too convenient) because that was the date of his death in 1616, as well as the date of St. George's Day, the annual feast day of England's patron saint. It is possible Shakespeare was born on the 23rd; no doubt he was born within a day or two of that date. In a time of high rates of infant mortality, parents would not wait long after a baby's birth for the baptism. Twenty percent of all children would die before their first birthday.

Life in 1564, not just for infants, was conspicuously vulnerable. If one lived to age fifteen, one was likely to live into one's fifties, but probably no more than 60 percent of those born lived past their mid-teens. Whole towns could be ravaged by epidemic disease. In 1563, the year before Shakespeare was born, an outbreak of plague claimed over one third of the population of London. Fire, too, was a constant threat; the thatched roofs of many houses were highly flammable, as well as offering handy nesting places for insects and rats. Serious crop failures in several years of the decade of the 1560s created food shortages, severe enough in many cases to lead to the starvation of the elderly and the infirm, and lowering the resistances of many others so that between 1536 and 1560 influenza claimed over 200,000 lives.

Shakespeare's own family in many ways reflected these unsettling realities. He was one of eight children, two of whom did not survive their first year, one of whom died at age eight; one lived to twenty-seven, while the four surviving siblings died at ages ranging from Edmund's thirty-nine to William's own fifty-two years. William married at an unusually early age. He was only eighteen, though his wife was twenty-six, almost exactly the norm of the day for women, though men normally married also in their mid- to late twenties. Shakespeare's wife Anne was already pregnant at the time that the marriage was formally confirmed, and a daughter, Susanna, was born six months later, in May 1583. Two years later, she gave birth to twins, Hamnet and Judith. Hamnet would die in his eleventh year.

If life was always at risk from what Shakespeare would later call "the thousand natural shocks / That flesh is heir to" (*Hamlet*, 3.1.61–62), the incessant threats to peace were no less unnerving, if usually less immediately life threatening. There were almost daily rumors of foreign invasion and civil war as the Protestant Queen Elizabeth assumed the crown in 1558 upon the death of her Catholic half sister, Mary. Mary's reign had been marked by the public burnings of Protestant "heretics," by the seeming subordination of England to Spain, and by a commitment to a ruinous war with France, that, among its other effects, fueled inflation and encouraged a debasing of the currency. If, for many, Elizabeth represented the hopes for a peaceful and prosperous Protestant future, it seemed unlikely in the early days of her rule that the young monarch could hold her England together against the twin menace of the powerful Catholic monarchies of Europe and the significant part of her own population who were reluctant to give up their old faith. No wonder the Queen's principal secretary saw England in the early years of Elizabeth's rule as a land surrounded by "perils many, great and imminent."

In Stratford-upon-Avon, it might often have been easy to forget what threatened from without. The simple rural life, shared by about 90 percent of the English populace, had its reassuring natural rhythms and delights. Life was structured by the daily rising and setting of the sun, and by the change of seasons. Crops were planted and harvested; livestock was bred, its young delivered; sheep were sheared, some livestock slaughtered. Market days and fairs saw the produce and crafts of the town arrayed as people came to sell and shop—and be entertained by musicians, dancers, and troupes of actors. But even in Stratford, the lurking tensions and dangers could be daily sensed. A few months before Shakespeare was born, there had been a shocking "defacing" of images in the church, as workmen, not content merely to whitewash over the religious paintings decorating the interior as they were ordered, gouged large holes in those felt to be too "Catholic"; a few months after Shakespeare's birth, the register of the same church records another deadly outbreak of plague. The sleepy market town on the northern bank of the gently flowing river Avon was not immune from the menace of the world that surrounded it.

This was the world into which Shakespeare was born. England at his birth was still poor and backward, a fringe nation on the periphery of Europe. English itself was a minor language, hardly spoken outside of the country's borders. Religious tension was inescapable, as the old Catholic faith was trying determinedly to hold on, even as Protestantism was once again anxiously trying to establish itself as the national religion. The country knew itself vulnerable to serious threats both from without and from within. In 1562, the young Queen, upon whom so many people's hopes rested, almost fell victim to smallpox, and in 1569 a revolt of the Northern earls tried to remove her from power and restore Catholicism as the national religion. The following year, Pope

Pius V pronounced the excommunication of "Elizabeth, the pretended queen of England" and forbade Catholic subjects obedience to the monarch on pain of their own excommunication. "Now we are in an evil way and going to the devil," wrote one clergyman, "and have all nations in our necks."

It was a world of dearth, danger, and domestic unrest. Yet it would soon dramatically change, and Shakespeare's literary contribution would, for future generations, come to be seen as a significant measure of England's remarkable transformation. In the course of Shakespeare's life, England, hitherto an unsophisticated and underdeveloped backwater acting as a bit player in the momentous political dramas taking place on the European continent, became a confident, prosperous, global presence. But this new world was only accidentally, as it is often known today, "The Age of Shakespeare." To the degree that historical change rests in the hands of any individual, credit must be given to the Queen. This new world arguably was "The Age of Elizabeth," even if it was not the Elizabethan Golden Age, as it has often been portrayed.

The young Queen quickly imposed her personality upon the nation. She had talented councilors around her, all with strong ties to her of friendship or blood, but the direction of government was her own. She was strong willed and cautious, certain of her right to rule and convinced that stability was her greatest responsibility. The result may very well have been, as historians have often charged, that important issues facing England were never dealt with head-on and left to her successors to settle, but it meant also that she was able to keep her England unified and for the most part at peace.

Religion posed her greatest challenge, though it is important to keep in mind that in this period, as an official at Elizabeth's court said, "Religion and the commonwealth cannot be parted asunder." Faith then was not the largely voluntary commitment it is today, nor was there any idea of some separation of church and state. Religion was literally a matter of life and death, of salvation and damnation, and the Church was the Church of England. Obedience to it was not only a matter of conscience but also of law. It was the single issue on which the nation was most likely to be torn apart.

Elizabeth's great achievement was that she was successful in ensuring that the Church of England became formally a Protestant Church, but she did so without either driving most of her Catholic subjects to sedition or alienating the more radical Protestant community. The so-called "Elizabethan Settlement" forged a broad Christian community of what has been called prayer-book Protestantism, even as many of its practitioners retained, as a clergyman said, "still a smack and savor of popish principles." If there were forces on both sides who were uncomfortable with the Settlement—committed Protestants, who wanted to do away with all vestiges of the old faith, and convinced Catholics, who continued to swear their allegiance to Rome—the majority of the country, as she hoped, found ways to live comfortably both within the law and within their faith. In 1571, she wrote to the Duke of Anjou that the forms of worship she recommended would "not properly compel any man to alter his opinion in the great matters now in controversy in the Church." The official toleration of religious ambiguity, as well as the familiar experience of an official change of state religion accompanying the crowning of a new monarch, produced a world where the familiar labels of Protestant and Catholic failed to define the forms of faith that most English people practiced. But for Elizabeth, most matters of faith could be left to individuals, as long as the Church itself, and Elizabeth's position at its head, would remain unchallenged.

In international affairs, she was no less successful with her pragmatism and willingness to pursue limited goals. A complex mix of prudential concerns about religion, the economy, and national security drove her foreign policy. She did not have imperial ambitions; in the main, she wanted only to be sure there would be no invasion of England and to encourage English trade. In the event, both goals brought England into conflict with Spain, determining the increasingly anti-Catholic tendencies of English foreign policy and, almost accidentally, England's emergence as a world power. When Elizabeth came to the throne, England was in many ways a mere satellite nation to the Netherlands, which was part of the Hapsburg Empire that the Catholic Philip II (who had briefly and unhappily been married to her predecessor and half sister, Queen Mary) ruled from Spain; by the end of her reign England was Spain's most bitter rival.

The transformation of Spain from ally to enemy came in a series of small steps (or missteps), no one of which was intended to produce what in the end came to pass. A series of posturings and provocations on both sides led to the rupture. In 1568, things moved to their breaking point, as the English confiscated a large shipment of gold that the Spanish were sending to their troops in the Netherlands. The following year saw the revolt of the Catholic earls in Northern England, followed by the papal excommunication of the Queen in 1570, both of which were by many in England assumed to be at the initiative, or at very least with the tacit support, of Philip. In fact he was not involved, but England under Elizabeth would never again think of Spain as a loyal friend or reliable ally. Indeed, Spain quickly became its mortal enemy. Protestant Dutch rebels had been opposing the Spanish domination of the Netherlands since the early 1560s, but, other than periodic financial support, Elizabeth had done little to encourage them. But in 1585, she sent troops under the command of the Earl of Leicester to support the Dutch rebels against the Spanish. Philip decided then to launch a full-scale attack on England, with the aim of deposing Elizabeth and restoring the Catholic faith. An English assault on Cadiz in 1587 destroyed a number of Spanish ships, postponing Philip's plans, but in the summer of 1588 the mightiest navy in the world, Philip's grand armada, with 132 ships and 30,493 sailors and troops, sailed for England.

By all rights, it should have been a successful invasion, but a combination of questionable Spanish tactics and a fortunate shift of wind resulted in one of England's greatest victories. The English had twice failed to intercept the armada off the coast of Portugal, and the Spanish fleet made its way to England, almost catching the English ships resupplying in Plymouth. The English navy was on its heels, when conveniently the Spanish admiral decided to anchor in the English Channel off the French port of Calais to wait for additional troops coming from the Netherlands. The English attacked with fireships, sinking four Spanish galleons, and strong winds from the south prevented an effective counterattack from the Spanish. The Spanish fleet was pushed into the North Sea, where it regrouped and decided its safest course was to attempt the difficult voyage home around Scotland and Ireland, losing almost half its ships on the way. For many in England the improbable victory was a miracle, evidence of God's favor for Elizabeth and the Protestant nation. Though war with Spain would not end for another fifteen years, the victory over the armada turned England almost overnight into a major world power, buoyed by confidence that they were chosen by God and, more tangibly, by a navy that could compete for control of the seas.

From a backward and insignificant Hapsburg satellite, Elizabeth's England had become, almost by accident, the leader of Protestant Europe. But if the victory over the armada signaled England's new place in the world, it hardly marked the end of England's travails. The economy, which initially was fueled by the military buildup, in the early 1590s fell victim to inflation, heavy taxation to support the war with Spain, the inevitable wartime disruptions of trade, as well as crop failures and a general economic downturn in Europe. Ireland, over which England had been attempting to impose its rule since 1168, continued to be a source of trouble and great expense (in some years costing the crown nearly one fifth of its total revenues). Even when the most organized of the rebellions, begun in 1594 and led by Hugh O'Neill, Earl of Tyrone, formally ended in 1603, peace and stability had not been achieved.

But perhaps the greatest instability came from the uncertainty over the succession, an uncertainty that marked Elizabeth's reign from its beginning. Her near death from smallpox in 1562 reminded the nation that an unmarried queen could not insure the succession, and Elizabeth was under constant pressure to marry and produce an heir. She was always aware of and deeply resented the pressure, announcing as early as 1559: "this shall be for me sufficient that a marble stone shall declare that a queen, having reigned such a time, lived and died a virgin." If, however, it was for her "sufficient," it was not so for her advisors and for much of the nation, who hoped she would wed. Arguably Elizabeth was the wiser, knowing that her unmarried hand was a political advantage, allowing her to diffuse threats or create alliances with the seeming possibility of a match. But as with so much in her reign, the strategy bought temporary stability at the price of longer-term solutions.

By the mid 1590s, it was clear that she would die unmarried and without an heir, and various candidates were positioning themselves to succeed her. Enough anxiety was produced that all published debate about the succession was forbidden by law. There was no direct descendant of the English crown to claim rule, and all the claimants had to reach well back into their family history to find some legitimacy. The best genealogical claim belonged to King James VI of Scotland. His mother, Mary, Queen of Scots, was the granddaughter of James IV of Scotland and Margaret Tudor, sister to Elizabeth's father, Henry VIII. Though James had right on his side, he was, it must be remembered, a foreigner. Scotland shared the island with England but was a separate nation. Great Britain, the union of England and Scotland, would not exist formally until 1707, but with Elizabeth's death early in the morning of March 24, 1603, surprisingly uneventfully the thirty-seven-year-old James succeeded to the English throne. Two nations, one king: King James VI of Scotland, King James I of England.

Most of his English subjects initially greeted the announcement of their new monarch with delight, relieved that the crown had successfully been transferred without any major disruption and reassured that the new King was married with two living sons. However, quickly many became disenchanted with a foreign King who spoke English with a heavy accent, and dismayed even further by the influx of Scots in positions of power. Nonetheless, the new King's greatest political liability may well have been less a matter of nationality than of temperament: he had none of Elizabeth's skill and ease in publicly wooing her subjects. The Venetian ambassador wrote back to the doge that the new King was unwilling to "caress the people, nor make them that good cheer the late Queen did, whereby she won their loves."

He was aloof and largely uninterested in the daily activities of governing, but he was interested in political theory and strongly committed to the cause of peace. Although a steadfast Protestant, he lacked the reflexive anti-Catholicism of many of his subjects. In England, he achieved a broadly consensual community of Protestants. The so-called King James Bible, the famous translation published first in 1611, was the result of a widespread desire to have an English Bible that spoke to all the nation, transcending the religious divisions that had placed three different translations in the hands of his subjects. Internationally, he styled himself *Rex Pacificus* (the peace-loving king). In 1604, the Treaty of London brought Elizabeth's war with Spain formally to an end, and over the next decade he worked to bring about political marriages that might cement stable alliances. In 1613, he married his daughter to the leader of the German Protestants, while the following year he began discussions with Catholic Spain to marry his son to the Infanta Maria. After some ten years of negotiations, James's hopes for what was known as the Spanish match were finally abandoned, much to the delight of the nation, whose long-felt fear and hatred for Spain outweighed the subtle political logic behind the plan.

But if James sought stability and peace, and for the most part succeeded in his aims (at least until 1618, when the bitter religio-political conflicts on the European continent swirled well out of the King's control), he never really achieved concord and cohesion. He ruled over two kingdoms that did not know, like, or even want to understand one another, and his rule did little to bring them closer together. His England remained separate from his Scotland, even as he ruled over both. And even his England remained self divided, as in truth it always was under Elizabeth, ever more a nation of prosperity and influence but still one forged out of deep-rooted divisions of means, faiths, and allegiances that made the very nature of English identity a matter of confusion and concern. Arguably this is the very condition of great drama—sufficient peace and prosperity to support a theater industry and sufficient provocation in the troubling uncertainties about what the nation was and what fundamentally mattered to its people to inspire plays that would offer tentative solutions or at the very least make the troubling questions articulate and moving.

Nine years before James would die in 1625, Shakespeare died, having returned from London to the small market town in which he was born. If London, now a thriving modern metropolis of well over 200,000 people, had, like the nation itself, been transformed in the course of his life, the Warwickshire market town still was much the same. The house in which Shakespeare was born still stood, as did the church in which he was baptized and the school in which he learned to read and write. The river Avon still ran slowly along the town's southern limits. What had changed was that Shakespeare was now its most famous citizen, and, although it would take more than another 100 years to fully achieve this, he would in time become England's, for having turned the great ethical, social, and political issues of his own age into plays that would live forever.

William Shakespeare: A Chronology

1558 **November 17: Queen Elizabeth crowned**

1564 April 26: Shakespeare baptized, third child born to John Shakespeare and Mary Arden

1564 **May 27: Death of Jean Calvin in Geneva**

1565 John Shakespeare elected alderman in Stratford-upon-Avon

1568 **Publication of the Bishops' Bible**

1568 September 4: John Shakespeare elected Bailiff of Stratford-upon-Avon

1569 **Northern Rebellion**

1570 **Queen Elizabeth excommunicated by the Pope**

1572 **August 24: St. Bartholomew's Day Massacre in Paris**

1576 **The Theatre is built in Shoreditch**

1577–1580 **Sir Francis Drake sails around the world**

1582 November 27: Shakespeare and Anne Hathaway married (Shakespeare is 18)

1583 Queen's Men formed

1583 May 26: Shakespeare's daughter, Susanna, baptized

1584 **Failure of the Virginia Colony**

1585 February 2: Twins, Hamnet and Judith, baptized (Shakespeare is 20)

1586 Babington Plot to dethrone Elizabeth and replace her with Mary, Queen of Scots

1587 February 8: Execution of Mary, Queen of Scots

1587 Rose Theatre built

1588 August: Defeat of the Spanish armada (Shakespeare is 24)

1588 September 4: Death of Robert Dudley, Earl of Leicester

1590 First three books of Spenser's *Faerie Queene* published; Marlowe's *Tamburlaine* published

1592 March 3: *Henry VI, Part One* performed at the Rose Theatre (Shakespeare is 27)

1593 February–November: Theaters closed because of plague

1593 Publication of *Venus and Adonis*

1594 Publication of *Titus Andronicus*, first play by Shakespeare to appear in print (though anonymously)

1594 Lord Chamberlain's Men formed

1595 March 15: Payment made to Shakespeare, Will Kemp, and Richard Burbage for performances at court in December, 1594

1595 Swan Theatre built

1596 Books 4–6 of *The Faerie Queene* published

1596 August 11: Burial of Shakespeare's son, Hamnet (Shakespeare is 32)

1596–1599 Shakespeare living in St. Helen's, Bishopsgate, London

1596 October 20: Grant of Arms to John Shakespeare

1597 May 4: Shakespeare purchases New Place, one of the two largest houses in Stratford (Shakespeare is 33)

1598 Publication of *Love's Labor's Lost*, first extant play with Shakespeare's name on the title page

1598 Publication of Francis Meres's *Palladis Tamia*, citing Shakespeare as "the best for Comedy and Tragedy" among English writers

1599 Opening of the Globe Theatre

1601 February 7: Lord Chamberlain's Men paid 40 shillings to play *Richard II* by supporters of the Earl of Essex, the day before his abortive rebellion

1601 February 17: Execution of Robert Devereaux, Earl of Essex

1601 September 8: Burial of John Shakespeare

1602 May 1: Shakespeare buys 107 acres of farmland in Stratford

1603 March 24: Queen Elizabeth dies; James VI of Scotland succeeds as James I of England (Shakespeare is 39)

1603 May 19: Lord Chamberlain's Men reformed as the King's Men

1604 Shakespeare living with the Mountjoys, a French Huguenot family, in Cripplegate, London

1604 First edition of Marlowe's *Dr. Faustus* published (written c. 1589)

1604 March 15: Shakespeare named among "players" given scarlet cloth to wear at royal procession of King James

1604 Publication of authorized version of *Hamlet* (Shakespeare is 40)

1605 Gunpowder Plot

1605 June 5: Marriage of Susanna Shakespeare to John Hall

1608 Publication of *King Lear* (Shakespeare is 44)

1608–1609 Acquisition of indoor Blackfriars Theatre by King's Men

1609 *Sonnets* published

1611 King James Bible published (Shakespeare is 47)

1612 November 6: Death of Henry, eldest son of King James

1613 February 14: Marriage of King James's daughter Elizabeth to Frederick, the Elector Palatine

1613 March 10: Shakespeare, with some associates, buys gatehouse in Blackfriars, London

1613 June 29: Fire burns the Globe Theatre

1614 Rebuilt Globe reopens

1616 February 10: Marriage of Judith Shakespeare to Thomas Quiney

1616 March 25: Shakespeare's will signed

1616 April 23: Shakespeare dies (age 52)

1616 April 23: Cervantes dies in Madrid

1616 April 25: Shakespeare buried in Holy Trinity Church in Stratford-upon-Avon

1623 August 6: Death of Anne Shakespeare

1623 October: Prince Charles, King James's son, returns from Madrid, having failed to arrange his marriage to Maria Anna, Infanta of Spain

1623 First Folio published with 36 plays (18 never previously published)

Words, Words, Words: Understanding Shakespeare's Language

by David Scott Kastan

It is silly to pretend that it is easy to read Shakespeare. Reading Shakespeare isn't like picking up a copy of *USA Today* or *The New Yorker*, or even F. Scott Fitzgerald's *Great Gatsby* or Toni Morrison's *Beloved*. It is hard work, because the language is often unfamiliar to us and because it is more concentrated than we are used to. In the theater it is usually a bit easier. Actors can clarify meanings with gestures and actions, allowing us to get the general sense of what is going on, if not every nuance of the language that is spoken. "Action is eloquence," as Volumnia puts it in *Coriolanus*, "and the eyes of th' ignorant / More learnèd than the ears" (3.276–277). Yet the real greatness of Shakespeare rests not on "the general sense" of his plays but on the specificity and suggestiveness of the words in which they are written. It is through language that the plays' full dramatic power is realized, and it is that rich and robust language, often pushed by Shakespeare to the very limits of intelligibility, that we must learn to understand. But we can come to understand it (and enjoy it), and this essay is designed to help.

Even experienced readers and playgoers need help. They often find that his words are difficult to comprehend. Shakespeare sometimes uses words no longer current in English or with meanings that have changed. He regularly multiplies words where seemingly one might do as well or even better. He characteristically writes sentences that are syntactically complicated and imaginatively dense. And it isn't just we, removed by some 400 years from his world, who find him difficult to read; in his own time, his friends and fellow actors knew Shakespeare was hard. As two of them, John Hemings and Henry Condell, put it in their prefatory remarks to Shakespeare's First Folio in 1623, "read him, therefore, and again and again; and if then you do not like him, surely you are in some manifest danger not to understand him."

From the very beginning, then, it was obvious that the plays both deserve and demand not only careful reading but continued re-reading—and that not to read Shakespeare with all the attention a reader can bring to bear on the language is almost to guarantee that a reader will not "understand him" and remain among those who "do not like him." But Shakespeare's colleagues were nonetheless confident that the plays exerted an attraction strong enough to ensure and reward the concentration of their readers, confident, as they say, that in them "you will find enough, both to draw and hold you." The plays do exert a kind of magnetic pull, and have successfully drawn in and held readers for over 400 years.

Once we are drawn in, we confront a world of words that does not always immediately yield its delights; but it will—once we learn to see what is demanded of us. Words in Shakespeare do a lot, arguably more than anyone else has ever asked them to do. In part, it is because he needed his words to do many things at once. His stage had no sets and few props, so his words are all we have to enable us to imagine what his characters see. And they also allow us to see what the characters don't see, especially about themselves. The words are vivid and immediate, as well as complexly layered and psychologically suggestive. The difficulties they pose are not the "thee's" and "thou's" or "prithee's" and "doth's" that obviously mark the chronological distance between Shakespeare and us. When Gertrude says to Hamlet, "thou hast thy father much offended"

(3.4.8), we have no difficulty understanding her chiding, though we might miss that her use of the "thou" form of the pronoun expresses an intimacy that Hamlet pointedly refuses with his reply: "Mother, *you* have my father much offended" (3.4.9; italics mine).

Most deceptive are words that look the same as words we know but now mean something different. Words often change meanings over time. When Horatio and the soldiers try to stop Hamlet as he chases after the Ghost, Hamlet pushes past them and says, "I'll make a ghost of him that lets me" (1.4.85). It seems an odd thing to say. Why should he threaten someone who "lets" him do what he wants to do? But here "let" means "hinder," not, as it does today, "allow" (although the older meaning of the word still survives, for example, in tennis, where a "let serve" is one that is hindered by the net on its way across). There are many words that can, like this, mislead us: "his" sometimes means "its," "an" often means "if," "envy" means something more like "malice," "cousin" means more generally "kinsman," and there are others, though all are easily defined. The difficulty is that we may not stop to look thinking we already know what the word means, but in this edition a ° following the word alerts a reader that there is a gloss in the left margin, and quickly readers get used to these older meanings.

Then, of course, there is the intimidation factor—strange, polysyllabic, or Latinate words that not only are foreign to us but also must have sounded strange even to Shakespeare's audiences. When Macbeth wonders whether all the water in all the oceans of the world will be able to clean his bloody hands after the murder of Duncan, he concludes: "No; this my hand will rather / The multitudinous seas incarnadine, / Making the green one red" (2.2.64–66). Duncan's blood staining Macbeth's murderous hand is so offensive that, not merely does it resist being washed off in water, but it will "the multitudinous seas incarnadine": that is, turn the sea-green oceans blood-red. Notes will easily clarify the meaning of the two odd words, but it is worth observing that they would have been as odd to Shakespeare's readers as they are to us. The *Oxford English Dictionary* (*OED*) shows no use of "multitudinous" before this, and it records no use of "incarnadine" before 1591 (*Macbeth* was written about 1606). Both are new words, coined from the Latin, part of a process in Shakespeare's time where English adopted many Latinate words as a mark of its own emergence as an important vernacular language. Here they are used to express the magnitude of Macbeth's offense, a crime not only against the civil law but also against the cosmic order, and then the simple monosyllables of turning "the green one red" provide an immediate (and needed) paraphrase and register his own sickening awareness of the true hideousness of his deed.

As with "multitudinous" in *Macbeth*, Shakespeare is the source of a great many words in English. Sometimes he coined them himself, or, if he didn't invent them, he was the first person whose writing of them has survived. Some of these words have become part of our language, so common that it is hard to imagine they were not always part of it: for example, "assassination" (*Macbeth*, 1.7.2), "bedroom" (*A Midsummer Night's Dream*, 2.2.57), "countless" (*Titus Andronicus*, 5.3.59), "fashionable" (*Troilus and Cressida*, 3.3.165), "frugal" (*The Merry Wives of Windsor*, 2.1.28), "laughable" (*The Merchant of Venice*, 1.1.56), "lonely" (*Coriolanus*, 4.1.30), and "useful" (*King John*, 5.2.81). But other words that he originated were not as, to use yet another Shakespearean coinage, "successful" (*Titus Andronicus*, 1.1.66). Words like "crimeless" (*Henry VI, Part Two*, 2.4.63, meaning "innocent"), "facinorous" (*All's Well That Ends Well*, 2.3.30, meaning "extremely wicked"), and "recountment" (*As You Like It*, 4.3.141, meaning "narrative" or "account") have, without much resistance, slipped into oblivion. Clearly Shakespeare liked words, even unwieldy ones. His working vocabulary, about 18,000 words, is staggering, larger than almost any other English writer, and he seems to be the first person to use in print about 1,000 of these. Whether he coined the new words himself or was intrigued by the new words he heard in the streets of London doesn't really matter; the point is that he was remarkably alert to and engaged with a dynamic language that was expanding in response to England's own expanding contact with the world around it.

But it is neither new words nor old ones that are the source of the greatest difficulty of Shakespeare's language. The real difficulty (and the real delight) comes in trying to see how he uses the words, how he endows them with more than their denotative meanings. Why, for example, does Macbeth say that he hopes that the "sure and firm-set earth" (2.1.56) will not hear his steps as he goes forward to murder Duncan? Here "sure" and "firm-set" mean virtually the same thing: stable, secure, fixed. Why use two words? If this were a student paper, no doubt the teacher would circle one of them and write "redundant." But the redundancy is exactly what Shakespeare wants. One word would do if the purpose were to describe the solidity of the earth, but here the redundancy points to something different. It reveals something about Macbeth's mind, betraying through the doubling how deep is his awareness of the world of stable values that the terrible act he is about to commit must unsettle.

Shakespeare's words usually work this way: in part describing what the characters see and as often betraying what they feel. The example from *Macbeth* is a simple example of how this works. Shakespeare's words are carefully patterned. How one says something is every bit as important as what is said, and the conspicuous patterns that are created alert us to the fact that something more than the words' lexical sense has been put into play. Words can be coupled, as in the example above, or knit into even denser metaphorical constellations to reveal something about the speaker (which often the speaker does not know), as in Prince Hal's promise to his father that he will outdo the rebels' hero, Henry Percy (Hotspur):

> Percy is but my factor, good my lord,
> To engross up glorious deeds on my behalf.
> And I will call him to so strict account
> That he shall render every glory up,
> Yea, even the slightest worship of his time,
> Or I will tear the reckoning from his heart.
>
> *(Henry IV, Part One,* 3.2.147–152)

The Prince expresses his confidence that he will defeat Hotspur, but revealingly in a reiterated language of commercial exchange ("factor," "engross," "account," "render," "reckoning") that tells us something important both about the Prince and the ways in which he understands his world. In a play filled with references to coins and counterfeiting, the speech demonstrates not only that Hal has committed himself to the business at hand, repudiating his earlier, irresponsible tavern self, but also that he knows it is a business rather than a glorious world of chivalric achievement; he inhabits a world in which value (political as well as economic) is not intrinsic but determined by what people are willing to invest, and he proves himself a master of producing desire for what he has to offer.

Or sometimes it is not the network of imagery but the very syntax that speaks, as when Claudius announces his marriage to Hamlet's mother:

> Therefore our sometime sister, now our Queen,
> Th' imperial jointress to this warlike state,
> Have we—as 'twere with a defeated joy,
> With an auspicious and a dropping eye,
> With mirth in funeral and with dole in marriage,
> In equal scale weighing delight and dole—
> Taken to wife. *(Hamlet,* 1.2.8–14)

All he really wants to say here is that he has married Gertrude, his former sister-in-law: "Therefore our sometime sister . . . Have we . . . Taken to wife." But the straightforward sentence gets interrupted and complicated, revealing his own discomfort with the announcement. His elaborations and intensifications of Gertrude's role ("sometime sister," "Queen," "imperial jointress"), the self-conscious rhetorical balancing of the middle three lines (indeed "in equal scale weighing delight and dole"), all declare by the all-too obvious artifice how desperate he is to hide the awkward facts behind a veneer of normalcy and propriety. The very unnaturalness of the sentence is what alerts us that we are meant to understand more than the simple relation of fact.

Why doesn't Shakespeare just say what he means? Well, he does—exactly what he means. In the example from *Hamlet* just above, Shakespeare shows us something about Claudius that Claudius doesn't know himself. Always Shakespeare's words will offer us an immediate sense of what is happening, allowing us to follow the action, but they also offer us a counterplot, pointing us to what might be behind the action, confirming or contradicting what the characters say. It is a language that shimmers with promise and possibility, opening the characters' hearts and minds to our view—and all we have to do is learn to pay attention to what is there before us.

Shakespeare's Verse

Another distinctive feature of Shakespeare's dramatic language is that much of it is in verse. Almost all of the plays mix poetry and prose, but the poetry dominates. *The Merry Wives of Windsor* has the lowest percentage (only about 13 percent verse), while *Richard II* and *King John* are written entirely in verse (the only examples, although *Henry VI, Part One* and *Part Three* have only a very few prose lines). In most of the plays, about 70 percent of the lines are written in verse.

Shakespeare's characteristic verse line is a non-rhyming iambic pentameter ("blank verse"), ten syllables with every second one stressed. In *A Midsummer Night's Dream*, Titania comes to her senses after a magic potion has led her to fall in love with an ass-headed Bottom: "Methought I was enamored of an ass" (4.1.76). Similarly, in *Romeo and Juliet*, Romeo gazes up at Juliet's window: "But soft, what light through yonder window breaks" (2.2.2). In both these examples, the line has ten syllables organized into five regular beats (each beat consisting of the stress on the second syllable of a pair, as in "But soft," the da-dum rhythm forming an "iamb"). Still, we don't hear these lines as jingles; they seem natural enough, in large part because this dominant pattern is varied in the surrounding lines.

The play of stresses indeed becomes another key to meaning, as Shakespeare alerts us to what is important. In *Measure for Measure*, Lucio urges Isabella to plead for her brother's life: "Oh, to him, to him, wench! He will relent" (2.2.129). The iambic norm (unstressed-stressed) tells us (and an actor) that the emphasis at the beginning of the line is on "to" not "him"—it is the action not the object that is being emphasized—and at the end of the line the stress falls on "will." Alternatively, the line can play against the established norm. In *Hamlet*, Claudius corrects Polonius's idea of what is bothering the Prince: "Love? His affections do not that way tend" (3.1.161). The iambic norm forces the emphasis onto "that" ("do not *that* way tend"), while the syntax forces an unexpected stress on the opening word, "Love." In the famous line, "The course of true love never did run smooth" (*A Midsummer Night's Dream*, 1.1.134), the iambic expectation is varied in both the middle and at the end of the line. Both "love" and the first syllable of "never" are stressed, as are both syllables at the end: "run smooth," creating a metrical foot in which both syllables are stressed (called a "spondee"). The point to notice is that the "da-dum, da-dum, da-dum, da-dum, da-dum" line is not inevitable; it merely sets an expectation against which many variations can be heard.

In fact, even the ten-syllable norm can be varied. Shakespeare sometimes writes lines with fewer or more syllables. Often there is an extra, unstressed syllable at the end of a line (a so-called "feminine ending"); sometimes there are verse lines with only nine. In *Henry IV, Part One*, King Henry replies incredulously to the rebel Worcester's claim that he hadn't "sought" the confrontation with the King: "You have not sought it. How comes it then?" (5.1.27). There are only nine syllables here (some earlier editors, seeking to "correct" the verse, added the word "sir" after the first question to regularize the line). But the pause where one expects a stressed syllable is dramatically effective, allowing the King's anger to be powerfully present in the silence.

As even these few examples show, Shakespeare's verse is unusually flexible, allowing a range of rhythmical effects. It should not be understood as a set of strict rules but as a flexible set of practices rooted in dramatic necessity. It is designed to highlight ideas and emotions, and it is based less upon rigid syllable counts than on an arrangement of stresses within an understood temporal norm, as one might expect from a poetry written to be heard in the theater rather than read on the page.

Here Follows Prose

Although the plays are dominated by verse, prose plays a significant role. Shakespeare's prose has its own rhythms, but it lacks the formal patterning of verse, and so is printed without line breaks and without the capitals that mark the beginning of a verse line. Like many of his fellow dramatists, Shakespeare tended to use prose for comic scenes, the shift from verse serving, especially in his early plays, as a social marker. Upper-class characters speak in verse; lower-class characters speak in prose. Thus, in *A Midsummer Night's Dream*, the Athenians of the court, as well as the fairies, all speak in verse, but the "rude mechanicals," Bottom and his artisan friends, all speak in prose, except for the comic verse they speak in their performance of "Pyramis and Thisbe."

As Shakespeare grew in experience, he became more flexible about the shifts from verse to prose, letting it, among other things, mark genre rather than class and measure various kinds of intensity. Prose becomes in the main the medium of comedy. The great comedies, like *Much Ado About Nothing*, *Twelfth Night*, and *As You Like It*, are all more than 50 percent prose. But even in comedy, shifts between verse and prose may be used to measure subtle emotional changes. In Act One, scene three of *The Merchant of Venice*, Shylock and Bassanio begin the scene speaking of matters of business in prose, but when Antonio enters and the deep conflict between the Christian and the Jew becomes evident, the scene shifts to verse. But prose may itself serve in moments of emotional intensity. Shylock's famous speech in Act Three, scene one, "Hath not a Jew eyes . . ." is all in prose, as is Hamlet's expression of disgust at the world ("I have of late—but wherefore I know not—lost all my mirth . . .") at 3.1.261–276. Shakespeare comes to use prose to vary the tone of a scene, as the shift from verse subtly alerts an audience or a reader to some new emotional register.

Prose becomes, as Shakespeare's art matures, not inevitably the mark of the lower classes but the mark of a salutary daily-ness. It is appropriately the medium in which letters are written, and it is the medium of a common sense that will at least challenge the potential self-deceptions of grandiloquent speech. When Rosalind mocks the excesses and artifice of Orlando's wooing in Act Four, scene one of *As You Like It*, it is in prose that she seeks something genuine in the expression of love:

> The poor world is almost six thousand years old, and in all this time there was not any man died in his own person, *videlicit* [i.e., namely], in a love cause. . . . Men have died from time to time, and worms have eaten them, but not for love.

Here the prose becomes the sound of common sense, an effective foil to the affectation of pinning poems to trees and thinking that it is real love.

It is not that prose is artless; Shakespeare's prose is no less self-conscious than his verse. The artfulness of his prose is different, of course. The seeming ordinariness of his prose is no less an effect of his artistry than is the more obvious patterning of his verse. Prose is no less serious, compressed, or indeed figurative. As with his verse, Shakespeare's prose performs numerous tasks and displays various, subtle formal qualities; and recognizing the possibilities of what it can achieve is still another way of seeing what Shakespeare puts right before us to show us what he has hidden.

Further Reading

N.F. Blake, *Shakespeare's Language: An Introduction* (New York: St. Martin's Press, 1983).

Jonathan Hope, *Shakespeare's Grammar* (London: Thomson, 2003).

Sister Miriam Joseph, *Shakespeare's Use of the Arts of Language* (New York: Columbia University Press, 1947).

M. M. Mahood, *Shakespeare's Wordplay* (London: Methuen, 1957).

Russ McDonald, *Shakespeare and the Arts of Language* (Oxford: Oxford University Press, 2001).

Brian Vickers, *The Artistry of Shakespeare's Prose* (London: Methuen, 1968).

George T. Wright, *Shakespeare's Metrical Art* (Berkeley: Univ. of California Press, 1991).

Key to the Play Text

Symbols

°	Indicates an explanation or definition in the left-hand margin.
1	Indicates a gloss on the page facing the play text.
[ ]	Indicates something added or changed by the editors (i.e., not in the early printed text that this edition of the play is based on).

Terms

F, Folio, or *First Folio*	The first collected edition of Shakespeare's plays, published in 1623.
Q, Quarto	The usual format in which the individual plays were first published. *Hamlet* was first published in an unauthorized quarto (Q1) in 1603. Q2, on which this edition is based, was published in 1604–5.

Hamlet

William Shakespeare

List of Roles

Hamlet	*Prince of Denmark*
Gertrude	*Hamlet's mother and Queen*
Claudius	*Hamlet's uncle and King*
Ghost	*Ghost of Hamlet's father, the former Danish King*
Polonius	*Counselor to Claudius*
Laertes	*his son*
Ophelia	*his daughter*
Reynaldo	*Polonius's servant*
Horatio	*Hamlet's friend from Wittenburg*
Rosencrantz	*fellow student*
Guildenstern	*fellow student*
Voltemand **Cornelius**	*Danish ambassadors*
Barnardo **Francisco** **Marcellus**	*sentinels*
Osric	*a courtier*
Players	*playing Player King, Player Queen, Prologue, and Lucianus*
Clowns	*as gravediggers*
Priest	
Gentleman	
Followers of Laertes	
Messengers	
Sailor	
Fortinbras	*Prince of Norway*
Captain	*in the Norwegian army*
Ambassadors	*from England*
Lord	

Courtiers, attendants, servants, lords, guards, musicians, soldiers, sailors, officers

1 *most carefully upon your hour*

Precisely at the assigned time

Act 1, Scene 1

Enter **Barnardo** *and* **Francisco**, *two sentinels.*

Barnardo

Who's there?

Francisco

identify Nay, answer me. Stand and unfold° yourself.

Barnardo

Long live the King!

Francisco

Barnardo?

Barnardo

He.

Francisco

You come most carefully upon your hour.[1]

Barnardo

'Tis now struck twelve. Get thee to bed, Francisco.

Francisco

For this relief much thanks. 'Tis bitter cold,
And I am sick at heart.

Barnardo

Have you had quiet guard?

Francisco

Not a mouse stirring.

Barnardo

Well, good night.
If you do meet Horatio and Marcellus,
companions The rivals° of my watch, bid them make haste.

Enter **Horatio** *and* **Marcellus**.

Francisco

I think I hear them.—Stand, ho! Who's there?

1 *A piece of him.*

I.e., what's left of him (the implication being that Horatio is shrinking in the freezing cold), though perhaps Horatio offers his hand as a literal *piece* of himself.

2 *speak to it*

Renaissance belief held that ghosts could not speak unless spoken to. As a scholar (see line 44), Horatio is deemed most fit to address the Ghost probably because his knowledge of Latin would allow him to perform an exorcism, should it prove to be a demon.

Horatio

Friends to this ground.

Marcellus

al citizens / Danish King And liegemen° to the Dane.°

Francisco

i.e., God give Give° you good night.

Marcellus

Oh, farewell, honest soldier. Who hath relieved you?

Francisco

Barnardo hath my place. Give you good night. *He exits.*

Marcellus

Holla, Barnardo.

Barnardo

Say, what, is Horatio there?

Horatio

A piece of him.[1]

Barnardo

Welcome, Horatio.—Welcome, good Marcellus.

Marcellus

What? Has this thing appeared again tonight?

Barnardo

I have seen nothing.

Marcellus

Horatio says 'tis but our fantasy
And will not let belief take hold of him
Concerning Touching° this dreaded sight twice seen of us.
Therefore I have entreated him along
With us to watch the minutes of this night,
That, if again this apparition come,
verify; corroborate He may approve° our eyes and speak to it.[2]

Horatio

Tush, tush, 'twill not appear.

1 *Last night of all*

Just last night

2 *harrows*

Distresses; torments; a *harrow* is a farm implement for breaking up clumps of earth.

3 *usurp'st*

Horatio accuses the Ghost of wrongfully appearing in the night as well as in the likeness of the dead King.

Barnardo

Sit down a while,
And let us once again assail your ears,
That are so fortified against our story,
What we have two nights seen.

Horatio

Well, sit we down,
And let us hear Barnardo speak of this.

Barnardo

Last night of all,[1]
North Star When yond same star that's westward from the pole°
its / illuminate Had made his° course t' illume° that part of Heaven
Where now it burns, Marcellus and myself,
striking The bell then beating° one—

Enter **Ghost**.

Marcellus

Peace; break thee off! Look where it comes again!

Barnardo

shape; appearance In the same figure° like the King that's dead.

Marcellus

[to **Horatio**] Thou art a scholar. Speak to it, Horatio.

Barnardo

he / Look at Looks 'a° not like the King? Mark° it, Horatio.

Horatio

Most like. It harrows[2] me with fear and wonder.

Barnardo

wants to It would° be spoke to.

Marcellus

Speak to it, Horatio.

Horatio

What art thou that usurp'st[3] this time of night

1 *sensible and true avouch*

I.e., the unimpeachable testimony

2 *As thou art to thyself.*

I.e., the Ghost resembles the King as much as you, Marcellus, resemble yourself.

3 *He smote the sledded Polacks*

He defeated the Polish military troops, who were equipped with sleds for traveling on ice. Other editors have taken Q2's "sledded pollax" to mean "sledded pole-axe," a weapon weighted with a sledge at the back, which old Hamlet slams down in anger.

4 *gone by our watch*

Moved past our sentry position

Together with that fair and warlike form
King of Denmark In which the majesty of buried Denmark°
formerly Did sometimes° march? By Heaven, I charge thee,
speak.

Marcellus

It is offended.

Barnardo

See, it stalks away.

Horatio

Stay! Speak, speak! I charge thee, speak!

Ghost *exits.*

Marcellus

'Tis gone and will not answer.

Barnardo

How now, Horatio? You tremble and look pale.
Is not this something more than fantasy?
of What think you on° 't?

Horatio

Before my God, I might not this believe
Without the sensible and true avouch[1]
Of mine own eyes.

Marcellus

Is it not like the King?

Horatio

As thou art to thyself.[2]
Such was the very armor he had on
King of Norway When he the ambitious Norway° combated.
meeting So frowned he once when, in an angry parle,°
He smote the sledded Polacks[3] on the ice.
'Tis strange.

Marcellus

precisely Thus twice before, and jump° at this dead hour,
strides With martial stalk° hath he gone by our watch.[4]

1 *In what particular thought to work I know not*

I.e., I cannot say why with any precision.

2 *in the gross and scope of mine opinion*

In my general view

3 *Why this same strict and most observant watch / So nightly toils the subject of the land*

Why the citizens of the state spend every night in this vigilant state of watchfulness

4 *foreign mart*

expenditure abroad

5 *divide*

Distinguish (i.e., the ship makers are not allowed a day of rest on Sundays).

6 *Doth make the night joint laborer with the day*

Makes the nighttime a period of labor, in addition to the working day

7 *by Fortinbras of Norway, / Thereto pricked on by a most emulate pride, / Dared to the combat*

Incited by his own competitive pride, Fortinbras (King) of Norway challenged him (old Hamlet) to combat.

8 *heraldry*

Conventions that governed the rules of combat

9 *stood seized of*

Had legal possession of

10 *a moiety competent*

An equivalent portion

11 *which had return / To the inheritance of Fortinbras / Had he been vanquisher*

Which (i.e., an equivalent amount of land) would have been given to Fortinbras if Norway had been victorious

12 *as, by the same comart / And carriage of the article designed, / His fell to Hamlet*

Just as, according to those same terms and the execution of the Kings' drawn-up contract, his (Fortinbras's) land would be forfeit to Hamlet

13 *young Fortinbras*

I.e., the son of old Fortinbras

Horatio

In what particular thought to work I know not,[1]
But in the gross and scope of mine opinion[2]
calamity This bodes some strange eruption° to our state.

Marcellus

Good now, sit down and tell me, he that knows,
Why this same strict and most observant watch
So nightly toils the subject of the land,[3]
brass And with such daily cost of brazen° cannon
And foreign mart[4] for implements of war;
forced labor / difficult Why such impress° of shipwrights, whose sore° task
Does not divide[5] the Sunday from the week.
impending What might be toward,° that this sweaty haste
Doth make the night joint laborer with the day?[6]
Who is 't that can inform me?

Horatio

That can I.
At least the whisper goes so: our last King,
Whose image even but now appeared to us,
Was, as you know, by Fortinbras of Norway,
Thereto pricked on by a most emulate pride,
i.e., the dead King Dared to the combat,[7] in which our valiant Hamlet°
(For so this side of our known world esteemed him)
agreement Did slay this Fortinbras, who by a sealed compact°
Well ratified by law and heraldry,[8]
Did forfeit, with his life, all these his lands
Which he stood seized of[9] to the conqueror,
Against the which a moiety competent[10]
wagered Was gagèd° by our King, which had return
To the inheritance of Fortinbras
Had he been vanquisher,[11] as, by the same comart
And carriage of the article designed,
His fell to Hamlet.[12] Now, sir, young Fortinbras,[13]

1 *Sharked up a list*

Indiscriminately gathered a band (as sharks gather food indiscriminately)

2 *lawless resolutes*

Determined criminals; the Folio prints "landless," a slightly different image, not, as here, a group of desperados, but a group of men willing to fight because, like Fortinbras, they have lost the right to their land.

3 *For food and diet to some enterprise / That hath a stomach in 't*

Two possible meanings: either the lawless men join Fortinbras's band because they will be given food as pay, or else the men themselves function as food, i.e., fodder for the war effort.

4 *strong hand*

Force; a pun on Fortinbras's name, which means "strong arm."

5 *posthaste and rummage*

Agitated activity and commotion

6 *I think it be no other but e'en so.*

I think that is precisely the reason.

7 *Well may it sort*

It would be fitting

8 *stars with trains of fire*

I.e., comets

9 *moist star*

The moon (often described as *moist* for its power to control the tides)

10 *Neptune's*

Roman god of the sea

11 *almost to doomsday*

It was believed that eclipses would portend the coming of the day of Judgment.

untested Of unimprovèd° mettle hot and full,
outskirts Hath in the skirts° of Norway here and there
Sharked up a list of[1] lawless resolutes[2]
For food and diet to some enterprise
which enterprise That hath a stomach in 't,[3] which° is no other—
clearly As it doth well° appear unto our state—
from But to recover of° us, by strong hand[4]
compulsory And terms compulsatory,° those foresaid lands
So by his father lost. And this, I take it,
Is the main motive of our preparations,
source The source of this our watch, and the chief head°
Of this posthaste and rummage[5] in the land.

Barnardo

I think it be no other but e'en so.[6]
Well may it sort[7] that this portentous figure
Comes armèd through our watch so like the King
reason; cause That was and is the question° of these wars.

Horatio

particle of dust A mote° it is to trouble the mind's eye.
flourishing In the most high and palmy° state of Rome,
before A little ere° the mightiest Julius fell,
shrouded The graves stood tenantless and the sheeted° dead
chatter Did squeak and gibber° in the Roman streets,
As stars with trains of fire[8] and dews of blood,
Ominous signs Disasters° in the sun; and the moist star,[9]
Upon whose influence Neptune's[10] empire stands,
Was sick almost to doomsday[11] with eclipse.
forerunner And even the like precurse° of feared events,
always As harbingers preceding still° the fates
i.e., disastrous event And prologue to the omen° coming on,
Have Heaven and Earth together demonstrated
regions Unto our climatures° and countrymen.

1 *cross it*

Cross its path; challenge it (perhaps, alternatively, make the sign of the cross as a means of protection)

2 *art privy to*

Have private information about

3 *partisan*

A long-handled spear with a laterally projecting blade

Enter **Ghost**.

wait But soft;° behold! Lo, where it comes again.
I'll cross it[1] though it blast me.—Stay, illusion!

It spreads his arms.

If thou hast any sound or use of voice,
Speak to me.
If there be any good thing to be done
That may to thee do ease and grace to me,
Speak to me.
If thou art privy to[2] thy country's fate,
perhaps; luckily Which happily° foreknowing may avoid,
Oh, speak!
i.e., hoarded Or if thou hast uphoarded° in thy life
illegally obtained Extorted° treasure in the womb of Earth,
For which, they say, your spirits oft walk in death,
Speak of it. Stay and speak!

The cock crows.

Stop it, Marcellus.

Marcellus

Shall I strike it with my partisan?[3]

Horatio

stop Do, if it will not stand.°

Barnardo

'Tis here.

Horatio

'Tis here. [**Ghost** *exits.*]

Marcellus

'Tis gone.
it being We do it wrong, being° so majestical,
To offer it the show of violence,

1 *the god of day*

I.e., the god of the sun, Apollo

2 *extravagant and erring*

Wandering out of its proper bounds

3 *of the truth herein / This present object made probation*

I.e., our experience with this ghost confirms the supposition (that at the cock's crow all ghosts must vanish from sight).

4 *ever 'gainst the season*

Always in anticipation of Christmas

5 *bird of dawning*

I.e., the cock

6 *strike*

Exert evil influence on individuals

For it is, as the air, invulnerable,
And our vain blows malicious mockery.

Barnardo

crowed It was about to speak when the cock crew.°

Horatio

And then it started, like a guilty thing
Upon a fearful summons. I have heard
herald; trumpeter The cock, that is the trumpet° to the morn,
Doth with his lofty and shrill-sounding throat
Awake the god of day,[1] and, at his warning,
Whether in sea or fire, in earth or air,
hurries Th' extravagant and erring[2] spirit hies°
confinement To his confine,° and of the truth herein
This present object made probation.[3]

Marcellus

It faded on the crowing of the cock.
Some say that ever 'gainst that season[4] comes
Wherein our savior's birth is celebrated,
This bird of dawning[5] singeth all night long.
And then, they say, no spirit dare stir abroad.
The nights are wholesome: then no planets strike,[6]
bewitches No fairy takes,° nor witch hath power to charm,
holy So hallowed° and so gracious is that time.

Horatio

So have I heard and do in part believe it.
reddish brown But look, the morn, in russet° mantle clad,
Walks o'er the dew of yon high eastward hill.
Break we our watch up, and, by my advice,
Let us impart what we have seen tonight
Unto young Hamlet, for, upon my life,

1 *As needful in our loves*

As is required by our love (for Hamlet)

2 *convenient*

I.e., conveniently; the word could be used, as here, adverbially in Shakespeare's time.

This spirit, dumb to us, will speak to him.
Do you consent we shall acquaint him with it,
As needful in our loves,[1] fitting our duty?

Marcellus

Let's do 't, I pray, and I this morning know
Where we shall find him most convenient.[2] *They exit.*

1 with others

In the Folio, Ophelia enters here as well.

2 **Claudius**

Claudius's speech displays his conspicuous control of the arts of formal rhetoric. An audience in 1600 would have recognized that training especially in the balancing of his clauses, e.g., *With* mirth *in* funeral *and with* dirge *in* marriage (1.2.12): the jarring ceremonial and political transition is gracefully overcome by the rhythmic symmetry. (Rhetoricians call this device of balanced clauses *isocolon*.) Such polish was prized in men of state; compare its elegant premeditation with the spontaneous, self-interrupting style of Hamlet's soliloquies. Notice also that Shakespeare seems to have been aware that Denmark, unlike England, was an elective monarchy. Young Hamlet is treated throughout the play as the likely next king, but there is no violation of Danish law or custom in the fact that Claudius follows his brother on the throne; he was presumably elected by the nobles to the role. Hamlet later complains that Claudius *Popped in between th' election and my hopes* (5.2.64), possibly meaning that Claudius preempted the election, but more likely that the new King blocked his path to advancement.

3 *it us befitted*

It was appropriate for us

4 *To be contracted in one brow of woe*

To be brought together in one shared expression of grief

5 *we with wisest sorrow think on him / Together with remembrance of ourselves*

While I think about him sorrowfully, I also have myself in mind

6 *sometime sister*

Former sister-in-law

7 *now our Queen*

English law prohibited marriage between a man and his brother's wife, viewing such a marriage as technically incestuous. Henry VIII used this rationale to annul his marriage to Katherine of Aragon, his brother's widow, so he could marry Anne Boleyn. Under Germanic law, however, it was not uncommon for a new king to marry the former king's widow.

8 *an auspicious and a dropping eye*

With one eye looking up hopefully and one eye sadly downcast

9 *Now follows that you know*

Now I am going to turn to things about which you already know something.

10 *disjoint and out of frame*

Fractured and disordered

11 *Colleaguèd with the dream of his advantage*

Coupled with his fantasy that the Norwegian army is stronger than ours

Act 1, Scene 2

Flourish [of trumpets]. Enter **Claudius**, *King of Denmark;* **Gertrude** *the Queen; [the] Council, as* **Polonius** *and his son* **Laertes**; **Hamlet**, *with others*[1] *[including* **Cornelius** *and* **Voltemand**].

Claudius[2]

., my (royal pronoun) Though yet of Hamlet our° dear brother's death
i.e., fresh The memory be green,° and that it us befitted[3]
To bear our hearts in grief and our whole kingdom
To be contracted in one brow of woe,[4]
natural emotion Yet so far hath discretion fought with nature°
That we with wisest sorrow think on him
Together with remembrance of ourselves.[5]
Therefore our sometime sister,[6] now our Queen,[7]
oint owner; possessor Th' imperial jointress° to this warlike state,
Have we—as 'twere with a defeated joy,
With an auspicious and a dropping eye,[8]
With mirth in funeral and with dirge in marriage,
grief In equal scale weighing delight and dole°—
excluded Taken to wife. Nor have we herein barred°
Your better wisdoms, which have freely gone
With this affair along. For all, our thanks.
Now follows that you know:[9] young Fortinbras,
opinion Holding a weak supposal° of our worth,
because of Or thinking by° our late dear brother's death
Our state to be disjoint and out of frame,[10]
Colleaguèd with this dream of his advantage,[11]
He hath not failed to pester us with message
Concerning Importing° the surrender of those lands
binding agreements Lost by his father, with all bands° of law,
To our most valiant brother. So much for him.
Now for ourself and for this time of meeting
Thus much the business is: we have here writ

1 *in that the levies, / The lists, and full proportions are all made / Out of his subject*

I.e., since the money for the expedition, the men, and the equipment are all raised from those who are subject (to the King of Norway).

2 *Giving to you no further personal power / To business with the King more than the scope / Of these dilated articles allow*

Giving you no further permission to negotiate with the King than these detailed instructions permit

3 *let your haste commend your duty*

Let a speedy departure (rather than long farewells) demonstrate your loyalty

4 *We doubt it nothing.*

I do not doubt it.

5 *You cannot speak of reason to the Dane / And lose your voice.*

There is nothing reasonable that you can ask of me (*the Dane* = the Danish King) that will not be granted (*lose your voice* = speak to no purpose)

6 *That shall not be my offer, not thy asking*

That I would not offer before you even asked me

7 *leave and favor*

Kind permission

To Norway, uncle of young Fortinbras—
weak / bedridden Who, impotent° and bedrid,° scarcely hears
Of this his nephew's purpose—to suppress
progress His further gait° herein, in that the levies,
The lists, and full proportions are all made
Out of his subject;[1] and we here dispatch
You, good Cornelius, and you, Voltemand,
As For° bearers of this greeting to old Norway,
Giving to you no further personal power
To business with the King more than the scope
Of these dilated articles allow.[2] [*hands them documents*]
Farewell, and let your haste commend your duty.[3]

Cornelius, Voltemand

In that and all things will we show our duty.

Claudius

We doubt it nothing.[4] Heartily farewell.

[**Voltemand** *and* **Cornelius** *exit.*]

And now, Laertes, what's the news with you?
You told us of some suit. What is 't, Laertes?
You cannot speak of reason to the Dane
And lose your voice.[5] What wouldst thou beg, Laertes,
That shall not be my offer, not thy asking?[6]
., naturally connected The head is not more native° to the heart,
The hand more instrumental to the mouth,
Than is the throne of Denmark to thy father.
What wouldst thou have, Laertes?

Laertes

My dread lord,
Your leave and favor[7] to return to France,
From whence, though willingly, I came to Denmark
To show my duty in your coronation;
Yet now, I must confess, that duty done,
My thoughts and wishes bend again toward France

1 *bow them to your gracious leave and pardon*

Submit themselves to your permission and approval

2 *slow leave*

Reluctant permission

3 *Upon his will I sealed my hard consent*

I.e., I reluctantly agreed to his desire.

4 *Take thy fair hour*

I.e., enjoy your youthful days

5 *thy best graces spend it at thy will*

Let your best qualities make use of it (*time*) as they wish

6 *A little more than kin and less than kind.*

Hamlet's wordplay is aggressive (and could either be an aside or a deliberate confrontation). He grimly notes that he and Claudius have become *a little more than kin* with Claudius's marriage to Hamlet's mother, as the two men are now more intimately related than they were previously. However, the feelings between Hamlet and Claudius are *less than kind*, meaning both "less than affectionate" and "less than natural." Hamlet's riddling line is a variation on the proverb "The nearer in kin the less in kindness."

7 *too much i' the sun*

I.e., too much in your royal favor (with a sarcastic pun on *sun/son*)

8 *nighted color*

Black clothes worn for mourning; also, melancholy, gloomy behavior

9 *Denmark*

Either Claudius, the King of Denmark, or the nation of Denmark itself

10 *vailèd lids*

Downcast eyes

11 *cold*

The Folio text prints "good," and many editors follow, though Hamlet seems to be implicitly accusing her of being cold, that is, of failing to display the grief he feels.

And bow them to your gracious leave and pardon.[1]

Claudius

Have you your father's leave? What says Polonius?

Polonius

He hath, my lord, wrung from me my slow leave[2]
diligent By laborsome° petition, and at last
Upon his will I sealed my hard consent.[3]
I do beseech you, give him leave to go.

Claudius

Take thy fair hour,[4] Laertes. Time be thine,
And thy best graces spend it at thy will.[5]
kinsman —But now, my cousin° Hamlet, and my son—

Hamlet

A little more than kin and less than kind.[6]

Claudius

i.e., sadness How is it that the clouds° still hang on you?

Hamlet

Not so much, my lord; I am too much in the sun.[7]

Gertrude

Good Hamlet, cast thy nighted color[8] off
And let thine eye look like a friend on Denmark.[9]
Do not forever with thy vailèd lids[10]
Seek for thy noble father in the dust.
Thou know'st 'tis common: all that lives must die,
Passing through nature to eternity.

Hamlet

Ay, madam, it is common.

Gertrude

If it be,
special; personal Why seems it so particular° with thee?

Hamlet

"Seems," madam? Nay, it is. I know not "seems."
only 'Tis not alone° my inky cloak, cold[11] mother,

1 *windy suspiration of forced breath*

Frequent insincere sighing

2 *shapes*

Appearances; the Folio prints "shows."

3 *a will most incorrect to Heaven*

A will that refuses to submit itself to God's will

4 *As any the most vulgar thing to sense*

I.e., as any ordinary thing that is easily perceived by the senses

5 *first corpse*

A reference to Abel, who, according to the Bible, was the first human to die, with an ironic undertone, as he was killed by his brother Cain, see Genesis 4:11–12.

6 *most immediate*

Next in succession; although Denmark was formally an elective monarchy, the successor was inevitably the eldest son of the monarch, and the election by the nobles merely ratified the obvious lineal choice.

Nor customary suits of solemn black,
Nor windy suspiration of forced breath,[1]
copious No, nor the fruitful° river in the eye,
behavior; expression Nor the dejected 'havior° of the visage,
Together with all forms, moods, shapes[2] of grief,
That can denote me truly. These indeed "seem,"
For they are actions that a man might play.
surpasses But I have that within which passes° show,
These but the trappings and the suits of woe.

Claudius

'Tis sweet and commendable in your nature, Hamlet,
To give these mourning duties to your father.
But you must know your father lost a father;
That father lost, lost his; and the survivor bound
In filial obligation for some term
dutiful; proper To do obsequious° sorrow. But to persever
grieving In obstinate condolement° is a course
Of impious stubbornness. 'Tis unmanly grief.
disobedient It shows a will most incorrect° to Heaven,[3]
lacking strength A heart unfortified,° or mind impatient,
An understanding simple and unschooled:
For what we know must be and is as common
As any the most vulgar thing to sense.[4]
Why should we in our peevish opposition
offence Take it to heart? Fie! 'Tis a fault° to Heaven,
A fault against the dead, a fault to nature,
To reason most absurd, whose common theme
always Is death of fathers, and who still° hath cried,
From the first corpse[5] till he that died today,
"This must be so." We pray you, throw to earth
futile This unprevailing° woe and think of us
As of a father, for let the world take note:
You are the most immediate[6] to our throne,

1 *Wittenberg*

German city with a famous university attended by many Danes after its founding in 1502. Martin Luther was its professor of theology in 1512, and Wittenberg became known as the birthplace of Protestantism.

2 *in all my best*

To the best of my abilities

3 *Sits smiling to*

Pleases

4 *in grace whereof / No jocund health that Denmark drinks today / But the great cannon to the clouds shall tell, / And the King's rouse the Heaven shall bruit again, / Respeaking earthly thunder*

I.e., in honor of this, every joyous toast that I (the King of Denmark) drink will be counted off by firing of cannon, and Heaven will echo the toast with its answering thunder.

5 *sallied*

Assailed, besieged. This is a much debated crux. Both Q1 and Q2 (the text on which this edition is based) print *sallied*, though many editors amend this to "sullied," meaning "defiled" or "desecrated." The Folio reads "solid," which provides a nice contrast with *melt*, though is perhaps a compositor's effort to make sense of an unfamiliar word.

6 *the Everlasting had not fixed / His canon 'gainst self-slaughter*

God had not prohibited suicide (*canon* = law)

preeminence And with no less nobility° of love
Than that which dearest father bears his son
Do I impart toward you. For your intent
In going back to school in Wittenberg,[1]
contrary It is most retrograde° to our desire,
agree And we beseech you, bend° you to remain
Here in the cheer and comfort of our eye,
Our chiefest courtier, cousin, and our son.

Gertrude

Let not thy mother lose her prayers, Hamlet;
I pray thee, stay with us. Go not to Wittenberg.

Hamlet

I shall in all my best[2] obey you, madam.

Claudius

Why, 'tis a loving and a fair reply.
Behave Be° as ourself in Denmark.—Madam, come.
agreement This gentle and unforced accord° of Hamlet
Sits smiling to[3] my heart, in grace whereof
joyful No jocund° health that Denmark drinks today
But the great cannon to the clouds shall tell,
echo And the King's rouse the Heaven shall bruit° again,
Respeaking earthly thunder.[4] Come away.

Flourish. All but **Hamlet** *exit.*

Hamlet

Oh, that this too, too sallied[5] flesh would melt,
Thaw, and resolve itself into a dew,
Or that the Everlasting had not fixed
His canon 'gainst self-slaughter![6] O God, God!
How weary, stale, flat, and unprofitable
activities Seem to me all the uses° of this world!
Fie on 't, ah fie! 'Tis an unweeded garden
offensive That grows to seed. Things rank° and gross in nature
entirely Possess it merely.° That it should come thus:

1 *that was to this / Hyperion to a satyr*

I.e., when compared with the current King, my father is *Hyperion* (the ancient Greek sun god) and Claudius a *satyr* (a mythological creature, half man and half goat, associated with drunken lust).

2 *might not beteem*

Would not permit

3 *As if increase of appetite had grown / By what it fed on*

I.e., as though she became hungrier the more she ate

4 *Niobe*

A tragic figure from Greek mythology, Niobe's children were killed by Apollo and Diana, and the gods then turned her to stone. Her grief, however, was so great that she continued to weep (in the form of a spring that ran from the rock).

5 *wants discourse of reason*

Lacks the faculties of rational thought

6 *Hercules*

Hero in Greek mythology famous for his extraordinary strength

7 *left the flushing in her gallèd eyes*

I.e., stopped making her eyes red and sore

8 *post / With such dexterity*

Rush so nimbly

9 *incestuous sheets*

In the period incest was understood to include marriage to a brother's wife, which was proscribed in the *Book of Common Prayer*, found in every English church and many households; see also Leviticus 18:16 and 18:20.

But two months dead—nay, not so much, not two—
So excellent a King, that was to this
Hyperion to a satyr,[1] so loving to my mother
That he might not beteem[2] the winds of Heaven
Visit her face too roughly. Heaven and Earth,
Must I remember? Why, she should hang on him
As if increase of appetite had grown
By what it fed on,[3] and yet, within a month—
Let me not think on 't. Frailty, thy name is woman!—
before A little month, or ere° those shoes were old
With which she followed my poor father's body,
Like Niobe,[4] all tears. Why, she—
O God, a beast that wants discourse of reason[5]
Would have mourned longer!—married with my uncle,
My father's brother, but no more like my father
Than I to Hercules.[6] Within a month,
insincere Ere yet the salt of most unrighteous° tears
Had left the flushing in her gallèd eyes,[7]
She married. O most wicked speed, to post
With such dexterity[8] to incestuous sheets![9]
It is not nor it cannot come to good—
But break, my heart, for I must hold my tongue.

Enter **Horatio**, **Marcellus**, *and* **Barnardo**.

Horatio

Hail to your Lordship.

Hamlet

I am glad to see you well.
Horatio? Or I do forget myself.

Horatio

The same, my lord, and your poor servant ever.

1 *change*

Exchange. Hamlet wants to exchange Horatio's word, *servant*, for his own word, *friend*.

2 *what make you from Wittenberg*

What has brought you here from Wittenberg?

3 *truster of*

I.e., entrusted with

4 *hard upon*

Soon after

5 *The funeral baked meats / Did coldly furnish forth the marriage tables.*

The leftovers from the funeral feast provided the meal for the marriage celebration.

6 *Or ever*

Before

Hamlet

Sir, my good friend, I'll change[1] that name with you.
And what make you from Wittenberg,[2] Horatio?
—Marcellus!

Marcellus

My good lord.

Hamlet

I am very glad to see you. [*to* **Bernardo**] Good ev'n, sir.
—But what, in faith, make you from Wittenberg?

Horatio

idle A truant° disposition, good my lord.

Hamlet

I would not hear your enemy say so,
Nor shall you do mine ear that violence,
To make it truster of[3] your own report
Against yourself. I know you are no truant.
But what is your affair in Elsinore?
We'll teach you for to drink ere you depart.

Horatio

My lord, I came to see your father's funeral.

Hamlet

I prithee, do not mock me, fellow student;
I think it was to see my mother's wedding.

Horatio

Indeed, my lord, it followed hard upon.[4]

Hamlet

Thrift, thrift, Horatio! The funeral baked meats
Did coldly furnish forth the marriage tables.[5]
most hated Would I had met my dearest° foe in Heaven
Or ever[6] I had seen that day, Horatio.
My father—methinks I see my father.

1 *take him for all in all*

I.e., who seems perfect in every particular

2 *Season your admiration*

Restrain your amazement

3 *dead waste*

Barren stillness

4 *at point exactly, cap-à-pie*

In every exact detail, from head to foot

5 *oppressed and fear-surprisèd*

I.e., overcome with fear

Horatio

Where, my lord?

Hamlet

In my mind's eye, Horatio.

Horatio

He I saw him once. 'A° was a goodly king.

Hamlet

'A was a man, take him for all in all.[1]
I shall not look upon his like again.

Horatio

My lord, I think I saw him yesternight.

Hamlet

Saw who?

Horatio

My lord, the King your father.

Hamlet

The King my father?

Horatio

Season your admiration[2] for a while
attentive With an attent° ear, till I may deliver,
Upon the witness of these gentlemen,
This marvel to you.

Hamlet

For God's love, let me hear.

Horatio

Two nights together had these gentlemen,
Marcellus and Barnardo, on their watch,
In the dead waste[3] and middle of the night,
Been thus encountered: a figure like your father,
Armed at point exactly, cap-à-pie,[4]
Appears before them and with solemn march
Goes slow and stately by them. Thrice he walked
By their oppressed and fear-surprisèd[5] eyes

1 *his truncheon's length*

I.e., no farther away than the length of his commander's baton

2 *These hands are not more like*

I.e., my two hands are not more like one another than the Ghost was like your father.

3 *address / Itself to motion, like as it would speak*

Began to move, as though it wanted to speak

4 *writ down in*

Required by

reduced Within his truncheon's length,[1] whilst they, distilled°
effect Almost to jelly with the act° of fear,
Stand dumb and speak not to him. This to me
terrified In dreadful° secrecy impart they did,
And I with them the third night kept the watch,
reported Where, as they had delivered,° both in time,
Form of the thing, each word made true and good,
The apparition comes. I knew your father;
These hands are not more like.[2]

Hamlet

But where was this?

Marcellus

battlements My lord, upon the platform° where we watch.

Hamlet

Did you not speak to it?

Horatio

My lord, I did,
But answer made it none. Yet once methought
It lifted up its head and did address
Itself to motion, like as it would speak.[3]
just But even° then the morning cock crew loud,
And at the sound it shrunk in haste away
And vanished from our sight.

Hamlet

'Tis very strange.

Horatio

As I do live, my honored lord, 'tis true,
And we did think it writ down in[4] our duty
To let you know of it.

Hamlet

Indeed, sirs, but this troubles me.
Hold you the watch tonight?

1 *Then saw you not his face.*

The Folio punctuates this with a question mark, but Q2's period makes this an expression of Hamlet's sharp skepticism.

Marcellus, Barnardo

We do, my lord.

Hamlet

Armed, say you?

Marcellus, Barnardo

Armed, my lord.

Hamlet

From top to toe?

Marcellus, Barnardo

My lord, from head to foot.

Hamlet

Then saw you not his face.[1]

Horatio

helmet visor Oh yes, my lord. He wore his beaver° up.

Hamlet

What? Looked he frowningly?

Horatio

expression A countenance° more
In sorrow than in anger.

Hamlet

Pale or red?

Horatio

Nay, very pale.

Hamlet

And fixed his eyes upon you?

Horatio

Most constantly.

Hamlet

I would I had been there.

Horatio

It would have much amazed you.

1 *sable silvered*

Black mixed with gray

Hamlet

Very like. Stayed it long?

Horatio

count to While one with moderate haste might tell° a hundred.

Marcellus, Barnardo

Longer, longer.

Horatio

Not when I saw 't.

Hamlet

gray His beard was grizzled,° no?

Horatio

It was, as I have seen it in his life,
A sable silvered.[1]

Hamlet

I will watch tonight.
Perchance 'twill walk again.

Horatio

I warrant it will.

Hamlet

If it assume my noble father's person,
I'll speak to it, though Hell itself should gape
And bid me hold my peace. I pray you all,
If you have hitherto concealed this sight,
held; kept secret Let it be tenable° in your silence still.
happen And whatsomever else shall hap° tonight,
Give it an understanding but no tongue.
repay I will requite° your loves. So fare you well.
Upon the platform, 'twixt eleven and twelve,
I'll visit you.

Horatio, Marcellus, Barnardo

Our duty to your honor.

Hamlet

Your loves, as mine to you. Farewell.
[**Horatio**, **Marcellus**, *and* **Barnardo**] *exit.*
My father's spirit in arms. All is not well.
suspect I doubt° some foul play. Would the night were come!
Till then sit still, my soul. Foul deeds will rise,
Though all the earth o'erwhelm them, to men's eyes.
He exits.

1 *My necessaries are embarked.*

My luggage is aboard ship.

2 *as the winds give benefit / And convey is assistant*

As the winds are favorable and some means of transport is available

3 *Hold it a fashion and a toy in blood*

Consider it a passing phase and an amorous fancy

4 *For nature, crescent, does not grow alone / In thews and bulk, but, as this temple waxes, / The inward service of the mind and soul / Grows wide withal.*

I.e., for in the natural course of growth, a man does not grow in strength and size alone, but, as the body (the *temple* of the soul) grows larger, the life of the mind and soul matures as well.

5 *His greatness weighed*

I.e., considering his royalty

6 *Carve for himself*

I.e., choose for himself. (Literally, "select and *carve* out his own portion of meat," from the proverbial expression, "To be one's own carver.")

Act 1, Scene 3

Enter **Laertes** *and* **Ophelia**, *his sister.*

Laertes

My necessaries are embarked.[1] Farewell.
And, sister, as the winds give benefit
be remiss And convey is assistant,[2] do not sleep,°
But let me hear from you.

Ophelia

Do you doubt that?

Laertes

foolishness For Hamlet and the trifling° of his favor,
Hold it a fashion and a toy in blood,[3]
springlike A violet in the youth of primy° nature,
Premature Forward,° not permanent, sweet, not lasting,
diversion The perfume and suppliance° of a minute,
No more.

Ophelia

No more but so?

Laertes

Think it no more,
growing For nature, crescent,° does not grow alone
sinews In thews° and bulk, but, as this temple waxes,
The inward service of the mind and soul
Grows wide withal.[4] Perhaps he loves you now,
stain / deceit And now no soil° nor cautel° doth besmirch
The virtue of his will; but you must fear.
His greatness weighed,[5] his will is not his own.
unimportant He may not, as unvalued° persons do,
Carve for himself,[6] for on his choice depends
The safety and health of this whole state,

1 *therefore must his choice be circumscribed / Unto the voice and yielding of that body / Whereof he is the head*

Therefore his choice (of a wife) must be subject to the vote and consent of the nation that he rules.

2 *As he in his particular act and place / May give his saying deed*

As he, in his specific position and circumstance, may act on his promise.

3 *main voice*

General consent

4 *your chaste treasure*

I.e., your chastity

5 *unmastered importunity*

Uncontrolled pleading

6 *keep you in the rear of your affection*

Hold back, even if your feelings are moving forward (a military metaphor)

7 *The chariest maid is prodigal enough / If she unmask her beauty to the moon.*

The most cautious maiden takes a great enough risk if she exposes herself to the moon (an emblem of chastity).

8 *The canker galls the infants of the spring / Too oft before their buttons be disclosed*

Too often, the cankerworm destroys the young plants before their buds are open.

9 *Youth to itself rebels, though none else near.*

I.e., youth rebels of its own accord, even without a tempter.

10 *libertine*

One who lacks moral self-restraint; a philanderer or lecher

11 *recks not his own rede*

I.e., does not follow his own advice

And therefore must his choice be circumscribed
Unto the voice and yielding of that body
Whereof he is the head.[1] Then if he says he loves you,
befits It fits° your wisdom so far to believe it
As he in his particular act and place
May give his saying deed,[2] which is no further
along with Than the main voice[3] of Denmark goes withal.°
Then weigh what loss your honor may sustain
gullible / listen to If with too credent° ear you list° his songs,
Or lose your heart, or your chaste treasure[4] open
To his unmastered importunity.[5]
Fear it, Ophelia. Fear it, my dear sister,
And keep you in the rear of your affection,[6]
Out of the shot and danger of desire.
The chariest maid is prodigal enough
If she unmask her beauty to the moon.[7]
slanderous Virtue itself 'scapes not calumnious° strokes.
The canker galls the infants of the spring
Too oft before their buttons be disclosed,[8]
And in the morn and liquid dew of youth
blights Contagious blastments° are most imminent.
Be wary, then; best safety lies in fear.
Youth to itself rebels, though none else near.[9]

Ophelia

I shall the effect of this good lesson keep
As watchman to my heart. But, good my brother,
ungodly Do not, as some ungracious° pastors do,
Show me the steep and thorny way to Heaven
proud Whiles, like a puffed° and reckless libertine,[10]
Himself the primrose path of dalliance treads
And recks not his own rede.[11]

Laertes

Oh, fear me not.

1 *Occasion smiles upon a second leave.*

Favorable circumstances kindly allow me to take a second farewell

2 *sits in the shoulder*

Is at the back

3 *these few precepts in thy memory / Look thou character*

I.e., make sure you inscribe these principles in your memory. Polonius's speech to Laertes would have been familiar to audiences at a time when letters of advice from fathers to sons were published and widely read. Its style is marked by a constant use of maxims, or *sententiae*, concisely formulated rules for behavior that could be transcribed in the commonplace books that schoolboys were taught to keep. Hamlet himself keeps such a book: see 1.5.107.

4 *their adoption tried*

Having tested their suitability for friendship

5 *dull*

Make callous; desensitize

6 *unfledged courage*

Unproven young man (the image is of a baby bird, newly hatched and not yet prepared for flight).

7 *Costly thy habit as thy purse can buy*

Dress as expensively as you can afford

8 *they in France of the best rank and station / Are of a most select and generous chief in that*

I.e., those in France who are of the highest social station are skilled at displaying their nobility through their choice of clothing.

9 *husbandry*

Household economy, compared here to a knife used to pare away excessive spending

10 *season this in thee*

Help this advice take root and ripen in you

Enter **Polonius**.

I stay too long, but here my father comes.
A double blessing is a double grace:
Occasion smiles upon a second leave.[1]

Polonius

Still Yet° here, Laertes? Aboard, aboard, for shame!
The wind sits in the shoulder[2] of your sail,
waited And you are stayed° for. There, my blessing with thee,
And these few precepts in thy memory
Look thou character:[3] give thy thoughts no tongue,
inappropriate / its Nor any unproportioned° thought his° act.
friendly / coarse Be thou familiar° but by no means vulgar.°
Those friends thou hast, and their adoption tried,[4]
Grapple them unto thy soul with hoops of steel,
i.e., handshaking But do not dull[5] thy palm with entertainment°
Of each new-hatched, unfledged courage.[6] Beware
Of entrance to a quarrel, but being in,
Manage Bear° 't that th' opposèd may beware of thee.
Give every man thy ear but few thy voice.
opinion Take each man's censure° but reserve thy judgment.
Costly thy habit as thy purse can buy,[7]
showy fashion But not expressed in fancy°—rich, not gaudy—
For the apparel oft proclaims the man,
And they in France of the best rank and station
Are of a most select and generous chief in that.[8]
Neither a borrower nor a lender be,
For loan oft loses both itself and friend,
And borrowing dulleth th' edge of husbandry.[9]
This above all: to thine own self be true,
And it must follow, as the night the day,
Thou canst not then be false to any man.
Farewell. My blessing season this in thee.[10]

1 *of late*

recently

2 *'tis put on*

It has been suggested to

Laertes

Most humbly do I take my leave, my lord.

Polonius

waiting for you The time invites you. Go. Your servants tend.°

Laertes

Farewell, Ophelia, and remember well
What I have said to you.

Ophelia

'Tis in my memory locked,
And you yourself shall keep the key of it.

Laertes

Farewell. *He exits.*

Polonius

What is 't, Ophelia, he hath said to you?

Ophelia

concerning So please you, something touching° the Lord Hamlet.

Polonius

i.e., Indeed Marry,° well bethought:
'Tis told me he hath very oft of late[1]
Given private time to you, and you yourself
i.e., attention Have of your audience° been most free and bounteous.
If it be so as so 'tis put on[2] me—
And that in way of caution—I must tell you,
your place You do not understand yourself° so clearly
As it behooves my daughter and your honor.
What is between you? Give me up the truth.

Ophelia

offers He hath, my lord, of late made many tenders°
Of his affection to me.

Polonius

inexperienced "Affection?" Pooh, you speak like a green° girl,
Untested Unsifted° in such perilous circumstance.
Do you believe his "tenders," as you call them?

1 *Tender yourself more dearly*

Value yourself more highly

2 *not to crack the wind of the poor phrase, / Running it thus*

I.e., not to ruin the phrase with overuse (as one might make a horse broken winded by riding it too hard)

3 *you'll tender me a fool*

(1) make yourself look foolish in my eyes; (2) make me look foolish; (3) provide me with a grandchild

4 *springes to catch woodcocks*

Snares (*springes* rhymes with "hinges") to trap woodcocks, which were proverbially stupid birds easily caught

5 *scanter of*

Less free with

6 *Set your entreatments at a higher rate / Than a command to parley.*

I.e., value your person more highly than to show up whenever he wants. Polonius employs a military metaphor here, instructing Ophelia not to enter into negotiations (*entreatments*) with Hamlet simply because he calls for a wartime conference (*parley*).

Ophelia

I do not know, my lord, what I should think.

Polonius

Marry, I will teach you. Think yourself a baby
taken That you have ta'en° these tenders for true pay,
genuine currency Which are not sterling.° Tender yourself more dearly,[1]
Or—not to crack the wind of the poor phrase,
Running it thus[2]—you'll tender me a fool.[3]

Ophelia

courted My lord, he hath importuned° me with love
manner In honorable fashion.°

Polonius

flattery Ay, "fashion"° you may call it. Go to, go to.

Ophelia

authority And hath given countenance° to his speech, my lord,
With almost all the holy vows of Heaven.

Polonius

Ay, springes to catch woodcocks.[4] I do know,
lavishly When the blood burns, how prodigal° the soul
Lends the tongue vows. These blazes, daughter,
extinguished Giving more light than heat, extinct° in both
being made Even in their promise as it is a-making,°
You must not take for fire. From this time
Be something scanter of[5] your maiden presence.
Set your entreatments at a higher rate
Than a command to parley.[6] For Lord Hamlet,
concerning Believe so much in° him that he is young
And with a larger tether may he walk
short Than may be given you. In few,° Ophelia,
Do not believe his vows, for they are brokers
Not of that dye which their investments show,

1 *for they are brokers / Not of that dye which their investments show, / But mere implorators of unholy suits, / Breathing like sanctified and pious bonds, / The better to beguile*

I.e., for they are go-betweens, who are not as holy as their clerical vestments imply; rather they are solicitors of sinful actions, speaking as though holy and pious in their commitments in order to trick you.

2 *Come your ways.*

Come along.

But mere implorators of unholy suits,
Breathing like sanctified and pious bonds,
The better to beguile.[1] This is for all:
I would not, in plain terms, from this time forth,
disgrace Have you so slander° any moment's leisure
As to give words or talk with the Lord Hamlet.
Look to 't, I charge you. Come your ways.[2]

Ophelia

I shall obey, my lord. *They exit.*

1 *lacks of*

Is not yet

2 *The King doth wake tonight and takes his rouse, / Keeps wassail and the swaggering upspring reels*

The King stays up drinking tonight, holding a drinking contest and staggering through a drunken dance.

3 *The triumph of his pledge*

The celebration of his promise (see 1.2.125–128)

4 *Ay, marry, is 't.*

Yes, indeed, it is.

5 *More honored in the breach than the observance*

More honored by being broken than in following it

6 *east and west*

I.e., universally (modifies *traduced and taxed* in 1.4.18)

Act 1, Scene 4

Enter **Hamlet**, **Horatio**, *and* **Marcellus**.

Hamlet

harshly The air bites shrewdly;° it is very cold.

Horatio

bitter; sharp It is nipping and an eager° air.

Hamlet

What hour now?

Horatio

I think it lacks of[1] twelve.

Marcellus

No, it is struck.

Horatio

Indeed? I heard it not.
time It then draws near the season°
custom Wherein the spirit held his wont° to walk.

A flourish of trumpets and two pieces [of ordnance] goes off.

What does this mean, my lord?

Hamlet

The King doth wake tonight and takes his rouse,
Keeps wassail and the swaggering upspring reels,[2]
Rhine wine And, as he drains his draughts of Rhenish° down,
The kettle-drum and trumpet thus bray out
The triumph of his pledge.[3]

Horatio

Is it a custom?

Hamlet

Ay, marry, is 't.[4]
But to my mind, though I am native here
tradition And to the manner° born, it is a custom
More honored in the breach than the observance.[5]
This heavy-headed revel east and west[6]

1 *traduced and taxed of*

Misrepresented and censured by

2 *at height*

Excellently

3 *The pith and marrow of our attribute*

The heart and essence of our reputation

4 *By their o'ergrowth of some complexion*

I.e., by the disproportionate increase of one of the humors (the four bodily fluids that, according to Renaissance physiology, controlled a person's physical and emotional nature)

5 *Or by some habit that too much o'erleavens / The form of plausive manners*

Or by one habit that swells so large it ruins their better manners (like bread that has been overly leavened with excessive amounts of yeast)

6 *nature's livery or fortune's star*

I.e., either a natural defect or an accident determined by fate (*livery* meaning "clothing" or "uniform," while *star* is here the object rather than the agent of astrological influence)

7 *His virtues else*

His other virtues

8 *The dram of evil / Doth all the noble substance of a doubt, / To his own scandal.*

The tiny amount of evil obscures all the good in a man, to his shame.

9 *Be thou a spirit of health or goblin damned*

Opinions about the nature of the Ghost have always been divided. Here Hamlet wonders whether the phantom is a good or bad spirit: he has not yet decided for himself whether he will address it as his dead father or whether to trust what it says. At different moments the play seems to regard the Ghost as an omen of Denmark's destruction, a spirit come back from the grave to finish its business on Earth, a soul returned from purgatory to beg our remembrance, or—as Protestant viewers might have preferred—a devil in disguise who would lure the Prince to his death or a mere illusion or brainsick fantasy. This range of possibilities reflects a moment in English history when Catholic traditions (including the doctrine of purgatory: see note to 1.5.9–13), Protestant reforms, and tenacious folk beliefs in spirits and fairies all contended for the hearts and minds of Shakespeare's audience. The fact that scholars have never come to consensus only makes the question of which beliefs are advanced when, and by whom, more fertile and interesting.

10 *blasts*

Violent gusts of wind

Makes us traduced and taxed of[1] other nations.
call They clepe° us drunkards and with swinish phrase
reputation Soil our addition,° and indeed it takes
From our achievements, though performed at height,[2]
The pith and marrow of our attribute.[3]
happens So oft it chances° in particular men
blemish; fault That, for some vicious mole° of nature in them,
parentage As in their birth° (wherein they are not guilty,
its Since nature cannot choose his° origin),
By their o'ergrowth of some complexion[4]
fences Oft breaking down the pales° and forts of reason,
Or by some habit that too much o'erleavens
The form of plausive manners[5]—that these men,
Carrying, I say, the stamp of one defect,
(Being nature's livery or fortune's star[6]),
His virtues else,[7] be they as pure as grace,
sustain As infinite as man may undergo,°
opinion Shall in the general censure° take corruption
From that particular fault. The dram of evil
Doth all the noble substance of a doubt,
To his own scandal.[8]

Enter **Ghost**.

Horatio

Look, my lord, it comes!

Hamlet

Angels and ministers of grace defend us!
salvation / demon Be thou a spirit of health° or goblin° damned,[9]
breezes Bring with thee airs° from Heaven or blasts[10] from Hell,
Be thy intents wicked or charitable,
Thou com'st in such a questionable shape
That I will speak to thee. I'll call thee Hamlet,

1 *glimpses of the moon*

Flickering moonlight

2 *fools of nature*

I.e., mortals (playthings of *nature*)

3 *set my life at a pin's fee*

Consider my life to be worth no more than the cost of a pin (*at a pin's fee* was proverbial for "of little value")

King, father, royal Dane. Oh, answer me!
Let me not burst in ignorance, but tell
consecrated / coffined Why thy canonized° bones, hearsèd° in death,
burial clothes Have burst their cerements;° why the sepulcher,
buried Wherein we saw thee quietly interred,°
Hath oped his ponderous and marble jaws
To cast thee up again. What may this mean,
armor That thou, dead corpse, again in complete steel°
Revisits thus the glimpses of the moon,[1]
Making night hideous, and we fools of nature[2]
mental constitution So horridly to shake our disposition°
With thoughts beyond the reaches of our souls?
Why Say why is this? Wherefore?° What should we do?

[*The* **Ghost**] *beckons.*

Horatio

It beckons you to go away with it,
communication As if it some impartment° did desire
To you alone.

Marcellus

Look with what courteous action
It waves you to a more removèd ground.
But do not go with it.

Horatio

No, by no means.

Hamlet

It will not speak—then I will follow it.

Horatio

Do not, my lord.

Hamlet

Why? What should be the fear?
I do not set my life at a pin's fee,[3]
And for my soul—what can it do to that,
Being a thing immortal as itself?

1 *deprive your sovereignty of reason*

Unseat reason as the ruling power in your mind (although it is hard not to hear this as "deny your Highness your sanity")

2 *toys of desperation*

Thoughts of suicide

3 *As hardy as the Nemean lion's nerve*

As tough as the sinews of the Nemean lion, a ferocious mythical creature killed by Hercules as the first of his twelve labors.

It waves me forth again. I'll follow it.

Horatio

sea What if it tempt you toward the flood,° my lord,
Or to the dreadful summit of the cliff
hangs / its That beetles° o'er his° base into the sea,
And there assume some other horrible form
Which might deprive your sovereignty of reason[1]
And draw you into madness? Think of it:
The very place puts toys of desperation[2]
cause Without more motive° into every brain
That looks so many fathoms to the sea
And hears it roar beneath.

Hamlet

It waves me still. [*to* **Ghost**] Go on. I'll follow thee.

Marcellus

You shall not go, my lord.

Hamlet

Hold off your hands.

Horatio

Be ruled. You shall not go.

Hamlet

My fate cries out
And makes each petty artery in this body
As hardy as the Nemean lion's nerve.[3]
Still am I called.—Unhand me, gentlemen.
hinders By Heaven, I'll make a ghost of him that lets° me.
I say, away!—Go on. I'll follow thee.

Ghost *and* **Hamlet** *exit.*

Horatio

grows He waxes° desperate with imagination.

Marcellus

Let's follow. 'Tis not fit thus to obey him.

1 *it*

refers to the issue ("outcome") in 1.4.89.

Horatio

Let's go / end

Have° after. To what issue° will this come?

Marcellus

Something is rotten in the state of Denmark.

Horatio

Heaven will direct it.[1]

Marcellus

Nay, let's follow him. *They exit.*

1 *My hour*

I.e., dawn (the time when the Ghost must leave the Earth)

2 *sulfurous and tormenting flames*

The flames of purgatory, which in Catholic thought was a place where souls unready to enter Heaven were purged of their remaining sins (see lines 10–13 and note)

3 *lend thy serious hearing*

Listen carefully

4 *days of nature*

Natural life

5 *I am thy father's spirit, / Doomed for a certain term to walk the night / And for the day confined to fast in fires / Till the foul crimes done in my days of nature / Are burned and purged away.*

These lines suggest the Catholic doctrine of purgatory, which holds that the souls of the dead are kept for a time in a middle state where they are scourged for their sins on Earth before completing the voyage either to Heaven or to Hell. The soul's time in purgatory could be hastened by prayers from the living, and when England was a Catholic nation institutions called *chantries* were endowed by the wealthy to sponsor prayers on their behalf after death. The Protestant assault on this practice of remembrance closed down the chantries, but the belief was tenacious (and not only among recusant Catholics) even into the 17th century, seventy years after England's stop-and-start Reformation had begun. These lines are cited by partisans of a "Catholic" ghost, but see note to 1.4.40. Stephen Greenblatt's *Hamlet in Purgatory* is the most thorough discussion; see the For Further Reading section.

6 *harrow up*

Uproot; tear out

Act 1, Scene 5

Enter **Ghost** *and* **Hamlet**.

Hamlet

Whither wilt thou lead me? Speak! I'll go no further.

Ghost

Pay attention to Mark° me.

Hamlet

I will.

Ghost

My hour[1] is almost come
When I to sulfurous and tormenting flames[2]
Must render up myself.

Hamlet

Alas, poor ghost!

Ghost

Pity me not, but lend thy serious hearing[3]
To what I shall unfold.

Hamlet

Speak. I am bound to hear.

Ghost

So art thou to revenge when thou shalt hear.

Hamlet

What?

Ghost

I am thy father's spirit,
Doomed for a certain term to walk the night
do penance And for the day confined to fast° in fires
Till the foul crimes done in my days of nature[4]
Except Are burned and purged away.[5] But° that I am forbid
To tell the secrets of my prison house,
I could a tale unfold whose lightest word
Would harrow up[6] thy soul, freeze thy young blood,

1 *start from their spheres*

I.e., jump from their sockets. The image is from Renaissance astronomy, which held that stars and planets revolved around the Earth in a series of concentrically nested crystalline spheres.

2 *knotted and combinèd locks*

Hair matted and wound together (no longer, in his grief, caring about his appearance)

3 *eternal blazon*

List of supernatural mysteries

4 *Revenge*

The phrase "Hamlet, revenge!" seems to have been a cliché of the theater world long before Shakespeare wrote his *Hamlet*: it was probably famous from the lost *Ur-Hamlet* (see "*Hamlet* on the Early Stage," page 405) and certainly native to the fashion for revenge tragedies in the 1580s. Plays like Thomas Kyd's *The Spanish Tragedy* (which shares many features with *Hamlet*) tell the story of a crime, often the murder of a father or son, and its bloody consequences. Part of the genre's excitement is derived from the equivocal place of revenge in a Christian culture. Revenge had the sanction of ancient works like the plays of the Roman philosopher Seneca, which were models for their Elizabethan imitators, but the New Testament is unequivocal in its disapproval: "Dearly beloved, avenge not yourselves, but give place unto wrath: for it is written, Vengeance is mine; I will repay, saith the Lord" (Romans 12:19).

5 *in the best*

In the best cases

6 *Haste me to know 't*

Quickly inform me of it

7 *duller shouldst thou be than the fat weed / That roots itself in ease on Lethe wharf / Wouldst thou not stir in this*

You would have to be duller than the lazy reed that grows on the banks of the Lethe (the mythological river of forgetfulness) if you are not moved to action by this.

8 *given out*

Announced publicly

9 *forgèd process*

Fabricated story

10 *Rankly abused*

Disgracefully deceived

Make thy two eyes, like stars, start from their spheres,[1]
Thy knotted and combinèd locks[2] to part
And each particular hair to stand on end,
porcupine Like quills upon the fearful porpentine.°
i.e., be delivered But this eternal blazon[3] must not be°
Listen To ears of flesh and blood. List,° list, oh, list
If thou didst ever thy dear father love—

Hamlet

O God!

Ghost

Revenge[4] his foul and most unnatural murder.

Hamlet

Murder?

Ghost

Murder most foul, as in the best[5] it is,
But this most foul, strange, and unnatural.

Hamlet

Haste me to know 't,[6] that I, with wings as swift
thought As meditation° or the thoughts of love,
May sweep to my revenge.

Ghost

I find thee apt,
And duller shouldst thou be than the fat weed
That roots itself in ease on Lethe wharf
Wouldst thou not stir in this.[7] Now, Hamlet, hear:
garden 'Tis given out[8] that, sleeping in my orchard,°
A serpent stung me. So the whole ear of Denmark
Is by a forgèd process[9] of my death
Rankly abused.[10] But know, thou noble youth,
The serpent that did sting thy father's life
Now wears his crown.

Hamlet

O my prophetic soul!

1 *falling off*

Abandonment of devotion (or possibly "decline in standards")

2 *that dignity*

Such worthiness

3 *went hand in hand even with*

Perfectly agreed with

4 *But virtue, as it never will be moved*

But just like virtue, which cannot be shaken

5 *leprous distilment*

Poisonous distillation that causes symptoms like leprosy

6 *natural gates and alleys*

I.e., veins and arteries

7 *possess / And curd*

Take control of and curdle

8 *a most instant tetter barked about, / Most lazar-like*

I.e., instantly a scaly rash covered me like tree bark, as though I were a leper.

My uncle!

Ghost

adulterous Ay, that incestuous, that adulterate° beast,
With witchcraft of his wit, with traitorous gifts—
O wicked wit and gifts, that have the power
So to seduce!—won to his shameful lust
The will of my most seeming-virtuous Queen.
O Hamlet, what a falling off[1] was there
From me, whose love was of that dignity[2]
That it went hand in hand even with[3] the vow
descend I made to her in marriage, and to decline°
Upon a wretch whose natural gifts were poor
Compared with To° those of mine.
But virtue, as it never will be moved,[4]
Though lewdness court it in a shape of Heaven,
So lust, though to a radiant angel linked,
satisfy; satiate Will sate° itself in a celestial bed
And prey on garbage.
But soft! Methinks I scent the morning air.
Brief let me be. Sleeping within my orchard,
My custom always of the afternoon,
Upon my secure hour thy uncle stole
(a poison) With juice of cursed hebona° in a vial,
entrances And in the porches° of my ears did pour
The leprous distilment,[5] whose effect
hatred Holds such an enmity° wi' th' blood of man
mercury That swift as quicksilver° it courses through
The natural gates and alleys[6] of the body,
i.e., the poison And with a sudden vigor it° doth possess
sour And curd,[7] like eager° droppings into milk,
The thin and wholesome blood. So did it mine,
And a most instant tetter barked about,
Most lazar-like,[8] with vile and loathsome crust

1 *Unhouseled, disappointed, unaneled, / No reckoning made, but sent to my account / With all my imperfections on my head*

Without having received the Eucharist, unprepared for death, without being given last rites; I received no absolution and was sent to judgment with my sins unforgiven.

2 *Taint not thy mind, nor let your soul contrive / Against thy mother aught*

Do not let your mind be corrupted, and do not let your soul plot any kind of punishment against your mother

3 *swiftly*

Hamlet asks for immediate help to keep him from collapsing; the Folio prints the simpler "stiffly."

4 *distracted globe*

(1) confused head; (2) disordered world; (3) a reference to the Globe Theatre, where *Hamlet* was first performed.

5 *wipe away all trivial, fond records*

Erase (from the writing tablet, *table*, that Hamlet imagines as his memory) all insignificant and foolish recollections (*trivial* comes from the "trivium" of scholastic university studies, i.e., grammar, rhetoric, and logic, so Hamlet's erasure is not inconsequential).

6 *All saws of books, all forms, all pressures past*

All maxims copied from books, all principles, all past impressions

All my smooth body.
Thus was I, sleeping, by a brother's hand
deprived Of life, of crown, of queen at once dispatched,°
Cut off even in the blossoms of my sin,
Unhouseled, disappointed, unaneled,
judgment No reckoning made, but sent to my account°
With all my imperfections on my head.[1]
Oh, horrible, oh, horrible, most horrible!
natural feeling If thou hast nature° in thee, bear it not.
Let not the royal bed of Denmark be
lust A couch for luxury° and damned incest.
But howsomever thou pursues this act,
Taint not thy mind, nor let thy soul contrive
Against thy mother aught.[2] Leave her to Heaven
And to those thorns that in her bosom lodge
To prick and sting her. Fare thee well at once.
morning The glowworm shows the matin° to be near
begins / ineffectual And 'gins° to pale his uneffectual° fire.
Adieu, adieu, adieu. Remember me. *[He exits.]*

Hamlet

O all you host of Heaven! O Earth! What else?
add And shall I couple° Hell? Oh, fie! Hold, hold, my heart,
immediately And you, my sinews, grow not instant° old
But bear me swiftly[3] up. Remember thee?
Ay, thou poor ghost, whiles memory holds a seat
In this distracted globe.[4] Remember thee!
tablet Yea, from the table° of my memory
I'll wipe away all trivial, fond records,[5]
All saws of books, all forms, all pressures past[6]
That youth and observation copied there,
And thy commandment all alone shall live
Within the book and volume of my brain,
Unmixed with baser matter. Yes, by Heaven!

1 *tables*

Writing tablets, whether an ordinary paper book or perhaps one with erasable leaves. This is Hamlet the student, trained to pick out useful sayings and transcribe them in his commonplace book for meditation and reuse. Here there may be something slightly ridiculous, or frantic, or self-parodying about the gesture, momentarily reducing the Ghost's refrain "Remember me!" to the trivial motto, "one may smile, and smile, and be a villain" (line 108). See the note on Polonius's maxims at 1.3.58.

2 *Illo*

Like *Hillo* in line 118, this is a call, a variant of "hallo."

3 *bird*

Hamlet mockingly compares Marcellus's call to the cry of a falconer summoning his bird back to his fist.

wicked O most pernicious° woman!
O villain, villain, smiling, damnèd villain!
Fitting / write My tables![1]—Meet° it is I set° it down
That one may smile, and smile, and be a villain—
At least I am sure it may be so in Denmark.
watchword So, uncle, there you are. Now to my word.°
It is "Adieu, adieu. Remember me."
I have sworn 't.

Enter **Horatio** *and* **Marcellus**.

Horatio

My lord, my lord!

Marcellus

Lord Hamlet—

Horatio

Heavens secure him!

Hamlet

So be it.

Horatio

Illo,[2] ho, ho, my lord!

Hamlet

Hillo, ho, ho, boy. Come, bird,[3] come.

Marcellus

How is 't, my noble lord?

Horatio

What news, my lord?

Hamlet

Oh, wonderful!

Horatio

Good my lord, tell it.

Hamlet

No. You will reveal it.

1 *But he's*

Who isn't

2 *Saint Patrick*

Believed to guard the entrance to purgatory (where souls must remain until they have atoned for their sins and are prepared for Heaven)

Horatio

Not I, my lord, by Heaven.

Marcellus

Nor I, my lord.

Hamlet

ever How say you, then? Would heart of man once° think it?
But you'll be secret?

Both

Ay, by Heaven.

Hamlet

There's never a villain dwelling in all Denmark
thorough But he's[1] an arrant° knave.

Horatio

to come There needs no ghost, my lord, come° from the grave
To tell us this.

Hamlet

Why, right; you are in the right.
discussion And so, without more circumstance° at all,
I hold it fit that we shake hands and part.
You, as your business and desire shall point you—
For every man hath business and desire,
Such as it is—and for my own poor part,
I will go pray.

Horatio

These are but wild and whirling words, my lord.

Hamlet

I'm sorry they offend you, heartily.
Yes faith, heartily.

Horatio

There's no offense, my lord.

Hamlet

Yes, by Saint Patrick,[2] but there is, Horatio,
concerning And much offense too, touching° this vision here.

1 *O'ermaster 't*

Control it (i.e., *your desire to know*)

2 *not I*

I.e., I will not tell it

3 *Upon my sword.*

Oaths were frequently sworn on swords because the crossguard and blade form a cross.

4 *cellarage*

Cellar. Probably a reference to the empty space underneath the Globe stage, known as *Hell* (conceptually paired with the rafters above the stage, known as *Heaven* or the *heavens*).

well-intentioned It is an honest° ghost, that let me tell you.
For your desire to know what is between us,
O'ermaster 't[1] as you may.—And now, good friends,
As you are friends, scholars, and soldiers,
Give me one poor request.

Horatio

What is 't, my lord? We will.

Hamlet

Never make known what you have seen tonight.

Both

My lord, we will not.

Hamlet

Nay, but swear 't.

Horatio

In faith, my lord, not I.[2]

Marcellus

Nor I, my lord, in faith.

Hamlet

Upon my sword.[3]

Marcellus

We have sworn, my lord, already.

Hamlet

Indeed, upon my sword, indeed.

Ghost

(*cries under the stage*) Swear!

Hamlet

trusty fellow Ha, ha, boy! Say 'st thou so? Art thou there, truepenny?°
—Come on, you hear this fellow in the cellarage.[4]
Consent to swear.

Horatio

Propose the oath, my lord.

Hamlet

Never to speak of this that you have seen.

1 Hic et ubique

Here and everywhere (Latin)

2 *pioneer*

Trench digger

3 *as a stranger give it welcome*

Show it the hospitality due to a guest

4 *your philosophy*

Probably not referring to Horatio's specific philosophic belief, but rather used in a colloquial sense to mean philosophy in general.

5 *put an antic disposition on*

Adopt the appearance and behavior of a madman

6 *an if*

If

7 *There be an if they might*

I.e., there are those who might speak if they could

8 *giving out*

Expression; pronouncement

9 *So grace and mercy at your most need help you*

I.e., exactly as you look for grace and mercy to help you in your times of greatest need

Swear by my sword.

Ghost

[*below*] Swear.

Hamlet

location *Hic et ubique?*[1] Then we'll shift our ground.°
—Come hither, gentlemen, and lay your hands
Again upon my sword. Swear by my sword
Never to speak of this that you have heard.

Ghost

[*below*] Swear by his sword.

Hamlet

Well said, old mole! Canst work i' th' earth so fast?
move yourselves A worthy pioneer![2]—Once more remove,° good friends.

Horatio

O day and night, but this is wondrous strange!

Hamlet

And therefore as a stranger give it welcome.[3]
There are more things in Heaven and Earth, Horatio,
Than are dreamt of in your philosophy.[4] But come.
Here, as before: never, so help you mercy,
whatsoever How strange or odd some'er° I bear myself
i.e., it useful (As I perchance hereafter shall think meet°
To put an antic disposition on),[5]
That you, at such times seeing me, never shall—
folded With arms encumbered° thus, or this headshake,
ambiguous Or by pronouncing of some doubtful° phrase,
As "Well, well, we know," or "We could an if[6] we would,"
wished Or "If we list° to speak," or "There be an if they might,"[7]
Or such ambiguous giving out[8]—to note
anything That you know aught° of me. This do swear,
So grace and mercy at your most need help you.[9]

1 *out of joint*

Dislocated; disordered

Ghost

[*below*] Swear!

Hamlet

Rest, rest, perturbèd spirit!—So, gentlemen,
With all my love I do commend me to you,
And what so poor a man as Hamlet is
friendliness May do t' express his love and friending° to you,
God willing, shall not lack. Let us go in together,
always And still° your fingers on your lips, I pray.
The time is out of joint.[1] O cursèd spite,
That ever I was born to set it right!
Nay, come; let's go together. *They exit.*

1 [**Reynaldo**]

The stage direction in Q2 reads "his man or two," perhaps suggesting that Shakespeare was unsure as he wrote about the precise staging, though the scene as written demands only one "man," Reynaldo.

2 *encompassment and drift of question*

I.e., roundabout and indirect method of asking

3 *come you more nearer / Than your particular demands will touch it*

I.e., you will get closer to the truth about Laertes than you would by asking direct questions

4 *Take you*

Pretend that you have

5 *put on him*

Ascribe to him

Act 2, Scene 1

Enter old **Polonius** *with his man* [**Reynaldo**].[1]

Polonius

messages Give him this money and these notes,° Reynaldo.

Reynaldo

I will, my lord.

Polonius

very You shall do marvelous° wisely, good Reynaldo,
inquiries Before you visit him, to make inquire°
Of his behavior.

Reynaldo

My lord, I did intend it.

Polonius

Marry, well said, very well said. Look you, sir,
for me / Danes Inquire me° first what Danskers° are in Paris,
income / stay And how, and who, what means,° and where they keep,°
What company, at what expense; and finding
By this encompassment and drift of question[2]
That they do know my son, come you more nearer
Than your particular demands will touch it.[3]
Take you,[4] as 'twere, some distant knowledge of him,
As thus: "I know his father and his friends,
And, in part, him." Do you mark this, Reynaldo?

Reynaldo

Ay, very well, my lord.

Polonius

"And in part him, but," you may say, "not well.
But, if 't be he I mean, he's very wild.
Addicted so and so—" And there put on him[5]
false stories / foul What forgeries° you please. Marry, none so rank°
care As may dishonor him—take heed° of that—

1 *usual slips / As are companions noted and most known / To youth and liberty*

Common flaws that are well known to exist in those who are young and able to do as they please

2 *as you may season it in the charge*

I.e., for you can mitigate the harmful effects of this slander through careful presentation

3 *open to incontinency*

Inclined to sexual excess

4 *taints of liberty*

Faults that result from independence

5 *A savageness in unreclaimèd blood, / Of general assault*

I.e., a wildness in unchecked will, to which all youths are subject

6 *fetch of wit*

Clever scheme

7 *a little soiled with working*

I.e., like a cloth made slightly dirty as it is used

8 *party in converse*

Partner in conversation

failings But, sir, such wanton, wild, and usual slips°
As are companions noted and most known
To youth and liberty.[1]

Reynaldo

gambling As gaming,° my lord?

Polonius

Ay, or drinking, fencing, swearing,
whoring Quarreling, drabbing°—you may go so far.

Reynaldo

My lord, that would dishonor him!

Polonius

'Faith, no, as you may season it in the charge.[2]
You must not put another scandal on him,
That he is open to incontinency.[3]
speak of That's not my meaning. But breathe° his faults so
subtly quaintly°
That they may seem the taints of liberty,[4]
The flash and outbreak of a fiery mind,
A savageness in unreclaimèd blood,
Of general assault.[5]

Reynaldo

But, my good lord—

Polonius

Why Wherefore° should you do this?

Reynaldo

Ay, my lord. I would know that.

Polonius

Marry, sir, here's my drift,
And I believe it is a fetch of wit:[6]
criticisms You, laying these slight sallies° on my son
As 'twere a thing a little soiled with working[7]—
question; sound out Mark you, your party in converse[8] (him you would sound°)

1 *Having ever seen in the prenominate crimes / The youth you breathe of guilty, be assured / He closes with you in this consequence*

I.e., if he has ever seen the young man that you speak about (i.e., Laertes) commit the aforesaid wrongs, be assured he will confirm your suspicions as follows

2 *o'ertook in 's rouse*

Overcome with drink (i.e., drunk)

3 *falling out at*

Quarreling over

4 *Your bait of falsehood take this carp of truth*

By telling small lies (about Laertes), you will be able to obtain the truth (about Laertes' behavior, as a fisherman uses tiny pieces of *bait* to catch the larger *carp*).

5 *assays of bias*

Tests that pursue an indirect route to reach their goal (like a weighted bowling ball that rolls along a curved line, or *bias*, to come to its target)

Having ever seen in the prenominate crimes
The youth you breathe of guilty, be assured
agrees He closes° with you in this consequence:[1]
"Good sir" or so, or "Friend," or "Gentleman,"
manner of address According to the phrase or the addition°
Of man and country.

Reynaldo

Very good, my lord.

Polonius

he And then, sir, does 'a° this, 'a does—What was I about to say? By the mass, I was about to say something. Where did I leave?

Reynaldo

At "closes in the consequence."

Polonius

At "closes in the consequence." Ay, marry.
He closes thus: "I know the gentleman;
I saw him yesterday"—or "th' other day,"
Or then, or then, with such or such—"and, as you say,
There was 'a gaming, there o'ertook in 's rouse,[2]
There falling out at[3] tennis," or, perchance,
"I saw him enter such a house of sale"—
Namely (Latin) *Videlicet*,° a brothel, or so forth. See you now,
Your bait of falsehood take this carp of truth,[4]
comprehension And thus do we of wisdom and of reach,°
roundabout paths With windlasses° and with assays of bias,[5]
real tendencies By indirections find directions° out;
So by my former lecture and advice
understand Shall you my son. You have° me, have you not?

Reynaldo

My lord, I have.

1 *Ungartered, and down-gyvèd to his ankle*

Without his garters, and with his stockings around his ankles like a prisoner's chains (*gyves*)

Polonius

i.e., be with God by° ye. Fare you well.

Reynaldo

Good my lord.

Polonius

for Observe his inclination in° yourself.

Reynaldo

I shall, my lord.

Polonius

practice And let him ply° his music.

Reynaldo

Well, my lord.

Polonius

Farewell. **Reynaldo** *exits.*

Enter **Ophelia**.

How now, Ophelia? What's the matter?

Ophelia

O my lord, my lord, I have been so affrighted!

Polonius

With what, i' th' name of God?

Ophelia

private chamber My lord, as I was sewing in my closet,°
jacket / unfastened Lord Hamlet, with his doublet° all unbraced,°
dirtied No hat upon his head, his stockings fouled,°
Ungartered, and down-gyvèd to his ankle,[1]
Pale as his shirt, his knees knocking each other,
expression And with a look so piteous in purport°
released As if he had been loosèd° out of Hell
To speak of horrors—he comes before me.

1 *As 'a*

As if he

2 *a little shaking of mine arm*

Giving my arm a small shake

3 *bended their light*

Directed their gaze

4 *Whose violent property fordoes itself*

Whose tendency to violence results in its own ruin

Polonius

Mad for thy love?

Ophelia

My lord, I do not know,
But truly, I do fear it.

Polonius

What said he?

Ophelia

He took me by the wrist and held me hard;
Then goes he to the length of all his arm,
And, with his other hand thus o'er his brow,
He falls to such perusal° of my face *[scrutiny]*
As 'a[1] would draw it. Long stayed he so.
At last, a little shaking of mine arm,[2]
And thrice his head thus waving° up and down, *[moving]*
He raised a sigh so piteous and profound
As it did seem to shatter all his bulk° *[i.e., body]*
And end his being. That done, he lets me go,
And, with his head over his shoulder turned,
He seemed to find his way without his eyes,
For out o' doors he went without their helps,
And to the last bended their light[3] on me.

Polonius

Come; go with me. I will go seek the King.
This is the very ecstasy° of love, *[madness]*
Whose violent property fordoes itself[4]
And leads the will to desperate undertakings
As oft as any passions under Heaven
That does afflict our natures. I am sorry.
What, have you given him any hard words of late?

Ophelia

No, my good lord, but as you did command
I did repel his letters and denied

1 *beshrew my jealousy*

Curse my suspiciousness

2 *it is as proper to our age / To cast beyond ourselves in our opinions*

I.e., it is as characteristic of old men to misinterpret (like old dogs that can no longer properly *cast*, or follow the scent of a trail)

3 *might move / More grief to hide than hate to utter love*

Might cause more distress to hide this love than anger (either from Hamlet for having his secret revealed, or from Claudius who may not approve of the match) in revealing it

4 *Come.*

Three times at the end of this scene Polonius tells her to come with him to the King, but neither in Q2 nor the Folio does she appear in the following scene.

His access to me.

Polonius

That hath made him mad.
attention I am sorry that with better heed° and judgment
observed I had not quoted° him. I feared he did but trifle
ruin And meant to wrack° thee—But beshrew my jealousy![1]
By Heaven, it is as proper to our age
To cast beyond ourselves in our opinions[2]
As it is common for the younger sort
To lack discretion. Come; go we to the King.
secret This must be known, which, being kept close,° might move
More grief to hide than hate to utter love.[3]
Come.[4] *They exit.*

1 *Sith nor*

Since neither

2 *of so young days*

Since your youth

3 *sith so neighbored to his youth and 'havior*

Since you are so familiar with his youth and usual behavior

4 *vouchsafe your rest*

Consent to stay

5 *lies within our remedy*

Can be remedied by us

6 *the supply and profit of our hope*

The help and advancement of our desire (i.e., for information about Hamlet's condition)

Act 2, Scene 2

Flourish. Enter King [**Claudius**] *and Queen* [**Gertrude**], **Rosencrantz** *and* **Guildenstern** [*, and other attendants*].

Claudius

Welcome, dear Rosencrantz and Guildenstern.
Besides Moreover° that we much did long to see you,
The need we have to use you did provoke
summons Our hasty sending.° Something have you heard
Of Hamlet's "transformation"—so call it
Sith nor[1] th' exterior nor the inward man
Resembles that it was. What it should be,
Other More° than his father's death, that thus hath put him
So much from th' understanding of himself,
I cannot dream of. I entreat you both
That, being of so young days[2] brought up with him
And sith so neighbored to his youth and 'havior,[3]
That you vouchsafe your rest[4] here in our court
Some little time, so by your companies
To draw him on to pleasures and to gather,
opportunity So much as from occasion° you may glean,
anything Whether aught° to us unknown afflicts him thus
revealed That, opened,° lies within our remedy.[5]

Gertrude

Good gentlemen, he hath much talked of you,
And sure I am two men there is not living
is attached to To whom he more adheres.° If it will please you
generosity To show us so much gentry° and good will
As to expend your time with us awhile
For the supply and profit of our hope,[6]
Your visitation shall receive such thanks
As fits a king's remembrance.

1 *Put your dread pleasures more into command / Than to entreaty*

Command us to execute your reverend desires rather than request us to do so

2 *in the full bent*

Completely (literally used to describe a bow that is fully drawn)

Rosencrantz

Both your Majesties
over Might, by the sovereign power you have of° us,
Put your dread pleasures more into command
Than to entreaty.[1]

Guildenstern

But we both obey
And here give up ourselves, in the full bent,[2]
To lay our service freely at your feet
To be commanded.

Claudius

Thanks, Rosencrantz and gentle Guildenstern.

Gertrude

Thanks, Guildenstern and gentle Rosencrantz,
And I beseech you instantly to visit
My too much changèd son.—Go, some of you,
And bring these gentlemen where Hamlet is.

Guildenstern

actions Heavens make our presence and our practices°
Pleasant and helpful to him!

Gertrude

Ay, amen!

Rosencrantz *and* **Guildenstern** *exit* [*, with attendants*].

Enter **Polonius**.

Polonius

Th' ambassadors from Norway, my good lord,
Are joyfully returned.

Claudius

always Thou still° hast been the father of good news.

Polonius

Have I, my lord? I assure my good liege,

1 *I hold my duty as I hold my soul, / Both to my God and to my gracious King.*

I consider my duty to God and my King to be as important as my soul.

2 *Hunts not the trail of policy so sure*

Does not so reliably follow the path of cunning

3 *I doubt it is no other but the main*

I fear it is nothing other than the obvious cause.

4 *sift him*

Examine him (i.e., Polonius) closely

5 *Upon our first*

When we first brought up the issue

6 *better looked into*

More carefully examined

I hold my duty as I hold my soul,
Both to my God and to my gracious King.[1]
And I do think—or else this brain of mine
Hunts not the trail of policy so sure[2]
As it hath used to do—that I have found
true The very° cause of Hamlet's lunacy.

Claudius

Oh, speak of that. That do I long to hear.

Polonius

Give first admittance to th' ambassadors.
dessert My news shall be the fruit° to that great feast.

Claudius

honor Thyself do grace° to them and bring them in.

[**Polonius** *exits*].

He tells me, my dear Gertrude, he hath found
origin The head° and source of all your son's distemper.

Gertrude

I doubt it is no other but the main:[3]
His father's death and our hasty marriage.

Enter [**Polonius** *with the*] *ambassadors,* [**Voltemand** *and* **Cornelius**].

Claudius

Well, we shall sift him.[4]—Welcome, my good friends!
Say, Voltemand, what from our brother Norway?

Voltemand

Most fair return of greetings and desires.
Upon our first,[5] he sent out to suppress
His nephew's levies, which to him appeared
King of Poland To be a preparation 'gainst the Polack,°
But, better looked into,[6] he truly found
It was against your Highness. Whereat, grieved

1 *Was falsely borne in hand*

Was taken advantage of

2 *arrests / On Fortinbras*

Orders that young Fortinbras cease his preparations

3 *give th' assay of arms*

Mount an attack

4 *three score thousand crowns in annual fee*

Sixty thousand crowns in annual payment (it is a very large sum of money, and the Folio's "three thousand" may be correct)

5 *such regards of safety and allowance*

Such terms guaranteeing the safety of Denmark and granting Fortinbras permission

6 *at our more considered time*

When we have more time for thought

weakness That so his sickness, age, and impotence°
Was falsely borne in hand,[1] sends out arrests
On Fortinbras,[2] which he, in brief, obeys,
conclusion Receives rebuke from Norway, and, in fine,°
Makes vow before his uncle never more
To give th' assay of arms[3] against your Majesty.
Whereon old Norway, overcome with joy,
Gives him three score thousand crowns in annual fee[4]
And his commission to employ those soldiers,
So levied as before, against the Polack,
With an entreaty—herein further shown —

[*gives* **Claudius** *a letter*]

passage That it might please you to give quiet pass°
Through your dominions for this enterprise,
On such regards of safety and allowance[5]
As therein are set down.

Claudius

pleases It likes° us well,
And at our more considered time[6] we'll read,
Answer, and think upon this business.
Meantime we thank you for your well-took labor.
Go to your rest. At night we'll feast together;
Most welcome home!

[**Voltemand** *and* **Cornelius**] *exit.*

Polonius

This business is well ended.
consider My liege and madam, to expostulate°
What majesty should be, what duty is,
Why day is day, night night, and time is time,
Were nothing but to waste night, day, and time.
Therefore, since brevity is the soul of wit
ornaments And tediousness the limbs and outward flourishes,°
I will be brief: your noble son is mad.

1 *More matter, with less art.*

(Give us) more substance with fewer artful turns of speech.

2 *For this effect defective comes by cause*

I.e., for the result is a defect (Hamlet's madness), which comes from the cause

3 *while she is mine*

I.e., until she marries

4 *gather and surmise*

Put this together and draw your conclusion

5 *I will be faithful*

I.e., I will read out the letter's contents exactly.

6 *But never doubt I love*

The final line of the poem seems to promise certainty with regard to Hamlet's feelings, but due to the multiple meanings of the word *doubt* the sentiment is ambiguous. One may *doubt* (question) the classical astronomical beliefs that the stars are made of fire and that the sun revolves around the Earth, or one may *doubt* (suspect) that truth is actually a liar. Thus, Hamlet may mean that (1) Ophelia should never disbelieve the truth of his love for her; or that (2) Ophelia should not imagine that Hamlet loves her.

7 *I am ill at these numbers*

(1) I am incompetent at writing metrical verse; (2) I am lovesick while writing these lines

8 *reckon my groans*

(1) count my sighs; (2) convert my sighs into verse

Mad call I it, for, to define true madness,
What is 't but to be nothing else but mad?
But let that go.

Gertrude

More matter, with less art.[1]

Polonius

Madam, I swear I use no art at all.
That he 's mad, 'tis true. Tis true, 'tis pity,
figure of speech And pity 'tis 'tis true—a foolish figure,°
to it But farewell it,° for I will use no art.
Mad let us grant him then; and now remains
That we find out the cause of this effect,
disability Or rather say, the cause of this defect,°
For this effect defective comes by cause.[2]
Consider Thus it remains, and the remainder thus. Perpend:°
I have a daughter—have while she is mine[3]—
notice Who in her duty and obedience, mark,°
Hath given me this. Now gather and surmise.[4]
[*reads*] "To the celestial and my soul's idol, the most beautified Ophelia"—That's an ill phrase, a vile phrase; "beautified" is a vile phrase. But you shall hear. Thus: "In her excellent white bosom, these" etc.—

Gertrude

Came this from Hamlet to her?

Polonius

wait Good madam, stay° a while; I will be faithful.[5]
[*reads*] "Doubt thou the stars are fire,
Doubt that the sun doth move,
Doubt truth to be a liar,
But never doubt I love.[6]
O dear Ophelia, I am ill at these numbers.[7] I have not art to reckon my groans,[8] but that I love thee best, oh, most best, believe it. Adieu. Thine evermore, most dear lady

1 *whilst this machine is to him*

While this physical frame, the body, belongs to him (i.e., while he is alive)

2 *fell out*

Happened

3 *If I had played the desk or table-book, / Or given my heart a winking, mute and dumb, / Or looked upon this love with idle sight*

I.e., if I had acted as a go-between for them, or made my heart shut its eyes and remain silent about these events, or looked upon this love without realizing its importance. (To *play the desk or table-book* means "to serve as a means of communication between the two of them.")

4 *out of thy star*

Above your social station

5 *lock herself from his resort*

Prohibit him from visiting her

6 *took the fruits of*

I.e., obeyed

whilst this machine is to him,[1] Hamlet."
This in obedience hath my daughter shown me,
And, more about, hath his solicitings,
As they fell out[2] by time, by means, and place,
All given to mine ear.

Claudius

                                        But how hath she
Received his love?

Polonius

                                    What do you think of me?

Claudius

As of a man faithful and honorable.

Polonius

gladly I would fain° prove so; but what might you think,
When I had seen this hot love on the wing—
As I perceived it, I must tell you that,
Before my daughter told me—what might you,
Or my dear Majesty your Queen here, think,
If I had played the desk or table-book,
Or given my heart a winking, mute and dumb,
Or looked upon this love with idle sight?[3]
quickly What might you think? No, I went round° to work,
address And my young mistress thus I did bespeak:°
"Lord Hamlet is a prince out of thy star;[4]
instructions This must not be." And then I prescripts° gave her,
That she should lock herself from his resort,[5]
Admit no messengers, receive no tokens;
Which done, she took the fruits of[6] my advice;
And he, repelled—a short tale to make—
Fell into a sadness, then into a fast,
sleeplessness Thence to a watch,° thence into a weakness,
headedness / decline Thence to a lightness,° and, by this declension,°
Into the madness wherein now he raves,

1 *Take this from this*

Polonius probably gestures first to his head and then his shoulders; the implication being that if he is wrong, Claudius should have him beheaded (or, less melodramatically, he may point to some sign of office that might be removed from his person).

2 *assistant for a state*

Government official

of us And all we° mourn for.

Claudius

Do you think this?

Gertrude

It may be, very like.

Polonius

Hath there been such a time—I would fain know that—
That I have positively said, "'Tis so,"
When it proved otherwise?

Claudius

Not that I know.

Polonius

Take this from this[1] if this be otherwise.
If circumstances lead me, I will find
Where truth is hid, though it were hid indeed
center of the Earth Within the center.°

Claudius

test How may we try° it further?

Polonius

at a time You know sometimes he walks four hours together°
Here in the lobby.

Gertrude

So he does indeed.

Polonius

let loose At such a time I'll loose° my daughter to him.
tapestry Be you and I behind an arras° then;
Mark the encounter. If he love her not
on that account And be not from his reason fall'n thereon,°
Let me be no assistant for a state[2]
wagon drivers But keep a farm and carters.°

Claudius

We will try it.

1 *board him presently*

I.e., address him immediately

2 *give me leave*

Excuse me

3 *God-'a'-mercy*

God have mercy on you (a conventional response to a greeting)

4 *fishmonger*

Editors have argued whether *fishmonger* might be slang for "flesh peddlar," but there is little convincing evidence of this. Hamlet seems to be deliberately taunting the self-important Polonius with the erroneous identification, under the cover of Hamlet's feigned madness.

5 *good kissing carrion*

Flesh good for kissing. It was a common belief in Shakespeare's time that the sun, shining on a corpse or other dead matter, would breed maggots. *Carrion* has the meaning "carcass," but can also be used to refer contemptuously to living flesh, particularly when engaged in sinful behavior.

Enter **Hamlet** [*reading a book*].

Gertrude

seriously But look where sadly° the poor wretch comes reading.

Polonius

Away, I do beseech you, both away.
I'll board him presently.[1] Oh, give me leave.[2]

[**Claudius** *and* **Gertrude**] *exit.*

How does my good Lord Hamlet?

Hamlet

Well, God-'a'-mercy.[3]

Polonius

Do you know me, my lord?

Hamlet

Excellent well. You are a fishmonger.[4]

Polonius

Not I, my lord.

Hamlet

Then I would you were so honest a man.

Polonius

Honest, my lord?

Hamlet

Ay, sir. To be honest, as this world goes, is to be one man picked out of ten thousand.

Polonius

That's very true, my lord.

Hamlet

For if the sun breed maggots in a dead dog, being a good kissing carrion[5]—Have you a daughter?

Polonius

I have, my lord.

1 *walk i' th' sun*

Hamlet suggests not only that the sun may *breed maggots* (line 178) but also that the sun (or son) may cause her to breed.

2 *Conception*

(1) thinking; (2) pregnancy

3 *Between who?*

Hamlet takes Polonius's question about the *matter* (i.e., content of the book) to mean "What is the point of contention?"

4 *purging thick amber*

Discharging thick resin

5 *walk out of the air*

Go indoors (fresh air was believed to be dangerous for those who were ill)

Hamlet

Let her not walk i' th' sun.[1] Conception[2] is a blessing, but, as your daughter may conceive—friend, look to 't.

Polonius

[*aside*] How say you by that? Still harping on my daughter. Yet he knew me not at first; 'a° said I was a fishmonger. 'A is far gone; and, truly, in my youth I suffered much extremity° for love, very near this. I'll speak to him again.—What do you read, my lord?

he
distress

Hamlet

Words, words, words.

Polonius

What is the matter, my lord?

Hamlet

Between who?[3]

Polonius

I mean the matter that you read, my lord.

Hamlet

Slanders, sir; for the satirical rogue says here that old men have gray beards, that their faces are wrinkled, their eyes purging thick amber[4] and plum-tree gum, and that they have a plentiful lack of wit together with most weak hams°—all which, sir, though I most powerfully and potently believe, yet I hold it not honesty° to have it thus set° down, for yourself, sir, shall grow old as I am—if, like a crab, you could go backward.

thighs
decent / written

Polonius

[*aside*] Though this be madness, yet there is method in 't.—Will you walk out of the air,[5] my lord?

Hamlet

Into my grave.

1 *a happiness that often madness hits on, which reason and sanity could not so prosperously be delivered of*

A relevance that sometimes madmen fortuitously express, which reasonable, sane men cannot achieve as effectively. *Be delivered of* (give birth to) continues the metaphor begun by Hamlet's references to *conception* and Polonius's own use of *pregnant*.

2 *and my daughter*

The Folio is much more precise about Polonius's thinking here: "I will leave him and suddenly contrive the means of meeting / Between him and my daughter." Perhaps Q2 accidently omitted the words between *and* and *my*, or it may be evidence of an earlier stage of Shakespeare's thinking about the meeting.

3 *As the indifferent children of the Earth.*

As ordinary mortals

Polonius

pertinent Indeed, that's out of the air. [*aside*] How pregnant° sometimes his replies are, a happiness that often madness hits on, which reason and sanity could not so prosperously be delivered of.[1] I will leave him and my daughter.[2] —My lord, I will take my leave of you.

Hamlet

with You cannot take from me anything that I will more willingly part withal°—except my life, except my life, except my life.

Enter **Guildenstern** *and* **Rosencrantz**.

Polonius

Fare you well, my lord.

Hamlet

These tedious old fools!

Polonius

[*to* **Rosencrantz** *and* **Guildenstern**] You go to seek the Lord Hamlet? There he is.

Rosencrantz

God save you, sir! [**Polonius** *exits.*]

Guildenstern

My honored lord!

Rosencrantz

My most dear lord!

Hamlet

My excellent good friends! How dost thou, Guildenstern? Ah, Rosencrantz! Good lads, how do you both?

Rosencrantz

As the indifferent children of the Earth.[3]

1 *very button*

Highest point (like the *button* on the top of a hat)

2 *privates*

Punning on multiple meanings: intimate friends; private citizens; genitalia

3 *secret parts*

Genitalia (and the sexual joking continues in calling fortune *a strumpet*, i.e., a prostitute).

4 *But your news is not true.*

The Folio text follows with 27 lines not in the Quarto; see page 389.

5 *beaten way*

Well-worn track. Hamlet wants to be serious now instead of continuing their joking.

6 *make you*

Are you doing

7 *too dear*

Not worth

Guildenstern

Fortunate Happy° in that we are not over happy. On Fortune's cap we are not the very button.[1]

Hamlet

Nor the soles of her shoe?

Rosencrantz

Neither, my lord.

Hamlet

Then you live about her waist, or in the middle of her favors?

Guildenstern

Faith, her privates[2] we.

Hamlet

In the secret parts[3] of Fortune? Oh, most true: she is a strumpet. What news?

Rosencrantz

None, my lord, but the world's grown honest.

Hamlet

Then is doomsday near. But your news is not true.[4] But in the beaten way[5] of friendship, what make you[6] at Elsinore?

Rosencrantz

To visit you, my lord; no other occasion.

Hamlet

voluntary truthfully Beggar that I am, I am even poor in thanks; but I thank you, and sure, dear friends, my thanks are too dear[7] a halfpenny. Were you not sent for? Is it your own inclining? Is it a free° visitation? Come, come, deal justly° with me. Come, come. Nay, speak.

Guildenstern

What should we say, my lord?

1 *your modesties have not craft enough to color*

I.e., you, in your basic decency, are not cunning enough to disguise

2 *by what more dear a better proposer can charge you withal*

By whatever more compelling claims that someone better than I at proposing oaths could impose on you

3 *hold not off*

Do not refrain (from telling me)

4 *So shall my anticipation prevent your discovery, and your secrecy to the King and Queen molt no feather.*

I.e., thus my speaking first will keep you from revealing your secret, and your vow of secrecy to the King and Queen will remain intact (literally, "won't have to shed its feathers.")

5 *forgone all custom of exercises*

Abandoned all my usual pursuits

6 *it goes so heavily with my disposition*

I.e., my mood is so melancholic

7 *fretted with golden fire*

Adorned with bright lights (i.e., the stars); the account of the sky, would also, for the audience at the Globe, suggest the decorated roof over the stage called "Heaven" or "the heavens."

Hamlet

Anything but to th' purpose: you were sent for, and there is a kind of confession in your looks which your modesties have not craft enough to color.[1] I know the good King and Queen have sent for you.

Rosencrantz

To what end, my lord?

Hamlet

request
harmony
straightforward

That you must teach me. But let me conjure° you, by the rights of our fellowship, by the consonancy° of our youth, by the obligation of our ever-preserved love, and by what more dear a better proposer can charge you withal:[2] be even° and direct with me whether you were sent for or no.

Rosencrantz

What say you?

Hamlet

on

Nay, then, I have an eye of° you. If you love me, hold not off.[3]

Guildenstern

My lord, we were sent for.

Hamlet

why
structure
sky
gathering

I will tell you why. So shall my anticipation prevent your discovery, and your secrecy to the King and Queen molt no feather.[4] I have of late—but wherefore° I know not—lost all my mirth, forgone all custom of exercises,[5] and, indeed, it goes so heavily with my disposition[6] that this goodly frame,° the Earth, seems to me a sterile promontory; this most excellent canopy, the air—look you, this brave o'erhanging firmament,° this majestical roof fretted with golden fire[7]—why, it appeareth nothing to me but a foul and pestilent congregation° of vapors. What a piece of work is a man:

1 *quintessence of dust*

In classical and medieval philosophy, *quintessence* was the superior, heavenly fifth element (in addition to the material earth, air, fire, and water) latent in all earthly things. Any object could conceivably be refined to its quintessence, or most intrinsic, elemental quality. The book of Genesis describes how God initially formed humans out of dust (2.7), so Hamlet scornfully calls humanity "dust at its dustiest," or "the most perfect example of dust."

2 *Lenten entertainment*

Poor welcome. The season of Lent is a time of penance and fasting in the Christian church, and during the Renaissance, London theaters were closed for its duration.

3 *foil and target*

Sword and shield

4 *the humorous man shall end his part in peace*

The eccentric character will be able to speak his part without interruption.

5 *the lady shall say her mind freely, or the blank verse shall halt for 't*

The female character will not be interrupted, or she will lose the rhythm of the verse.

6 *their inhibition comes by the means of the late innovation*

I.e., their prohibition is because of the recent unrest. In Renaissance England, theaters were closed at the death of a monarch or a prince and at times of significant political turmoil.

capabilities how noble in reason, how infinite in faculties;° in *well framed* form and moving how express° and admirable; in *understanding* action how like an angel; in apprehension° how like a god—the beauty of the world, the paragon of animals! And yet, to me, what is this quintessence of dust?[1] Man delights not me—nor women neither, though by your smiling you seem to say so.

Rosencrantz

My lord, there was no such stuff in my thoughts.

Hamlet

Why did ye laugh then, when I said "man delights not me"?

Rosencrantz

To think, my lord, if you delight not in man, what *actors* Lenten entertainment[2] the players° shall receive from *passed* you. We coted° them on the way, and hither are they coming to offer you service.

Hamlet

He that plays the king shall be welcome; his majesty *from* shall have tribute on° me. The adventurous knight shall *for free* use his foil and target,[3] the lover shall not sigh gratis,° the humorous man shall end his part in peace,[4] and the lady shall say her mind freely, or the blank verse shall halt for 't.[5] What players are they?

Rosencrantz

accustomed Even those you were wont° to take such delight in: the tragedians of the city.

Hamlet

i.e., in the city How chances it they travel? Their residence,° both in reputation and profit, was better both ways.

Rosencrantz

I think their inhibition comes by the means of the late innovation.[6]

1 *No, indeed are they not.*

The Folio text has 23 additional lines following line 302 in which Rosencrantz explains that it is because of competition from the children's acting companies; see page 393.

2 *picture in little*

Miniature portrait

3 *Your hands, come then.*

Here, Hamlet shakes Rosencrantz's and Guildenstern's hands.

4 *Let me comply with you in this garb, lest my extent to the players—which, I tell you, must show fairly outwards—should more appear like entertainment than yours.*

I.e., let me greet you in this fashion (i.e., by shaking hands), so that my extension of welcome to the players—which must appear very courteous—does not seem to be a more gracious reception than I give to you.

5 *north-north-west*

I.e., only occasionally (when the wind is blowing in the right direction)

6 *I know a hawk from a handsaw*

I.e., I can differentiate between things that are not at all alike (a proverbial expression); a warning to Rosencrantz and Guildenstern that Hamlet can distinguish friend from foe

Hamlet

esteem

Do they hold the same estimation° they did when I was in the city? Are they so followed?

Rosencrantz

No, indeed are they not.[1]

Hamlet

mocking faces

God's blood (an oath)

It is not very strange. For my uncle is King of Denmark, and those that would make mouths° at him while my father lived give twenty, forty, fifty, a hundred ducats apiece for his picture in little.[2] 'Sblood,° there is something in this more than natural, if philosophy could find it out.

A flourish [of trumpets].

Guildenstern

There are the players.

Hamlet

roper accompaniment

exchange greetings

welcome

Gentlemen, you are welcome to Elsinore.—Your hands, come then.[3] Th' appurtenance° of welcome is fashion and ceremony. Let me comply° with you in this garb, lest my extent° to the players—which, I tell you, must show fairly outwards—should more appear like entertainment than yours.[4] You are welcome, but my uncle-father and aunt-mother are deceived.

Guildenstern

In what, my dear lord?

Hamlet

I am but mad north-north-west.[5] When the wind is southerly, I know a hawk from a handsaw.[6]

Enter **Polonius**.

Polonius

Well be with you, gentlemen.

1 *Roscius*

A famous Roman actor from the first century B.C.

2 *Buzz, buzz.*

An expression of contempt, here intended for a messenger who brings outdated news

3 *scene individable*

Either (1) a play with no breaks during its performance; or (2) a play that observes the classical unities of action, time, and place (i.e., the narrative features a single, central storyline; the events in the play take place over a period of time roughly equivalent to that of the play itself; the stage represents a single physical space, and the location does not shift drastically between scenes)

4 *poem unlimited*

A dramatic poem not bound by classical rules

5 *Seneca*

Famous Roman tragedian, c. 3 B.C.–A.D. 65

6 *Plautus*

Famous Roman comedic playwright, c. 254–184 B.C.

7 *For the law of writ and the liberty*

I.e., for both plays that follow the classical rules and plays that do not

8 *O Jephthah, judge of Israel, what a treasure hadst thou!*

Hamlet quotes a ballad popular in England at the time, "Jephthah Judge of Israel," which tells the story of the Old Testament father whose rash vow costs him his daughter's life (Judges 11:21–40). Ballads and allusions to ballads are frequent in the play; see also 3.2.267 and Ophelia's songs in her madness (beginning at 4.5.22). They are a point of contact between the Prince and the popular culture of his day, and hence a way of unnerving his aristocratic companions (as Claudius will later observe at 4.3.4, Hamlet is "loved of the distracted multitude"). Like all quotations, these ballads can also be a way of saying things without having to take full responsibility for them: hence they are common to expressions of political dissent and to madness.

Hamlet

Hark you, Guildenstern, and you too—at each ear a hearer. That great baby you see there is not yet out of his swaddling-clouts.° *clothes*

Rosencrantz

Haply° *Perhaps* he is the second time come to them, for they say an old man is twice a child.

Hamlet

[*aside to* **Rosencrantz** *and* **Guildenstern**] I will prophesy he comes to tell me of the players. Mark it.—You say right, sir. O' Monday morning, 'twas then indeed.

Polonius

My lord, I have news to tell you.

Hamlet

My lord, I have news to tell you. When Roscius[1] was an actor in Rome—

Polonius

The actors are come hither, my lord.

Hamlet

Buzz, buzz.[2]

Polonius

Upon my honor—

Hamlet

Then came each actor on his ass—

Polonius

The best actors in the world, either for tragedy, comedy, history, pastoral, pastoral-comical, historical-pastoral, scene individable,[3] or poem unlimited.[4] Seneca[5] cannot be too heavy, nor Plautus[6] too light. For the law of writ and the liberty,[7] these are the only men.

Hamlet

O Jephthah, judge of Israel, what a treasure hadst thou![8]

1 *that follows not*

I.e., your claim that you love your daughter does not logically follow my having called you Jephthah (since Jephthah, in Judges 11, sacrifices his daughter to keep his vow to God that he would sacrifice the first thing he saw on his return home if he was victorious against the Ammonites).

2 *The first row of the pious chanson will show you more, for look where my abridgement comes*

You will have to look to the rest of the opening stanza of this holy ballad to learn more, for look, I am about to be cut off (i.e., by the players; *abridgement* could also mean "entertainment".)

3 *my young lady and mistress*

Addressed to the boy actor who played the women's roles

4 *By 'r Lady*

I.e., by Our Lady (i.e., the Virgin Mary); a mild oath

5 *your Ladyship is nearer to Heaven than when I saw you last, by the altitude of a chopine*

I.e., you are taller than when I last saw you, by the length of a high platform shoe

Polonius

What a treasure had he, my lord?

Hamlet

Why, [*sings*] One fair daughter and no more,
exceedingly The which he lovèd passing° well.

Polonius

[*aside*] Still on my daughter.

Hamlet

Am I not i' th' right, old Jephthah?

Polonius

If you call me Jephthah, my lord; I have a daughter that I love passing well.

Hamlet

Nay, that follows not.[1]

Polonius

What follows, then, my lord?

Hamlet

Why,
chance / knows [*sings*] As by lot,° God wot°—
and then, you know,
[*sings*] It came to pass, as most like it was—
The first row of the pious chanson will show you more,
for look where my abridgement comes.[2]

Enter the **Players**.

fringed (i.e., bearded) *defy* You are welcome, masters; welcome, all! I am glad to see thee well. Welcome, good friends.—Oh, old friend, why, thy face is valenced° since I saw thee last. Com'st thou to beard° me in Denmark?—What, my young lady and mistress![3] By 'r Lady,[4] your Ladyship is nearer to Heaven than when I saw you last, by the altitude of a chopine.[5] Pray God your voice, like a piece of

1 *uncurrent gold*

A gold coin was rendered uncurrent (i.e., no longer certified as legal tender) if a crack extended from the coin edge through the circle that surrounded the monarch's image. Hamlet hopes that the boy actor's voice has not yet broken, which would prohibit him from playing the women's parts.

2 *e'en to 't*

Get to work

3 *French falconers*

The French were considered experts at training falcons that would enthusiastically pursue any kind of prey.

4 *'twas caviary to the general*

I.e., it was too rich for the taste of the masses.

5 *cried in the top of*

Excelled

6 *sallets*

Salads (i.e., mixture of ingredients)

7 *more handsome than fine*

I.e., well crafted rather than gaudy

8 *Aeneas' talk to Dido*

In Book 2 of Virgil's Latin epic *The Aeneid*, the Trojan hero Aeneas comes to Queen Dido's court at Carthage and tells her about the fall of Troy and the death of King Priam.

9 *"The rugged Pyrrhus, . . .*

The speech Hamlet recites (lines 2.2.381–395) is in a higher style than the dialogue around it: note the complicated syntax (we wait three lines for the main verb, *Hath . . . smeared*), the frequent doubling of adjectives (*dread and black, Baked and impasted, tyrannous and damnèd*), and the penchant for Latinate words (*complexion, coagulate*). Scholars have argued about the effect: is Hamlet parodying the stiff diction of an older generation? Or is the speech meant to have a kind of epic grandeur that rises above the latter-day intrigues of the play? Certainly it is carefully fitted to the play around it, narrating an episode from the fall of Troy that features the death of a father, the grief of a mother, and a violent young man who briefly stays his hand, then lets it fall.

10 *Hyrcanian beast*

Tiger from Hyrcania on the Caspian Sea; *Hyrcanian* tigers were renowned for their ferocity.

11 *the ominous horse*

I.e., the Trojan horse. Greek soldiers entered the city of Troy by hiding in a massive, hollow, horse-shaped statue, which the Trojans were led to believe had been left behind by the departing Greek fleet.

12 *Hath now his dread and black complexion smeared / With heraldry more dismal*

I.e, has now painted his already frightening and dark appearance with more dire heraldic colors (i.e., blood)

13 *total gules*

Wholly red

uncurrent gold,[1] be not cracked within the ring.
—Masters, you are all welcome. We'll e'en to 't[2] like
French falconers:[3] fly at anything we see. We'll have a
at once / talent speech straight.° Come; give us a taste of your quality.°
Come, a passionate speech.

Player

What speech, my good lord?

Hamlet

I heard thee speak me a speech once, but it was never
more than acted, or, if it was, not above° once, for the play, I
remember, pleased not the million; 'twas caviary to the
general.[4] But it was—as I received it, and others,
whose judgments in such matters cried in the top of[5]
organized mine—an excellent play, well digested° in the scenes,
decorum set down with as much modesty° as cunning. I remember one said there were no sallets[6] in the lines to make
acceptable the matter savory,° nor no matter in the phrase that
might indict the author of affectation, but called it
straightforward an honest° method, as wholesome as sweet, and by
very much more handsome than fine.[7] One speech in 't
I chiefly loved. 'Twas Aeneas' talk to Dido[8] and there-
about of it, especially when he speaks of Priam's
slaughter. If it live in your memory, begin at this line—
Let me see, let me see—
"The rugged Pyrrhus,[9] like th' Hyrcanian beast[10]—"
'Tis not so. It begins with Pyrrhus—
black "The rugged Pyrrhus, he whose sable° arms,
Black as his purpose, did the night resemble
hidden When he lay couchèd° in th' ominous horse,[11]
Hath now this dread and black complexion smeared
With heraldry more dismal[12] head to foot.
marked Now is he total gules,[13] horridly tricked°
With blood of fathers, mothers, daughters, sons,

1 *Baked and impasted with the parching streets*

I.e., cooked and encrusted by (the heat and smoke from) the burning houses

2 *o'ersizèd*

Covered with *size*, a viscous substance used to prepare canvases for paint

3 *carbuncles*

Red jewels believed to glow in the dark

4 *Repugnant to command*

Resisting his order

5 *senseless Ilium, / Seeming to feel this blow, with flaming top / Stoops to his base, and with a hideous crash / Takes prisoner Pyrrhus' ear.*

The inanimate citadel seems itself to respond to the attack (on Priam), toppling in flames, and with a terrible noise captures Pyrrhus's attention.

6 *as a painted tyrant*

Unmoving, like a painting of a tyrant

7 *like a neutral to his will and matter*

I.e., like one who is unable to act in spite of his desire and provocation

8 *Cyclops' hammers*

In classical mythology, the Cyclopses were three one-eyed giants who worked as armorers for the gods.

Baked and impasted with the parching streets[1]
That lend a tyrannous and a damnèd light
To their lord's murder. Roasted in wrath and fire,
And thus o'ersizèd[2] with coagulate° gore, *congealed*
With eyes like carbuncles,[3] the hellish Pyrrhus
Old grandsire Priam seeks."
So, proceed you.

Polonius

'Fore God, my lord, well spoken, with good accent and good discretion.° *understanding*

Player

"Anon° he° finds him, *Soon / i.e., Priam*
Striking too short° at Greeks. His antique sword, *i.e., ineffectually*
Rebellious to his arm, lies where it falls,
Repugnant to command.[4] Unequal matched,
Pyrrhus at Priam drives, in rage strikes wide,
But with the whiff and wind of his fell° sword *cruel*
Th' unnerved° father falls. Then senseless Ilium, *strengthless*
Seeming to feel this blow, with flaming top
Stoops to his° base, and with a hideous crash *its*
Takes prisoner Pyrrhus' ear.[5] For, lo, his sword,
Which was declining° on the milky° head *descending / white*
Of reverend Priam, seemed i' th' air to stick.
So as a painted tyrant[6] Pyrrhus stood,
And, like a neutral to his will and matter,[7]
Did nothing.
But as we often see against° some storm *before*
A silence in the heavens, the rack° stand still, *high clouds*
The bold winds speechless, and the orb° below *i.e., Earth*
As hush as death, anon the dreadful thunder
Doth rend the region,° so, after Pyrrhus' pause, *sky*
A rousèd vengeance sets him new a-work,
And never did the Cyclops' hammers[8] fall

1 *Mars's*

Belonging to the Roman god of war (two syllables)

2 *forged for proof eterne*

I.e., made to be permanently invulnerable

3 *fellies*

Curved sections of a wheel rim

4 *her wheel*

Fortune was commonly depicted as a woman turning a wheel, which controlled the lives of mortals by raising up some and lowering others.

5 *bowl the round nave*

I.e., roll the central part of the wheel

6 *It shall to the barber's*

I.e., it will be cut shorter

7 *jig*

Lively, comic entertainment, usually including a dance (often performed as a short piece following a tragedy)

8 *bisson rheum*

blinding tears

9 *lank and all o'erteemèd*

Withered and worn out by childbearing (according to legend, Hecuba had at least seventeen children)

On Mars's[1] armor, forged for proof eterne,[2]
With less remorse than Pyrrhus' bleeding sword
Now falls on Priam.
Out, out, thou strumpet Fortune! All you gods
assembly In general synod° take away her power,
Break all the spokes and fellies[3] from her wheel,[4]
And bowl the round nave[5] down the hill of Heaven
As low as to the fiends!"

Polonius

This is too long.

Hamlet

Polonius is / lewdness It shall to the barber's,[6] with your beard.—Prithee, say on. He's° for a jig[7] or a tale of bawdry,° or he sleeps. Say on. Come to Hecuba.

Player

veiled "But who, ah woe, had seen the moblèd° Queen—"

Hamlet

"The moblèd Queen"?

Polonius

That's good.

Player

"Run barefoot up and down, threatening the flames
cloth With bisson rheum,[8] a clout° upon that head
recently / crown Where late° the diadem° stood, and, for a robe,
About her lank and all o'erteemèd[9] loins,
A blanket, in the alarm of fear caught up—
i.e., Anyone who Who° this had seen, with tongue in venom steeped,
power 'Gainst fortune's state° would treason have pronounced.
But if the gods themselves did see her then,
When she saw Pyrrhus make malicious sport
In mincing with his sword her husband's limbs,
The instant burst of clamor that she made,
(Unless things mortal move them not at all)

1 *the burning eyes of Heaven*

I.e., the heavenly bodies (sun, moon, stars, and planets)

2 *made . . . passion*

Aroused strong emotion

3 *Look where*

See whether

4 *turned his color*

Changed his complexion (i.e., gone pale)

5 *God's bodkin*

By God's dear body (an oath)

6 *for need*

If necessary

i.e., teary Would have made milch° the burning eyes of Heaven[1]
And passion[2] in the gods."

Polonius

Look where[3] he has not turned his color[4] and has
tears in 's eyes.—Prithee, no more.

Hamlet

'Tis well. I'll have thee speak out the rest of this soon.—Good
lodged my lord, will you see the players well bestowed?° Do
treated you hear; let them be well used,° for they are the
summary abstract° and brief chronicles of the time. After your
death you were better have a bad epitaph than their ill
report while you live.

Polonius

deserving My lord, I will use them according to their desert.°

Hamlet

according to God's bodkin,[5] man, much better! Use every man after°
his desert, and who shall 'scape whipping? Use them
after your own honor and dignity. The less they deserve
kindness the more merit is in your bounty.° Take them in.

Polonius

Come, sirs.

Hamlet

Follow him, friends. We'll hear a play tomorrow.
[**Polonius** *and three players start to exit.*]—Dost thou hear
me, old friend? Can you play *The Murder of Gonzago*?

Player

Ay, my lord.

Hamlet

have We'll ha° 't tomorrow night. You could, for need,[6]
study a speech of some dozen or sixteen lines which I
would set down and insert in 't, could you not?

Player

Ay, my lord.

1 *Could force his soul so to his own conceit / That from her working all the visage wanned*

I.e., could make his soul so completely embrace his fictional situation that his face grew pale

2 *distraction in his aspect*

Mental disorder in his appearance

3 *his whole function suiting / With forms to his conceit*

I.e., everything about him reflecting his imagined situation

4 *that*

I.e., that strong cause; the Folio text prints "the cue," and many editors follow it.

5 *peak / Like John-a-dreams, unpregnant of my cause*

Lay around, like an idle dreamer, not moved to action by the provocation before me

6 *damned defeat*

Overthrow deserving of damnation

Hamlet

Very well. Follow that lord, and look you mock him not. [*to the* **Players**] My good friends, I'll leave you till night. You are welcome to Elsinore.

Polonius *and* **Players** *exit.*

Rosencrantz

Good my lord.

[**Rosencrantz and Guildenstern**] *exit.*

Hamlet

Ay, so. Good-bye to you.—Now I am alone.
Oh, what a rogue and peasant slave am I!
Is it not monstrous that this player here,
Merely But° in a fiction, in a dream of passion,
Could force his soul so to his own conceit
That from her working all the visage wanned,[1]
Tears in his eyes, distraction in his aspect,[2]
A broken voice, and his whole function suiting
With forms to his conceit?[3] And all for nothing—
For Hecuba!
What's Hecuba to him, or he to her
That he should weep for her? What would he do
Had he the motive and that[4] for passion
That I have? He would drown the stage with tears
iversal / frightening And cleave the general° ear with horrid° speech,
innocent Make mad the guilty and appall the free,°
overwhelm Confound the ignorant, and amaze° indeed
The very faculties of eyes and ears. Yet I,
weak-spirited A dull and muddy-mettled° rascal, peak
Like John-a-dreams, unpregnant of my cause,[5]
And can say nothing—no, not for a king,
sovereignty Upon whose property° and most dear life
A damned defeat[6] was made. Am I a coward?

1 *gives me the lie i' th' throat / As deep as to the lungs*

I.e., calls me an inveterate liar (*As deep as to the lungs* is an intensifier.)

2 *pigeon-livered and lack gall*

I.e., cowardly. It was thought that pigeons had a gentle nature because their livers did not excrete *gall*, which supposedly produces anger.

3 *region kites*

Birds of prey in the sky

4 *stallion*

I.e., a male prostitute. The Folio prints "scullion," a kitchen servant, and many editors follow.

5 *tent him to the quick*

Probe his most vital parts

head Who calls me villain, breaks my pate° across,
Plucks off my beard and blows it in my face,
Tweaks me by the nose, gives me the lie i' th' throat
As deep as to the lungs?[1] Who does me this?
By God's wounds Ha! 'Swounds,° I should take it, for it cannot be
But I am pigeon-livered and lack gall[2]
To make oppression bitter, or ere this
I should ha' fatted all the region kites[3]
entrails With this slave's offal.° Bloody, bawdy villain!
unnatural Remorseless, treacherous, lecherous, kindless° villain!
excellent (sarcastic) Why, what an ass am I! This is most brave,°
That I, the son of a dear father murdered,
Prompted to my revenge by Heaven and Hell,
Must, like a whore, unpack my heart with words
whore And fall a-cursing like a very drab,°
A stallion![4] Fie upon 't, foh!
Get to work About,° my brains!—Hum, I have heard
That guilty creatures sitting at a play
artfulness Have, by the very cunning° of the scene,
immediately Been struck so to the soul that presently°
evil deeds They have proclaimed their malefactions,°
For murder, though it have no tongue, will speak
With most miraculous organ. I'll have these players
Play something like the murder of my father
Before mine uncle. I'll observe his looks.
flinch I'll tent him to the quick,[5] If 'a do blench,°
I know my course. The spirit that I have seen
May be a devil, and the devil hath power
T' assume a pleasing shape. Yea, and perhaps,
Out of my weakness and my melancholy,

1 *As he is very potent with such spirits, / Abuses me to damn me*

I.e., since he (the devil) has a great power over such melancholic states of mind, he might deceive me in order that I might be damned (for killing an innocent man).

As he is very potent with such spirits,
Abuses me to damn me.[1] I'll have grounds
More relative° than this. The play's the thing
Wherein I'll catch the conscience of the King. *He exits.*

substantial; pertinent

1 *drift of conference*

Steering of the conversation

2 *puts on this confusion*

Assumes the appearance of madness

3 *Grating so harshly all his days of quiet*

I.e., disrupting the quietness of his life

4 *distracted*

Mentally disturbed

5 *forward to be sounded*

Eager to be examined

6 *with much forcing of his disposition*

I.e., with a forced cheerfulness

7 *Niggard of question*

Reluctant to ask us questions

8 *assay him / To*

encourage him to try

Act 3, Scene 1

Enter King [**Claudius**], *Queen* [**Gertrude**], **Polonius, Ophelia, Rosencrantz, Guildenstern**, *Lords.*

Claudius

And can you by no drift of conference[1]
Get from him why he puts on this confusion,[2]
Grating so harshly all his days of quiet[3]
With turbulent and dangerous lunacy?

Rosencrantz

He does confess he feels himself distracted,[4]
he But from what cause 'a° will by no means speak.

Guildenstern

Nor do we find him forward to be sounded,[5]
feigned But with a crafty° madness keeps aloof
When we would bring him on to some confession
Of his true state.

Gertrude

Did he receive you well?

Rosencrantz

Most like a gentleman.

Guildenstern

But with much forcing of his disposition.[6]

Rosencrantz

Niggard of question,[7] but of our demands
forthcoming Most free° in his reply.

Gertrude

Did you assay him
To[8] any pastime?

Rosencrantz

Madam, it so fell out that certain players
overtook We o'erraught° on the way. Of these we told him,
And there did seem in him a kind of joy

1 *give him a further edge*

Encourage him further

2 *And gather by him, as he is behaved*

And learn from his behavior

To hear of it. They are here about the court,
And, as I think, they have already order°
This night to play before him.

i.e., a commission

Polonius

'Tis most true,
And he beseeched me to entreat your Majesties
To hear and see the matter.

Claudius

With all my heart, and it doth much content me
To hear him so inclined.
—Good gentlemen, give him a further edge[1]
And drive his purpose on to these delights.

Rosencrantz

We shall, my lord.

Rosencrantz *and* **Guildenstern** *exit* [*, with lords*].

Claudius

Sweet Gertrude, leave us too,
For we have closely° sent for Hamlet hither,
That he, as 'twere by accident, may here
Affront° Ophelia. Her father and myself,
We'll so bestow ourselves that, seeing unseen,
We may of their encounter frankly judge,
And gather by him, as he is behaved,[2]
If 't be th' affliction of his love or no
That thus he suffers for.

privately

Meet face to face

Gertrude

I shall obey you.
And for your part, Ophelia, I do wish
That your good beauties be the happy cause
Of Hamlet's wildness. So shall I hope your virtues
Will bring him to his wonted° way again
To both your honors.

normal; accustomed

1 *Read on this book / That show of such an exercise may color / Your loneliness.*

I.e., read this book (probably a prayer book) so that you have an excuse for being alone.

2 *'Tis too much proved*

It is too often shown

3 *devotion's visage*

The pretense of faith

4 *sugar o'er*

Sugarcoat; hide beneath false appearances

5 *The harlot's cheek, beautied with plast'ring art, / Is not more ugly to the thing that helps it / Than is my deed to my most painted word.*

Claudius compares the surface of a prostitute's face, covered with cosmetics, to the lies that cover and conceal his own deeds, claiming that the difference between her natural face and her falsified image is no greater than the difference between his deceptive public façade and his vile actions (that made him king).

6 *And, by opposing, end them*

And, by confronting those troubles, end their influence—Hamlet sees the alternative to enduring (to *suffer*) his present situation as the active confrontation of it, but in imagining his opponent as a *sea*, he admits that this course will not end in his victory but his death.

7 *To die, to sleep— / No more*

I.e., death is nothing worse than sleep

8 *natural shocks*

I.e., diseases and physical vulnerabilities

Ophelia

Madam, I wish it may. [**Gertrude** *exits.*]

Polonius

r Grace (i.e., Claudius) Ophelia, walk you here. —Gracious,° so please you,
We will bestow ourselves. —Read on this book
That show of such an exercise may color
Your loneliness.[1]—We are oft to blame in this;
'Tis too much proved,[2] that with devotion's visage[3]
And pious action we do sugar o'er[4]
The devil himself.

Claudius

Oh, 'tis too true!
stinging [*aside*] How smart° a lash that speech doth give my conscience!
The harlot's cheek, beautied with plast'ring art,
Is not more ugly to the thing that helps it
Than is my deed to my most painted word.[5]
O heavy burden!

Polonius

I hear him coming. Withdraw, my lord.

[**Claudius** *and* **Polonius** *hide.*]

Enter **Hamlet**.

Hamlet

To be, or not to be? That is the question—
endure Whether 'tis nobler in the mind to suffer°
The slings and arrows of outrageous fortune,
Or to take arms against a sea of troubles
And, by opposing, end them.[6] To die, to sleep—
No more[7]—and by a sleep to say we end
The heartache and the thousand natural shocks[8]
end That flesh is heir to. 'Tis a consummation°

1 *rub*

Obstacle (a term from the game of bowls, denoting any impediment that prevents the bowl from following its normal course)

2 *shuffled off this mortal coil*

(1) cast off this mortal flesh; (2) extricated ourselves from the turmoil of life

3 *makes calamity of so long life*

I.e., Allows adversity to be so long lived (instead of being terminated with the suicide of the sufferer)

4 *despised*

The Folio prints "dispriz'd" (undervalued)

5 *the spurns / That patient merit of th' unworthy takes*

The contempt that deserving people must patiently endure from less worthy persons

6 *When he himself might his quietus make / With a bare bodkin*

When he might settle his account (from the legal term *quietus est*, "laid to rest") with an unsheathed dagger (i.e., by killing himself)

7 *conscience*

Knowledge of right and wrong (though Hamlet is thinking more about punishment than morality)

8 *native hue*

Natural color (i.e., red)

9 *sicklied o'er with the pale cast of thought*

Unhealthily covered with the ashen tint of contemplation

10 *pitch and moment*

Scope and importance. The Folio prints "pith" for the Quarto's *pitch*.

11 *regard*

Consideration; *this regard* may either specifically refer to Hamlet's consideration of the problem he sees or merely mean "on this account"

12 *Soft you now*

Be quiet

13 *for this many a day*

This long time (i.e., since I last saw you)

Devoutly to be wished. To die, to sleep—
To sleep, perchance to dream—ay, there's the rub,[1]
For in that sleep of death what dreams may come
When we have shuffled off this mortal coil[2]
consideration Must give us pause. There's the respect°
That makes calamity of so long life.[3]
For who would bear the whips and scorns of time,
insult Th' oppressor's wrong, the proud man's contumely,°
The pangs of despised[4] love, the law's delay,
i.e., bureaucracy The insolence of office,° and the spurns
That patient merit of th' unworthy takes,[5]
When he himself might his quietus make
burdens With a bare bodkin?[6] Who would fardels° bear,
To grunt and sweat under a weary life,
But that the dread of something after death,
border The undiscovered country from whose bourn°
bewilders No traveler returns, puzzles° the will
And makes us rather bear those ills we have
Than fly to others that we know not of?
Thus conscience[7] does make cowards of us all,
And thus the native hue[8] of resolution
Is sicklied o'er with the pale cast of thought,[9]
And enterprises of great pitch and moment[10]
With this regard[11] their currents turn awry
And lose the name of action. Soft you now,[12]
prayers The fair Ophelia! [*to* **Ophelia**] Nymph, in thy orisons°
Be all my sins remembered.

Ophelia

Good my lord,
How does your honor for this many a day?[13]

Hamlet

I humbly thank you. Well.

1 *you should admit no discourse to your beauty*

I.e., you should allow your virtue no conversation with your beauty (although it could mean: "you should not allow those attracted to your beauty access to it"; but this is not how Ophelia understands it).

2 *commerce*

Interaction (though Hamlet seizes on its familiar economic sense)

3 *the power of beauty will sooner transform honesty from what it is to a bawd than the force of honesty can translate beauty into his likeness*

I.e., the force of beauty will transform a chaste woman into a prostitute more quickly than the appeal of chastity can remake a beautiful woman in its own image.

4 *the time gives it proof*

The current age proves it true

Ophelia

love tokens My lord, I have remembrances° of yours
That I have longèd long to redeliver.
I pray you now receive them.

Hamlet

anything No, not I. I never gave you aught.°

Ophelia

My honored lord, you know right well you did,
And, with them, words of so sweet breath composed
As made these things more rich. Their perfume lost,
Take these again, for to the noble mind
grow Rich gifts wax° poor when givers prove unkind.
There, my lord.

Hamlet

truthful; chaste Ha, ha! Are you honest?°

Ophelia

My lord?

Hamlet

Are you fair?

Ophelia

What means your lordship?

Hamlet

That if you be honest and fair, you should admit no discourse to your beauty.[1]

Ophelia

Could beauty, my lord, have better commerce[2] than with honesty?

Hamlet

Ay, truly, for the power of beauty will sooner transform honesty from what it is to a bawd than the force of honesty can translate beauty into his° (*its*) likeness.[3] This was sometime° (*formerly*) a paradox, but now the time gives it proof.[4] I did love you once.

1 *virtue cannot so inoculate our old stock but we shall relish of it*

I.e., virtue, when it is grafted (like a bud or branch) onto our inherently corrupt human nature, cannot completely remove the traces of our original nature

2 *indifferent honest*

Reasonably virtuous

3 *Where's your father?*

This line is often played as the moment when Hamlet realizes that Polonius is spying on him and Ophelia: perhaps because Ophelia's manner or a stray glance gives it away, perhaps because the old man coughs, or perhaps because Hamlet, in his fury, suddenly assumes it must be so.

4 *monsters*

I.e., cuckolds (men whose wives are unfaithful, commonly depicted with bull-like horns)

Ophelia

Indeed, my lord, you made me believe so.

Hamlet

You should not have believed me, for virtue cannot so inoculate our old stock but we shall relish of it.[1] I loved you not.

Ophelia

I was the more deceived.

Hamlet

Get thee to a nunnery.° Why wouldst thou be a breeder of sinners? I am myself indifferent honest,[2] but yet I could accuse me of such things that it were better my mother had not borne me. I am very proud, revengeful, ambitious, with more offences at my beck° than I have thoughts to put them in, imagination to give them shape, or time to act them in. What should such fellows as I do crawling between Earth and Heaven? We are arrant° knaves. Believe none of us. Go thy ways to a nunnery. Where's your father?[3]

convent

command

absolute

Ophelia

At home, my lord.

Hamlet

Let the doors be shut upon him, that he may play the fool nowhere but in 's own house. Farewell.

Ophelia

Oh, help him, you sweet heavens!

Hamlet

If thou dost marry, I'll give thee this plague for thy dowry: be thou as chaste as ice, as pure as snow, thou shalt not escape calumny.° Get thee to a nunnery. Farewell, or, if thou wilt needs marry, marry a fool, for wise men know well enough what monsters[4] you° make of them. To a nunnery go, and quickly too. Farewell.

slander

i.e., you women

1 *You jig and amble, and you lisp; you nick-name God's creatures and make your wan-tonness your ignorance.*

You dance and strut about, and you speak affectedly; you call creatures by suggestive names (see 4.7.167–168), and you use ignorance as the excuse for this provocative behavior.

2 *The courtier's, soldier's, scholar's eye, tongue, sword*

The ideal prince would simultaneously embody these three roles; Ophelia claims that, before he succumbed to madness, Hamlet epitomized the courtier's *eye* (aesthetic discernment), the soldier's *sword* (military prowess), and the scholar's *tongue* (rhetorical eloquence). His present mental disorder is perhaps glanced at in the disorder of the qualities in the line.

3 *expectation and rose of the fair state*

I.e., the hope and promise of the nation

4 *The glass of fashion and the mold of form*

The mirror of style and the model of conduct

5 *th' observed of all observers*

I.e., the object of every courtier's attention

6 *time*

Rhythm. The Folio prints "tune."

7 *Blasted with ecstasy*

Blighted with madness

8 Enter King [**Claudius**] and **Polonius**

Q2 prints this as an entry direction, although technically they have never exited, merely hidden themselves at line 54 and now move forward.

Ophelia

Heavenly powers, restore him!

Hamlet

plications of cosmetics I have heard of your paintings° well enough: God has
given you one face, and you make yourselves another.
You jig and amble, and you lisp; you nickname God's
creatures and make your wantonness your
of ignorance.[1] Go to, I'll no more on° 't. It hath made me
mad. I say we will have no more marriage. Those that
i.e., Claudius are married already, all but one,° shall live. The rest
shall keep as they are. To a nunnery, go. *He exits.*

Ophelia

Oh, what a noble mind is here o'erthrown!
The courtier's, soldier's, scholar's eye, tongue,
sword,[2]
Th' expectation and rose of the fair state,[3]
The glass of fashion and the mold of form,[4]
Th' observed of all observers,[5] quite, quite down!
And I, of ladies most deject and wretched,
sweetly spoken That sucked the honey of his musicked° vows,
Now see what noble and most sovereign reason
Like sweet bells jangled, out of time[6] and harsh;
blossoming That unmatched form and stature of blown° youth
Blasted with ecstasy.[7] Oh, woe is me,
T' have seen what I have seen, see what I see!

Enter King [**Claudius**] *and* **Polonius**.[8]

Claudius

emotions Love? His affections° do not that way tend;
Nor what he spake, though it lacked form a little,
Was not like madness. There's something in his soul
O'er which his melancholy sits on brood,

1 *There's something in his soul / O'er which his melancholy sits on brood, / And I do doubt the hatch and the disclose / Will be some danger*

Like a bird brooding on an egg, Hamlet's moody behavior conceals and incubates something in his soul that I fear will prove dangerous upon its emergence.

2 *set it down*

Resolved

3 *tribute*

Money paid by one country to another, usually as a sign of its submission. See 5.2.39.

4 *variable objects*

Different sights (i.e., change of scene)

5 *still beating*

Constantly focusing

6 *puts him thus / From fashion of himself*

I.e., divides him from his normal behavior

7 *in the ear*

Within hearing

8 *If she find him not*

I.e., if she is unable to find out his secret

And I do doubt the hatch and the disclose
Will be some danger[1]—which, for to prevent,
I have in quick determination
go to Thus set it down:[2] he shall with speed to° England
For the demand of our neglected tribute.[3]
Perhaps Haply° the seas and countries different
With variable objects[4] shall expel
nearly obsessive This something-settled° matter in his heart,
Whereon his brains still beating[5] puts him thus
From fashion of himself.[6] What think you on 't?

Polonius

It shall do well. But yet do I believe
The origin and commencement of his grief
unrequited Sprung from neglected° love.—How now, Ophelia?
You need not tell us what Lord Hamlet said;
We heard it all.—My lord, do as you please,
But, if you hold it fit, after the play
Let his Queen mother all alone entreat him
blunt To show his grief. Let her be round° with him,
And I'll be placed, so please you, in the ear[7]
Of all their conference. If she find him not,[8]
To England send him or confine him where
Your wisdom best shall think.

Claudius

It shall be so.
Madness in great ones must not unwatched go.

They exit.

1 *I had as lief*

I would rather

2 *groundlings*

Spectators at the London amphitheaters who stood on the ground directly in front of the raised performance stage (and who were proverbially common and vulgar)

3 *Termagant*

A supposed Muslim deity, imagined by medieval Europeans as overbearing and violent

4 *It out-Herods Herod*

Herod, King of Judea at the time of Christ's birth, was frequently depicted in medieval drama as a bombastic and domineering tyrant.

5 *I warrant your Honor.*

I assure you (that we will do as you say).

6 *the very age and body of the time his form and pressure*

I.e., show the present moment its own likeness and impression

7 *come tardy off*

Performed inadequately

8 *the censure of which one must in your allowance o'erweigh a whole theater of others*

I.e., the disapproval of one judicious person, you must admit, outweighs the approval of a whole theater full of undiscriminating people

Act 3, Scene 2

Enter **Hamlet** *and three of the* **Players**.

Hamlet

Speak the speech, I pray you, as I pronounced° it to you, trippingly on the tongue. But if you mouth° it, as many of our players do, I had as lief[1] the town crier spoke my lines. Nor do not saw the air too much with your hand, thus, but use all gently, for in the very torrent, tempest, and, as I may say, whirlwind of your passion, you must acquire and beget a temperance that may give it smoothness. Oh, it offends me to the soul to hear a robustious,° periwig-pated° fellow tear a passion to tatters, to very rags, to split the ears of the groundlings,[2] who for the most part are capable° of nothing but inexplicable dumb-shows° and noise. I would have such a fellow whipped for o'erdoing Termagant.[3] It out-Herods Herod.[4] Pray you, avoid it.

recited
declaim
rowdy / wig-wearing
appreciative
mimed scenes

Player

I warrant your Honor.[5]

Hamlet

Be not too tame neither, but let your own discretion be your tutor. Suit the action to the word, the word to the action, with this special observance: that you o'erstep not the modesty° of nature. For anything so o'erdone is from° the purpose of playing, whose end, both at the first and now, was and is to hold, as 'twere, the mirror up to nature: to show virtue her feature, scorn her own image, and the very age and body of the time his form and pressure.[6] Now this overdone or come tardy off,[7] though it makes the unskillful° laugh, cannot but make the judicious grieve, the censure of which one must in your allowance o'erweigh a whole theater of others.[8]

limits; moderation
contrary to
undiscriminating

1 *not to speak it profanely*

Not to be blasphemous (for suggesting that these actors are not made by God)

2 *accent of Christians*

I.e., speech of ordinary humans

3 *journeymen*

Hired assistants; the implication being that the actors who imitate human beings so poorly must have themselves been created by nature's less-skilled subordinates

4 *though in the meantime some necessary question of the play be then to be considered*

Even while an important aspect of the plot is being revealed on stage

Oh, there be players that I have seen play and heard others praise—and that highly—not to speak it profanely,[1] that, neither having th' accent of Christians[2] nor the gait of Christian, pagan, nor man, have so strutted and bellowed that I have thought some of nature's journeymen[3] had made men and not made them well, they imitated humanity so abominably.

Player

I hope we have reformed that indifferently° (*fairly well*) with us.

Hamlet

Oh, reform it altogether! And let those that play your clowns speak no more than is set° (*written*) down for them, for there be of° (*some among*) them that will themselves laugh to set on some quantity of barren° (*unthinking*) spectators to laugh too, though in the meantime some necessary question of the play be then to be considered.[4] That's villainous,° (*detestable*) and shows a most pitiful ambition in the fool that uses it. Go, make you ready. [**Players** *exit.*]

Enter **Polonius, Guildenstern,** *and* **Rosencrantz.**

How now, my lord! Will the King hear this piece of work?

Polonius

And the Queen too, and that presently.° (*immediately*)

Hamlet

Bid the players make haste.

[**Polonius** *exits.*]

Will you two help to hasten them?

Rosencrantz

Ay, my lord.

[**Rosencrantz** *and* **Guildenstern**] *exit.*

1 *thou art e'en as just a man / As e'er my conversation coped withal*

You are as honorable a man as I have ever dealt with

2 *let the candied tongue lick absurd pomp / And crook the pregnant hinges of the knee / Where thrift may follow fawning*

I.e., let flatterers save their sweet words for foolish rich people, and bow obsequiously, where a profit may be made from their actions.

3 *was mistress of her choice*

I.e., had the authority to make her own choices

4 *As one in suffering all that suffers nothing*

I.e., like a person experiencing all hardships who calmly manages to tolerate them all

5 *commeddled*

Mixed together

6 *they are not a pipe for Fortune's finger / To sound what stop she please*

I.e., that they cannot be swayed by the vicissitudes of fortune (literally, "they are not a pipe on which Fortune can play any note she chooses")

7 *Something too much of this.*

I.e., I have spoken altogether too much on this topic.

Hamlet

What ho, Horatio!

Enter **Horatio**.

Horatio

Here, sweet lord, at your service.

Hamlet

Horatio, thou art e'en as just a man
As e'er my conversation coped withal.[1]

Horatio

O my dear lord—

Hamlet

Nay, do not think I flatter,
favors For what advancement° may I hope from thee
That no revenue hast but thy good spirits
To feed and clothe thee? Why should the poor be
flattered?
No, let the candied tongue lick absurd pomp
And crook the pregnant hinges of the knee
Where thrift may follow fawning.[2] Dost thou hear?
Since my dear soul was mistress of her choice[3]
among And could of° men distinguish, her election
claimed Sh' hath sealed° thee for herself, for thou hast been—
As one in suffering all that suffers nothing[4]—
A man that Fortune's buffets and rewards
Hast ta'en with equal thanks. And blessed are those
passion Whose blood° and judgment are so well commeddled[5]
That they are not a pipe for Fortune's finger
To sound what stop she please.[6] Give me that man
That is not passion's slave, and I will wear him
In my heart's core, ay, in my heart of heart,
As I do thee. Something too much of this.[7]

1 *with the very comment of thy soul*

With all of your powers of concentration

2 *Vulcan's stithy*

Vulcan's forge. Vulcan, the Roman god of fire, was a blacksmith, and his forge was frequently associated with the fires of Hell.

3 *Give him heedful note*

Pay him careful attention

4 *In censure of his seeming*

In the judgment of his behavior

5 *pay the theft*

Repay what has been stolen (i.e., he won't get away with anything)

6 *be idle*

Either "act foolishly" so as to seem mad or "be doing nothing" so as not to be thought conspiring with Horatio.

7 *How fares*

The King means "How are you," but Hamlet takes *fares* in the sense of "eats."

8 *chameleon's dish*

It was believed that chameleons fed on air.

9 *I eat the air, promise-crammed.*

A pun on *air/heir*, and an allusion to Claudius's promise to make Hamlet the crown prince

10 *capons*

Castrated roosters, proverbially stupid, as they allow themselves to be fattened before being eaten. Hamlet's point is that capons cannot be fed with empty promises, though Claudius seems to believe he can feed Hamlet with them.

11 *I have nothing with this answer*

I.e., your reply bears no relation to the question I asked

There is a play tonight before the King;
One scene of it comes near the circumstance
Which I have told thee of my father's death.
I prithee, when thou see'st that act afoot,
Even with the very comment of thy soul,[1]
hidden Observe my uncle. If his occulted° guilt
reveal Do not itself unkennel° in one speech,
It is a damnèd ghost that we have seen,
suspicions And my imaginations° are as foul
As Vulcan's stithy.[2] Give him heedful note,[3]
fix intently For I mine eyes will rivet° to his face,
And after we will both our judgments join
In censure of his seeming.[4]

Horatio

Well, my lord.
anything If 'a steal aught° the whilst this play is playing,
being detected And 'scape detected,° I will pay the theft.[5]

Enter trumpets and kettle drums, King [**Claudius**], *Queen* [**Gertrude**], **Polonius**, **Ophelia** [, **Rosencrantz** *and* **Guildenstern**, *and Lords*].

Hamlet

[*to* **Horatio**] They are coming to the play. I must be idle.[6] Get you a place.

Claudius

How fares[7] our cousin Hamlet?

Hamlet

Excellent, i' faith. Of the chameleon's dish:[8] I eat the air, promise-crammed.[9] You cannot feed capons[10] so.

Claudius

I have nothing with this answer,[11] Hamlet; these words are not mine.

1 *nor mine now*

I.e., since Hamlet has spoken the words already, he cannot control nor recall them.

2 *Julius Caesar*

The first emperor of Rome, who was assassinated by his friend Brutus, and a reference to Shakespeare's own play, *Julius Caesar* (in which the actor who played Julius Caesar was probably the same one who first played Polonius).

3 *It was a brute part of him to kill so capital a calf there.*

It was a brutal (punning on *Brutus*) action for him (i.e., Brutus) to kill such a prize fool (i.e., Polonius, who was playing the part of Caesar). *Capital* (i.e., important) puns on "Capitol" in line 97, though Caesar was actually killed in the Senate building of Rome.

4 *stay upon your patience*

Wait for your permission to begin

5 *Here's metal more attractive.*

Hamlet adopts the language of a conventional lover; Ophelia is imagined as a magnet that draws Hamlet toward her.

6 *lie in your lap*

A sexual innuendo

7 *country*

I.e., sexual (with an aggressive pun on the first syllable of *country*, then, as now, a crude euphemism for female genitalia)

8 *nothing*

Thing could refer euphemistically to a man's penis; *nothing* to a woman's vagina. Hamlet's subsequent volley of sexual innuendo plays on these alternate meanings.

Hamlet

acted No, nor mine now.[1]—My lord, you played° once i' th' university, you say?

Polonius

That did I, my lord, and was accounted a good actor.

Hamlet

What did you enact?

Polonius

I did enact Julius Caesar.[2] I was killed i' th' Capitol. Brutus killed me.

Hamlet

It was a brute part of him to kill so capital a calf there.[3]—Be the players ready?

Rosencrantz

Ay, my lord. They stay upon your patience.[4]

Gertrude

Come hither, my dear Hamlet; sit by me.

Hamlet

No, good mother. Here's metal more attractive.[5]

Polonius

observe [*to* **King**] Oh, ho, do you mark° that?

Hamlet

Lady, shall I lie in your lap?[6]

Ophelia

No, my lord.

Hamlet

Do you think I meant country[7] matters?

Ophelia

I think nothing,[8] my lord.

Hamlet

pleasing That's a fair° thought to lie between maids' legs.

1 *your only jig-maker*

An unrivaled comic (i.e., I am the best comedian). Hamlet sardonically compares himself to the clown in a theatrical company, who traditionally performed a *jig* (see 2.2.430) at the end of the play.

2 *suit of sables*

Though it is black in color, sable is an expensive fur, the extravagance of which would be inappropriate for mourning clothes. Hamlet's sarcastic point seems to be that, since four months have passed since his father's death, obviously there's no further need to mourn.

3 *suffer not thinking on*

Endure being forgotten

4 *hobby-horse*

A dancer in a horse costume, a traditional role in May Day morris dances (a form of folk dance). In Shakespeare's time, the hobby-horse had become a conventional symbol of forgotten objects; the line Hamlet quotes is apparently a familiar catchphrase.

5 The trumpets [sound]. Dumb show follows.

The dumb show—a little play in pantomime—presents one of *Hamlet*'s most notorious problems. Does Claudius recognize the action—which follows the Ghost's description of the deed closely, down to pouring poison in the ear—as a representation of murder of his brother, the elder Hamlet? If he does, then why does he wait until the murder is represented again, in the play proper, to rise up and cry for light? Scholars have offered several explanations: perhaps Claudius is watching Hamlet too closely to see what is happening on stage; perhaps the Ghost's account is wrong, and the murder was committed by some other means; perhaps the dumb show is simply unintelligible (see Hamlet's remark about the genre at 3.2.12). Perhaps Claudius is more like Hamlet than we usually think, and needs to have the Prince's knowledge of the crime proven to him twice before he acts.

6 his

I.e., the sleeping King's

Ophelia

What is, my lord?

Hamlet

Nothing.

Ophelia

You are merry, my lord.

Hamlet

Who? I?

Ophelia

Ay, my lord.

Hamlet

these

O God, your only jig-maker.[1] What should a man do but be merry? For look you how cheerfully my mother looks, and my father died within 's° two hours.

Ophelia

Nay, 'tis twice two months, my lord.

Hamlet

he

So long? Nay then, let the devil wear black, for I'll have a suit of sables.[2] O heavens! Die two months ago and not forgotten yet? Then there's hope a great man's memory may outlive his life half a year. But, by 'r Lady, 'a° must build churches then, or else shall 'a suffer not thinking on,[3] with the hobby-horse[4] whose epitaph is "For, oh, For, oh! The hobby-horse is forgot!"

The trumpets [sound]. Dumb show follows.[5]

himself

*Enter [**Players** as] a King and a Queen, the Queen embracing him, and he her. He takes her up and declines his head upon her neck. He lies him° down upon a bank of flowers. She, seeing him asleep, leaves him. Anon come in another man, takes off his*[6] *crown, kisses it, pours poison in the sleeper's ears, and leaves him. The Queen returns, finds the*

1 passionate action

A great display of emotion

2 *miching* malhecho

Skulking wrongdoing (*malhecho*; Spanish for "misdeed")

3 *stooping to your clemency*

Bowing to beg your generosity

4 *posy of a ring*

A short, simple poem inscribed on the inside of a ring

King dead, makes passionate action.[1] *The poisoner with some three or four come in again; seem° to condole with her. The dead body is carried away. The poisoner woos the Queen with gifts. She seems harsh awhile, but in the end accepts love.*

they seem

[**Players** *exit.*]

Ophelia

What means this, my lord?

Hamlet

Marry, this miching *malhecho!*[2] It means mischief.

Ophelia

Perhaps / plot

Belike° this show imports the argument° of the play.

Enter **Prologue**.

Hamlet

We shall know by this fellow. The players cannot keep counsel. They'll tell all.

Ophelia

he

Will 'a° tell us what this show meant?

Hamlet

Ay, or any show that you will show him. Be not you ashamed to show, he'll not shame to tell you what it means.

Ophelia

wicked / watch

You are naught;° you are naught. I'll mark° the play.

Prologue

For us and for our tragedy,
Here stooping to your clemency,[3]
We beg your hearing patiently. *[He exits.]*

Hamlet

Is this a prologue or the posy of a ring?[4]

1 **King**

The Player King's diction is highly ornamented, even more so than that of the rugged Pyrrhus speech Hamlet calls for at 2.2.376–396. Note, for example, the mythological allusions of the opening lines, a periphrasis for the simple thought, "thirty years have passed." The rhymed couplets and frequently inverted syntax (*Discomfort you, my lord, it nothing must*, 3.2.153) are also marks of an elevated style. Hamlet has chosen a play that sounds older, ostentatiously formal, and mannered. His tastes, it seems, are still those of the scholar, even if his own idea of acting—his antic disposition—gives a much more radical sense of the potential of the theater.

2 *Phoebus' cart*

I.e., the sun, imagined in antiquity as being drawn across the sky by the god Phoebus Apollo's chariot

3 *Neptune's salt wash*

I.e., the sea (domain of the Roman god Neptune)

4 *Tellus' orbèd ground*

I.e., the Earth (domain of the Roman goddess Tellus)

5 *borrowed sheen*

Reflected radiance (from the sun)

6 *our*

The Folio prints "your."

7 *hold quantity*

Exist in equal proportions

8 *Either none, in neither aught, or in extremity*

I.e., either neither of them (fear nor love) is present, or else there is an excess of both.

9 *love*

Q2 prints "Lord," which makes little sense; *love* is the reading in the Folio.

10 *sized*

Of a certain size

11 *My operant powers their functions leave to do*

My vital powers stop functioning

Ophelia

'Tis brief, my lord.

Hamlet

As woman's love.

Enter [**Player**] **King**[1] *and* [**Player**] **Queen**.

[Player] King

Full thirty times hath Phoebus' cart[2] gone round
Neptune's salt wash[3] and Tellus' orbèd ground,[4]
And thirty dozen moons with borrowed sheen[5]
About the world have times twelve thirties been,
goddess of marriage Since love our hearts and Hymen° did our hands
reciprocally Unite commutual° in most sacred bands.

[Player] Queen

So many journeys may the sun and moon
Make us again count o'er ere love be done.
But woe is me! You are so sick of late,
So far from cheer and from our[6] former state,
fear for That I distrust° you. Yet though I distrust,
Sadden Discomfort° you, my lord, it nothing must.
For women fear too much, even as they love,
And women's fear and love hold quantity,[7]
Either none, in neither aught, or in extremity.[8]
experience Now what my love[9] is, proof° hath made you know,
i.e., its equal And, as my love is sized,[10] my fear is so°:
Where love is great, the littlest doubts are fear;
Where little fears grow great, great love grows there.

[Player] King

Faith, I must leave thee, love, and shortly too.
My operant powers their functions leave to do,[11]
And thou shalt live in this fair world behind,
perhaps Honored, beloved; and haply° one as kind

1 *None wed the second but who killed the first.*

I.e., no woman should marry a second time except one who has killed her first husband.

2 *The instances that second marriage move / Are base respects of thrift*

The motives that prompt a second marriage are vulgar considerations of financial advantage

3 *Purpose is but the slave to memory*

I.e., good intentions can only be kept if they are remembered

4 *Of violent birth but poor validity*

Robust at first but with little stamina

5 *To pay ourselves what to ourselves is debt*

To forget the promises we have made to ourselves

6 *The violence of either grief or joy / Their own enactures with themselves destroy.*

Extreme feelings of grief or joy, once they cease, undo the actions (*enactures*) made in their grip.

7 *slender accident*

The most insignificant event

8 *The great man down, you mark his favorite flies.*

When the great man is out of favor, observe how quickly his most favored supporter deserts him.

a husband For husband° shalt thou—

[Player] Queen

Oh, confound the rest!
Such love must needs be treason in my breast.
In second husband let me be accursed!
None wed the second but who killed the first.[1]

Hamlet

(A bitter herb) That's wormwood!°

[Player] Queen

The instances that second marriage move
Are base respects of thrift,[2] but none of love.
A second time I kill my husband dead
When second husband kisses me in bed.

[Player] King

I do believe you think what now you speak,
vow to do But what we do determine° oft we break.
Purpose is but the slave to memory,[3]
Of violent birth but poor validity,[4]
Which now, like fruit unripe, sticks on the tree,
But fall, unshaken, when they mellow be.
Most necessary 'tis that we forget
To pay ourselves what to ourselves is debt.[5]
What to ourselves in passion we propose,
The passion ending, doth the purpose lose.
The violence of either grief or joy
Their own enactures with themselves destroy.[6]
Where joy most revels, grief doth most lament;
Grief joys, joy grieves on slender accident.[7]
ever This world is not for aye,° nor 'tis not strange
That even our loves should with our fortunes change.
answer For 'tis a question left us yet to prove°
Whether love lead fortune, or else fortune love.
The great man down, you mark his favorite flies.[8]

1 *who not needs*

He who does not need (a friend)

2 *our devices still are overthrown*

Our plans are always disrupted

3 *Sport and repose lock from me day and night*

Let the day deny me pleasurable activity, and the night deny me rest.

4 *anchor's cheer in prison be my scope*

Let me be limited to an anchorite's (i.e., a hermit's) prison-like fare

5 *Meet what I would have well and it destroy*

Encounter and undo everything that I want to happen

or person / promoted The poor° advanced° makes friends of enemies.
this manner / attend And hitherto° doth love on fortune tend,°
For who not needs[1] shall never lack a friend,
need / test And who in want° a hollow friend doth try°
makes Directly seasons° him his enemy.
But, orderly to end where I begun,
in opposite directions Our wills and fates do so contrary° run
That our devices still are overthrown.[2]
outcomes Our thoughts are ours, their ends° none of our own:
So think thou wilt no second husband wed,
But die thy thoughts when thy first lord is dead.

[Player] Queen

Neither Nor° Earth to me give food, nor Heaven light;
Sport and repose lock from me day and night.[3]
To desperation turn my trust and hope,
And anchor's cheer in prison be my scope.[4]
obstacle / makes pale Each opposite° that blanks° the face of joy
Meet what I would have well and it destroy.[5]
i.e., in the next world Both here and hence° pursue me lasting strife
If, once I be a widow, ever I be a wife.

Hamlet

If she should break it now!

[Player] King

'Tis deeply sworn. Sweet, leave me here awhile.
gladly My spirits grow dull, and fain° I would beguile
The tedious day with sleep.

[Player] Queen.

Sleep rock thy brain,
And never come mischance between us twain.

[**Player Queen** *exits.* **Player King** *sleeps.*]

Hamlet

Madam, how like you this play?

1 *Marry, how tropically!*

I.e., Indeed, how metaphorically apt. Hamlet expresses his delight at his own wit.

2 *Let the galled jade wince; our withers are unwrung.*

Let the horse that is saddle sore wince in pain; our shoulders are not sore with chafing (i.e., this doesn't apply to us)

3 *chorus*

Actor who relates events that have occurred off stage

4 *I could interpret between you and your love, if i could see the puppets dallying.*

I could explain what is going on between you and your lover if I could see the actors (*puppets*) flirting

5 *Cost you a groaning to take off mine edge*

Playing off Ophelia's word *keen* (meaning "incisive" or "sharp"), Hamlet says that only *a groaning* (the cry of childbirth or perhaps of the loss of virginity) would take the *edge* off his jokes or off his sexual desire.

6 *Still better and worse.*

I.e., always sharper and more indecent.

Gertrude

The lady doth protest too much, methinks.

Hamlet

Oh, but she'll keep her word.

Claudius

plot Have you heard the argument?° Is there no offense in 't?

Hamlet

No, no, they do but jest. Poison in jest. No offense i' th' world.

Claudius

What do you call the play?

Hamlet

The Mousetrap. Marry, how tropically![1] This play is the
representation image° of a murder done in Vienna. Gonzago is the
soon Duke's name, his wife Baptista. You shall see anon.°
rascally 'Tis a knavish° piece of work, but what o' that? Your
innocent Majesty and we that have free° souls, it touches us not.
Let the galled jade wince; our withers are unwrung.[2]

Enter [Player as] **Lucianus**.

This is one Lucianus, nephew to the King.

Ophelia

You are as good as a chorus,[3] my lord.

Hamlet

what goes on between I could interpret between° you and your love, if I could
see the puppets dallying.[4]

Ophelia

You are keen, my lord; you are keen.

Hamlet

It would cost you a groaning to take off mine edge.[5]

Ophelia

Still better and worse.[6]

1 *So you mistake your husbands.*

With those words, you falsely take (mis-take) your husbands' (hands in marriage). Hamlet refers to the traditional wedding vows to take a spouse "for better or for worse," suggesting that women like Ophelia take their marriage oaths lightly.

2 *"The croaking raven doth bellow for revenge—"*

A slight misquotation from the anonymous play *The True Tragedy of Richard III* (1591): "The screeching raven sits croaking for revenge."

3 *Considerate season, else no creature seeing*

I.e., an appropriately chosen moment, with no one else present to see what is happening

4 *With Hecate's ban*

With the curse of Hecate (goddess of sorcery, pronounced with two syllables: Heck-it)

5 *On wholesome life usurps immediately*

I.e., let them act instantly to destroy *wholesome life*.

6 *Give o'er*

Stop

7 *let the stricken deer go weep*

It was believed that deer wept when wounded. These lines (255–258) perhaps derive from a ballad that has not survived.

8 *hart ungallèd*

Uninjured male deer

Hamlet

So you mistake your husbands.[1]—Begin, murderer.
grimacing Leave thy damnable faces° and begin. Come; "The
croaking raven doth bellow for revenge—"[2]

Lucianus

ready Thoughts black, hands apt,° drugs fit, and time agreeing,
Considerate season, else no creature seeing,[3]
Thou mixture rank, of midnight weeds collected,
With Hecate's ban[4] thrice blasted, thrice infected,
capability Thy natural magic and dire property°
On wholesome life usurps immediately.[5]

[*Pours poison into* **Player King**'*s ear.*]

Hamlet

..., the sleeping King's 'A poisons him i' th' garden for his estate. His° name's Gonzago. The story is extant, and written in very choice Italian. You shall see anon how the murderer gets the love of Gonzago's wife.

Ophelia

The King rises.

Gertrude

How fares my lord?

Polonius

Give o'er[6] the play!

Claudius

Give me some light, away!

Polonius

Lights, lights, lights!

All but **Hamlet** *and* **Horatio** *exit.*

Hamlet

Why, let the stricken deer go weep,[7]
The hart ungallèd[8] play,
stay awake For some must watch° while some must sleep:
Thus runs the world away.

1 *forest of feathers*

A reference to the long plumes decorating the hats of gallants, which had become a fashionable accessory in the theater.

2 *turn Turk with me*

I.e., betray me (to *turn Turk* literally meant to abandon Christianity)

3 *with Provincial roses on my razed shoes*

With decorative rosettes on my shoes with ornamental slits; *Provincial* here means 'in the style of Provence," a region in southern France; *razed* means "slashed."

4 *Damon*

Damon and his friend Pythias were the classical model of perfect friendship.

5 *pajock*

The meaning is uncertain, perhaps a variant of "patchcock," a word used to describe the degenerate English settlers in Ireland.

6 *You might have rhymed.*

Horatio expected Hamlet to say *ass*.

7 *perdy*

Indeed (from the French *per dieu*, "by God")

i.e., the play / *partnership / pack*

Would not this,° sir, and a forest of feathers[1]—if the rest of my fortunes turn Turk with me[2]—with Provincial roses on my razed shoes,[3] get me a fellowship° in a cry° of players?

Horatio

i.e., partnership

Half a share.°

Hamlet

i.e., I would say

A whole one, I.°

stripped; deprived

For thou dost know, O Damon[4] dear,
This realm dismantled° was
Of Jove himself. And now reigns here
A very, very—pajock.[5]

Horatio

You might have rhymed.[6]

Hamlet

O good Horatio, I'll take the Ghost's word for a thousand pound. Didst perceive?

Horatio

Very well, my lord.

Hamlet

Upon the talk of the poisoning?

Horatio

I did very well note him.

Hamlet

probably

Ah ha! Come; some music! Come; the recorders!
For if the King like not the comedy,
Why then, belike,° he likes it not, perdy.[7]
Come; some music!

Enter **Rosencrantz** *and* **Guildenstern**.

Guildenstern

grant

Good my lord, vouchsafe° me a word with you.

1 *Is in his retirement marvelous distempered.*

Is in his withdrawal (to his room) very upset .

2 *purgation*

(1) bloodletting; (2) spiritual purification; (3) legal clearing of guilt, acquittal

Hamlet

Sir, a whole history.

Guildenstern

The King, sir—

Hamlet

Ay, sir, what of him?

Guildenstern

Is in his retirement marvelous distempered.[1]

Hamlet

With drink, sir?

Guildenstern

anger No, my lord, with choler.°

Hamlet

resourceful / tell Your wisdom should show itself more richer° to signify° this to the doctor. For, for me to put him to his purgation[2] would perhaps plunge him into more choler.

Guildenstern

order Good my lord, put your discourse into some frame°
turn away and start° not so wildly from my affair.

Hamlet

calm I am tame,° sir. Pronounce.

Guildenstern

The Queen, your mother, in most great affliction of spirit, hath sent me to you.

Hamlet

You are welcome.

Guildenstern

Nay, good my lord, this courtesy is not of the right
kind / sensible breed.° If it shall please you to make me a wholesome°
answer, I will do your mother's commandment. If not,
permission to leave your pardon° and my return shall be the end of my business.

1 *pickers and stealers*

I.e., hands (a reference to the *Book of Common Prayer*, where the good Christian promises to "keep my hands from picking and stealing")

2 *surely*

Firmly; the Folio prints "freely" (of your own accord).

3 *your griefs*

Knowledge of your troubles

Hamlet

Sir, I cannot.

Guildenstern

What, my lord?

Hamlet

Make you a wholesome answer. My wit's diseased. But, sir, such answer as I can make, you shall command. Or, rather, as you say, my mother. Therefore no more but to the matter. My mother, you say?

Rosencrantz

Then thus she says: your behavior hath struck her into amazement and admiration.°

bewilderment

Hamlet

O wonderful son that can so 'stonish a mother! But is there no sequel at the heels of this mother's admiration? Impart.

Rosencrantz

She desires to speak with you in her closet° ere you go to bed.

private chamber

Hamlet

We shall obey, were she ten times our mother. Have you any further trade° with us?

business

Rosencrantz

My lord, you once did love me.

Hamlet

And do still, by these pickers and stealers.[1]

Rosencrantz

Good my lord, what is your cause of distemper? You do surely[2] bar the door upon your own liberty if you deny your griefs[3] to your friend.

Hamlet

Sir, I lack advancement.

1 *"While the grass grows—"*

A reference to the proverb, "While the grass grows, the horse starves." While Claudius's power grows, Hamlet's must waste away.

2 *something musty*

Somewhat old

3 *why do you go about to recover the wind of me, as if you would drive me into a toil?*

Why do you take a roundabout way to get downwind of me, as though you would force me into a trap?

4 *if my duty be too bold, my love is too unmannerly*

If in performing my duty toward you I have been too forward (in asking about your *distemper*), it is only as a result of the great love I have for you.

5 *know no touch of it*

Have no ability to play it

Rosencrantz

How can that be, when you have the voice of the King himself for your succession in Denmark?

Enter the **Players** *with recorders.*

Hamlet

Ay, sir, but "While the grass grows—"[1]; the proverb is something musty.[2]—Oh, the recorders! Let me see one.—To withdraw° with you: why do you go about to recover the wind of me, as if you would drive me into a toil?[3]

speak privately

Guildenstern

O my lord, if my duty be too bold, my love is too unmannerly.[4]

Hamlet

I do not well understand that. Will you play upon this pipe?

Guildenstern

My lord, I cannot.

Hamlet

I pray you.

Guildenstern

Believe me, I cannot.

Hamlet

I do beseech you.

Guildenstern

I know no touch of it,[5] my lord.

Hamlet

It is as easy as lying. Govern these ventages° with your fingers and thumb, give it breath with your mouth, and it will discourse most eloquent music. Look you, these are the stops.°

finger holes

finger holes

1 *sound me*

"Play me (like an instrument)"; also, "try to understand me"; "explore my depths"

2 *fret me*

(1) annoy me; (2) place your fingers on my frets (ridges to guide the placement of fingers on some instruments)

Guildenstern

But these cannot I command to any utterance of harmony. I have not the skill.

Hamlet

Why, look you now, how unworthy a thing you make of me! You would play upon me. You would seem to know my stops. You would pluck out the heart of my mystery. You would sound me[1] from my lowest note to the top of my compass.° *[range]* And there is much music, excellent voice, in this little organ,° *[i.e., the recorder]* yet cannot you make it speak? 'Sblood, do you think I am easier to be played on than a pipe? Call me what instrument you will, though you fret me,[2] you cannot play upon me.

Enter **Polonius**.

God bless you, sir.

Polonius

My lord, the Queen would speak with you, and presently.° *[immediately]*

Hamlet

Do you see yonder cloud that's almost in shape of a camel?

Polonius

By th' mass, and 'tis like a camel indeed.

Hamlet

Methinks it is like a weasel.

Polonius

It is backed like a weasel.

Hamlet

Or like a whale?

Polonius

Very like a whale.

1 *the top of my bent*

the limits of my endurance (for *bent*, see 2.2.30 and note)

2 *witching time*

The hour when witches come out to perform their sorcery

3 *breaks*

Lets; the Folio prints "breathes," which some editors adopt.

4 *drink hot blood*

Drinking blood was thought to be an incitement to murder.

5 *Nero*

First century A.D. Roman emperor who murdered his mother by ripping open her womb, according to some sources, to see where he had come from.

6 *How in my words somever she be shent, / To give them seals never my soul consent!*

However much she might be rebuked by my words, do not ever let my soul act upon them (*seals* were the imprinted wax that testified to the authority of a decree).

Hamlet

Then I will come to my mother by and by—They fool
me to the top of my bent.[1]—I will come by and by.
Leave me, friends. [*All but* **Hamlet** *exit.*]
I will say so; "by and by" is easily said.
'Tis now the very witching time[2] of night,
open wide When churchyards yawn° and Hell itself breaks[3] out
Contagion to this world. Now could I drink hot blood[4]
And do such business as the bitter day
Would quake to look on. Soft, now to my mother.
natural affection O heart, lose not thy nature;° let not ever
The soul of Nero[5] enter this firm bosom.
Let me be cruel, not unnatural:
I will speak daggers to her but use none.
My tongue and soul in this be hypocrites.
rebuked How in my words somever she be shent,°
To give them seals never my soul consent![6] *He exits.*

1 *stands it safe with us*

Is it safe for us (the royal first-person plural pronoun)

2 *forthwith dispatch*

Prepare at once

3 *terms of our estate*

I.e., responsibilities of my position

4 *brows*

(1) disordered thoughts; (2) threatening looks . The Folio prints the more obvious "lunacies."

5 *but much more / That spirit upon whose weal depends and rests / The lives of many*

I.e., but the person on whose well-being (*weal*) the multitudes rely must work even harder to keep himself from harm

6 *cess of majesty*

Ending (decease) of royalty

7 *Each small annexment, petty consequence*

Each little appendage (and each) unimportant matter connected to (the *massy wheel*)

Act 3, Scene 3

Enter King [**Claudius**], **Rosencrantz**, *and* **Guildenstern**.

Claudius

e., Hamlet's behavior I like him° not, nor stands it safe with us[1]
To let his madness range. Therefore prepare you.
I your commission will forthwith dispatch,[2]
go along And he to England shall along° with you.
The terms of our estate[3] may not endure
Hazard so near us as doth hourly grow
Out of his brows.[4]

Guildenstern

prepare; equip We will ourselves provide.°
care Most holy and religious fear° it is
To keep those many, many bodies safe
That live and feed upon your Majesty.

Rosencrantz

individual / private The single° and peculiar° life is bound
With all the strength and armor of the mind
harm To keep itself from noyance,° but much more
That spirit upon whose weal depends and rests
The lives of many.[5] The cess of majesty[6]
whirlpool Dies not alone, but, like a gulf,° doth draw
massive What's near it with it; or it is a massy° wheel
Fixed on the summit of the highest mount,
To whose huge spokes ten thousand lesser things
affixed Are mortised° and adjoined, which, when it falls,
Each small annexment, petty consequence,[7]
Accompanies Attends° the boisterous ruin. Never alone
universal Did the king sigh, but with a general° groan.

Claudius

Prepare Arm° you, I pray you, to this speedy voyage,
chains For we will fetters° put about this fear,

1 *I warrant she'll tax him home*

I guarantee she'll reprimand him thoroughly

2 *of vantage*

In addition (although it could mean "from an advantageous position," as it does in *Macbeth* 1.6.7)

3 *the primal eldest curse*

The first curse, which God placed upon Cain for having murdered his brother Abel (see Genesis 4:10–12)

4 *Though inclination be as sharp as will*

I.e., though I feel a natural impulse (to pray) as strong as my desire (to sin)

5 *to double business bound*

Contracted to perform two incompatible tasks

6 *Were thicker than itself with brother's blood*

Were covered with a layer of my brother's blood, thicker than my hand itself

7 *Whereto serves mercy / But to confront the visage of offence?*

I.e., why does mercy exist if not to confront (and pardon) the greatest sins?

Which now goes too free-footed.

Rosencrantz, Guildenstern

We will haste us.

[**Rosencrantz** *and* **Guildenstern**] *exit.*

Enter **Polonius**.

Polonius

My lord, he's going to his mother's closet.° *private chamber*
Behind the arras° I'll convey myself *wall tapestry*
To hear the process.° I'll warrant she'll tax him home,[1] *proceedings*
And, as you said (and wisely was it said),
'Tis meet° that some more audience than a mother— *fitting*
Since nature makes them partial—should o'erhear
The speech of vantage.[2] Fare you well, my liege.
I'll call upon you ere you go to bed
And tell you what I know.

Claudius

Thanks, dear my lord.

[**Polonius**] *exits.*

Oh, my offence is rank.° It smells to Heaven. *foul*
It hath the primal eldest curse[3] upon 't,
A brother's murder. Pray can I not;
Though inclination be as sharp as will,[4]
My stronger guilt defeats my strong intent,
And, like a man to double business bound,[5]
I stand in pause where° I shall first begin, *deciding where*
And both neglect. What if this cursèd hand
Were thicker than itself with brother's blood?[6]
Is there not rain enough in the sweet heavens
To wash it white as snow? Whereto serves mercy
But to confront the visage of offence?[7]

1 *And what's in prayer but this twofold force, / To be forestallèd ere we come to fall / Or pardoned being down?*

I.e., and what is the use of prayer except this double purpose: to prevent us from sinning, and to forgive us once we have sinned?

2 *mine own ambition*

I.e., the achievement of my ambition

3 *retain th' offense*

I.e., keep the profits of the crime

4 *Offense's gilded hand may show by justice*

I.e., the gold-filled hand of a criminal may exist side by side with justice. Q2's *show by* means "appear next to"; the Folio prints "shove by," meaning "push aside" or "evade," which many editors prefer.

5 *the action lies / In his true nature*

(1) legal proceedings are carried out properly; (2) deeds appear according to their true natures

6 *to the teeth and forehead of*

Face to face with

7 *To give in evidence*

To testify against ourselves

8 *limèd*

Caught in *lime*, a sticky compound spread on branches to catch birds

9 *would be scanned*

Requires careful examination

And what's in prayer but this twofold force,
To be forestallèd ere we come to fall
Or pardoned being down?[1] Then I'll look up.
My fault is past. But oh, what form of prayer
Can serve my turn? "Forgive me my foul murder"?
That cannot be, since I am still possessed
results Of those effects° for which I did the murder:
My crown, mine own ambition,[2] and my Queen.
May one be pardoned and retain th' offense?[3]
In the corrupted currents of this world
Offense's gilded hand may show by justice,[4]
And oft 'tis seen the wicked prize itself
Buys out the law. But 'tis not so above.
evasion There is no shuffling;° there the action lies
its In his° true nature,[5] and we ourselves compelled,
Even to the teeth and forehead of[6] our faults,
remains To give in evidence.[7] What then? What rests?°
can accomplish Try what repentance can.° What can it not?
Yet what can it when one cannot repent?
O wretched state! O bosom black as death!
O limèd[8] soul that, struggling to be free,
angled / an attempt Art more engaged!° Help, angels! Make assay.°
Bow, stubborn knees, and, heart with strings of steel,
Be soft as sinews of the newborn babe.
All may be well.

Enter **Hamlet** [*with drawn sword*].

Hamlet

he [*aside*] Now might I do it, but now 'a° is a-praying.
And now I'll do 't, and so 'a goes to Heaven,
And so am I revenged. That would be scanned:[9]
A villain kills my father, and, for that,

1 *base and silly*

Unworthy and pointless. The Folio prints "hire and salary" (i.e., as though Claudius had paid Hamlet to assassinate him during prayer, so that his soul might go to Heaven rather than Hell)

2 *grossly, full of bread*

I.e., as he was enjoying worldly pleasures, spiritually unprepared for death.

3 *broad blown*

In full bloom (see 1.5.76: "the blossoms of my sin")

4 *in our circumstance and course of thought / 'Tis heavy with him*

I.e., from my limited vantage point, it seems that he has many sins weighing against him

5 *know thou a more horrid hent*

Wait for a more horrible occasion

6 *physic*

Medicine (both Claudius's prayer and Hamlet's decision to spare him)

I, his sole son, do this same villain send
To Heaven.
Why, this is base and silly,[1] not revenge.
'A took my father grossly, full of bread,[2]
vigorous With all his crimes broad blown,[3] as flush° as May,
oul's account / except And how his audit° stands, who knows save° Heaven?
But in our circumstance and course of thought
'Tis heavy with him.[4] And am I then revenged
i.e., Claudius To take him° in the purging of his soul
prepared When he is fit and seasoned° for his passage?
No.
Up, sword, and know thou a more horrid hent:[5]
When he is drunk asleep, or in his rage,
Or in th' incestuous pleasure of his bed,
At game a-swearing, or about some act
trace That has no relish° of salvation in 't—
Then trip him, that his heels may kick at Heaven,
And that his soul may be as damned and black
is waiting As Hell, whereto it goes. My mother stays.°
This physic[6] but prolongs thy sickly days. *He exits.*

Claudius

My words fly up; my thoughts remain below.
Words without thoughts never to Heaven go. *He exits.*

1 *Look you lay home to him.*

Be sure you rebuke him thoroughly.

2 *your Grace hath screened and stood between / Much heat and him*

I.e., your Majesty has shielded him from much censure

3 *by the rood*

A mild oath, "by the cross" (*rood* is an Old English word for Christ's cross)

Act 3, Scene 4

Enter [Queen] **Gertrude** *and* **Polonius**

Polonius

immediately 'A will come straight.° Look you lay home to him.[1]
outrageous Tell him his pranks have been too broad° to bear with,
And that your Grace hath screened and stood between
Much heat and him.[2] I'll silence me even here.
blunt Pray you, be round.°

Gertrude

promise / Doubt I'll warrant° you. Fear° me not.
Withdraw; I hear him coming. [**Polonius** *hides behind the arras.*]

Enter **Hamlet**.

Hamlet

Now, mother, what's the matter?

Gertrude

Hamlet, thou hast thy father much offended.

Hamlet

Mother, you have my father much offended.

Gertrude

Come, come, you answer with an idle tongue.

Hamlet

Go, go, you question with a wicked tongue.

Gertrude

Why, how now, Hamlet?

Hamlet

What's the matter now?

Gertrude

Have you forgot me?

Hamlet

No, by the rood,[3] not so.

1 *set those to you that can speak*

I.e., find people to deal with you who can respond to your rudeness (i.e., the King)

2 *Dead for a ducat*

I.e., I'll bet a ducat I've killed it.

You are the Queen, your husband's brother's wife,
And—would it were not so!—you are my mother.

Gertrude

Nay then, I'll set those to you that can speak.[1]

Hamlet

Come, come, and sit you down. You shall not budge.
You go not till I set you up a glass° *mirror*
Where you may see the inmost part of you.

Gertrude

What wilt thou do? Thou wilt not murder me?
—Help, ho!

Polonius

[*behind the arras*] What, ho? Help!

Hamlet

How now, a rat? Dead for a ducat,[2] dead!

[*He stabs* **Polonius**.]

Polonius

Oh, I am slain.

Gertrude

O me, what hast thou done?

Hamlet

Nay, I know not. Is it the King?

Gertrude

Oh, what a rash and bloody deed is this!

Hamlet

A bloody deed? Almost as bad, good mother,
As kill a king and marry with his brother.

Gertrude

As kill a king?

Hamlet

Ay, lady, it was my word.
[*to the body of* **Polonius**] Thou wretched, rash, intruding fool, farewell.

1 *If damnèd custom have not brazed it so / That it be proof and bulwark against sense*

If your sinful habits have not turned it (your heart) as hard as brass, making it impregnable to natural feeling

2 *blister*

From a branding iron. Prostitutes were threatened with branding, though in fact it was never adopted as punishment.

3 *the body of contraction*

I.e., the marriage contract

4 *this solidity and compound mass*

I.e., the Earth (believed to be a solid *compound* of the four elements earth, air, fire, and water)

5 *heated visage*

A hot face (from shame and sickness)

6 *as against the doom*

As though anticipating the day of Judgment

7 *index*

Preface; prologue (as Hamlet has yet to name Gertrude's crime). The *index* of a book in Shakespeare's time was the table of contents.

8 *Look here upon this picture and on this*

Hamlet presumably produces two pictures, one of his father, and one of Claudius. It seems likely that these portraits were miniatures, which were popular in the day (see his comments at 2.2.300 about those who have bought his uncle's *picture in little* since the new King's accession). Some modern productions have both characters wearing these miniature portraits around their necks: Hamlet pulls one of his father out of his shirt and draws Gertrude near to make the comparison.

9 *counterfeit presentment*

Painted representation

10 *Hyperion's curls, the front of Jove himself*

The curly hair of the sun god; the forehead (i.e., face) of the king of gods himself

11 *Mercury*

Winged messenger of the gods

I took thee for thy better. Take thy fortune:
nosy Thou find'st to be too busy° is some danger.
Stop —Leave° wringing of your hands. Peace. Sit you down
And let me wring your heart. For so I shall
If it be made of penetrable stuff,
If damnèd custom have not brazed it so
That it be proof and bulwark against sense.[1]

Gertrude

What have I done, that thou dar'st wag thy tongue
In noise so rude against me?

Hamlet

Such an act
disfigures That blurs° the grace and blush of modesty,
Calls virtue hypocrite, takes off the rose
From the fair forehead of an innocent love
And sets a blister[2] there, makes marriage vows
gamblers' As false as dicers'° oaths—oh, such a deed
As from the body of contraction[3] plucks
The very soul, and sweet religion makes
jumble / blush A rhapsody° of words. Heaven's face does glow°
O'er this solidity and compound mass[4]
With heated visage,[5] as against the doom,[6]
Is thought-sick at the act.

Gertrude

Ay me, what act
That roars so loud and thunders in the index?[7]

Hamlet

Look here upon this picture and on this:[8]
The counterfeit presentment[9] of two brothers.
See. What a grace was seated on this brow?
Hyperion's curls, the front of Jove himself,[10]
god of war An eye like Mars° to threaten and command,
posture A station° like the herald Mercury[11]

1 *To give the world assurance of a man*

I.e., to make the world certain what a real man should be

2 *batten on this moor*

Feed yourself on this barren land

3 *The heyday in the blood*

I.e., sexual passion

4 *waits upon*

Is subordinate to

5 *Nor sense to ecstasy was ne'er so thralled, / But it reserved some quantity of choice / To serve in such a difference*

I.e., judgment is never so much in the sway of madness that it does not retain the capacity to distinguish between two men who are so different

6 *cozened you at hoodman-blind*

Cheated you in a game of blindmans' bluff (suggesting that Gertrude must have been artificially deprived of her senses when she took Claudius as her husband)

7 *Could not so mope*

Would not be so weak (i.e., even one of the five senses, working alone [and poorly], would have the ability to tell these two men apart)

8 *Rebellious Hell, / If thou canst mutine in a matron's bones, / To flaming youth let virtue be as wax / And melt in her own fire.*

Sin (which Hamlet sees itself as *Hell*, and as *Rebellious* because it causes us to rebel against our better sense), if you can make even an old woman's body mutiny against her judgment, then hot-blooded youth will turn chastity into wax, melting it with the heat of its passion.

9 *pardons*

I.e., makes excuses for. The Folio prints "panders," which there means "serves to gratify," and some editors adopt it.

10 *Proclaim no shame / When the compulsive ardor gives the charge, / Since frost itself as actively doth burn, / And reason pardons will.*

Do not label it a sin when irresistable passion attacks, since the elderly also burn (with desire), and their reason tries to justify their lust.

Recently landed New-lighted° on a Heaven-kissing hill—
A combination and a form indeed
approval Where every god did seem to set his seal°
To give the world assurance of a man.[1]
This was your husband. Look you now what follows:
i.e., ear of corn Here is your husband, like a mildewed ear°
Blighting Blasting° his wholesome brother. Have you eyes?
cease Could you on this fair mountain leave° to feed
And batten on this moor?[2] Ha, have you eyes?
You cannot call it love, for at your age
The heyday in the blood[3] is tame; it's humble
And waits upon[4] the judgment. And what judgment
Perceptual faculties Would step from this to this? Sense° sure you have,
Else could you not have motion, but sure that sense
paralyzed Is apoplexed,° for madness would not err,
Nor sense to ecstasy was ne'er so thralled,
But it reserved some quantity of choice
To serve in such a difference.[5] What devil was 't
That thus hath cozened you at hoodman-blind?[6]
Eyes without feeling, feeling without sight,
without (Latin) Ears without hands or eyes, smelling sans° all,
Or but a sickly part of one true sense
Could not so mope.[7] O shame, where is thy blush?
Rebellious Hell,
If thou canst mutine in a matron's bones,
To flaming youth let virtue be as wax
And melt in her own fire.[8] Proclaim no shame
When the compulsive ardor gives the charge,
Since frost itself as actively doth burn,
And reason pardons[9] will.[10]

Gertrude

O Hamlet, speak no more!
Thou turn'st my very eyes into my soul,

1 *grievèd*

I.e., grievous; the Folio prints "grained" (i.e., ingrained).

2 *twentieth part the tithe*

One twentieth of one tenth

3 *vice of kings*

I.e., perfect pattern of a vicious king

4 *shreds and patches*

I.e., inconsequential and inadequate pieces (as opposed to the *combination and a form indeed*, as Hamlet imagines his father in 3.4.60). Some editors find in this a reference to the patchwork costume worn by the stage fool, and in *vice* in line 98 a reference to the comic companion of the devil in the medieval morality plays; but Hamlet at this moment sees nothing clownish about Claudius, and a popular theatrical idiom would trivialize his disgust.

5 *lapsed in time and passion*

I.e., having wasted time and yielding to passion

And there I see such black and grievèd[1] spots
color As will leave there their tinct.°

Hamlet

Nay, but to live
greasy In the rank sweat of an enseamèd° bed,
Steeped Stewed° in corruption, honeying and making love
Over the nasty sty—

Gertrude

Oh, speak to me no more!
These words like daggers enter in my ears;
No more, sweet Hamlet.

Hamlet

A murderer and a villain,
A slave that is not twentieth part the tithe[2]
previous Of your precedent° lord, a vice of kings,[3]
thief A cutpurse° of the empire and the rule,
crown That from a shelf the precious diadem° stole
And put it in his pocket—

Gertrude

No more!

Hamlet

A king of shreds and patches[4]—

Enter **Ghost**.

Save me and hover o'er me with your wings,
You heavenly guards! [*to* **Ghost**] What would your
gracious figure?

Gertrude

Alas, he's mad!

Hamlet

Do you not come your tardy son to chide,
That, lapsed in time and passion,[5] lets go by

1 *Your bedded hair, like life in excrements*

Your hairs, which normally lay flat, as if such outgrowths (*excrement*) could have life of their own

2 *His form and cause conjoined, preaching to stones, / Would make them capable.*

His appearance and his motive, combined together, would make even stones respond to him.

3 *convert / My stern effects*

Change my serious intentions (i.e., that the pity Hamlet feels for the Ghost might temper his focus on revenge)

4 *Will want true color*

Will not be what it's supposed to be

urgent Th' important° acting of your dread command?
Oh, say!

Ghost

Do not forget. This visitation
sharpen Is but to whet° thy almost blunted purpose.
bewilderment But look: amazement° on thy mother sits.
Oh, step between her and her fighting soul.
Imagination Conceit° in weakest bodies strongest works.
Speak to her, Hamlet.

Hamlet

How is it with you, lady?

Gertrude

Alas, how is 't with you
empty air That you do bend your eye on vacancy°
insubstantial And with th' incorporal° air do hold discourse?
Forth at your eyes your spirits wildly peep,
call to arms And, as the sleeping soldiers in th' alarm,°
Your bedded hair, like life in excrements,[1]
Start up and stand on end. O gentle son,
madness Upon the heat and flame of thy distemper°
Sprinkle cool patience. Whereon do you look?

Hamlet

On him, on him! Look you, how pale he glares!
His form and cause conjoined, preaching to stones,
Would make them capable.[2]—Do not look upon me,
Lest with this piteous action you convert
My stern effects.[3] Then what I have to do
perhaps Will want true color,[4] tears perchance° for blood.

Gertrude

To whom do you speak this?

Hamlet

Do you see nothing there?

1 *This bodiless creation ecstasy / Is very cunning in.*

Madness (*ecstasy*) is very skillful (*cunning*) in producing such hallucinations.

2 *which madness / Would gambol from*

A task that a mad person would jump away from

3 *flattering unction*

Balm that soothes but does not heal

4 *skin and film*

Cover over (like skin growing over a wound)

Gertrude

Nothing at all, yet all that is I see.

Hamlet

Nor did you nothing hear?

Gertrude

No, nothing but ourselves.

Hamlet

Why, look you there! Look how it steals away—
characteristic clothing My father, in his habit° as he lived—
doorway Look where he goes, even now, out at the portal!°

Ghost *exits.*

Gertrude

invention This the very coinage° of your brain.
madness This bodiless creation ecstasy°
Is very cunning in.[1]

Hamlet

My pulse as yours doth temperately keep time
And makes as healthful music. It is not madness
That I have uttered. Bring me to the test,
repeat And I the matter will reword,° which madness
Would gambol from.[2] Mother, for love of grace,
Lay not that flattering unction[3] to your soul
That not your trespass but my madness speaks.
It will but skin and film[4] the ulcerous place
undermining Whiles rank corruption, mining° all within,
Infects unseen. Confess yourself to Heaven,
Repent what's past, avoid what is to come,
And do not spread the compost on the weeds
moral exhortation To make them ranker. Forgive me this my virtue,°
grossness / degenerate For in the fatness° of these pursy° times
Virtue itself of vice must pardon beg,
bow / permission Yea, curb° and woo for leave° to do him good.

1 *house*

Q2 has no verb here following *either*, but clearly something contrasting with *throw him out* is required both for sense and metrically. Shakespeare, in *The Comedy of Errors*, does write of "Satan, housed within this man" (4.4.51), and so this word is adopted here.

2 *me with this and this with me*

I.e., me with Polonius's death (which will result in Hamlet's punishment) and Polonius with me (by Hamlet's killing him)

3 *their scourge and minister*

Heaven's instrument of punishment

4 *answer well*

Take responsibility for

5 *This bad begins and worse remains behind.*

This is a bad beginning, and worse is yet to come.

Gertrude

O Hamlet, thou hast cleft my heart in twain.

Hamlet

Oh, throw away the worser part of it
And live the purer with the other half.
Good night—but go not to my uncle's bed.
Put on Assume° a virtue if you have it not.
habitual behavior That monster, custom,° who all sense doth eat,
Of habits devil, is angel yet in this:
practice That to the use° of actions fair and good
He likewise gives a frock or livery
quickly That aptly° is put on. Refrain tonight,
And that shall lend a kind of easiness
To the next abstinence, the next more easy.
imprint For use almost can change the stamp° of nature,
And either house[1] the devil or throw him out
With wondrous potency. Once more, good night,
And when you are desirous to be blessed,
I'll blessing beg of you. For this same lord
I do repent, but Heaven hath pleased it so
To punish me with this and this with me,[2]
That I must be their scourge and minister.[3]
hide I will bestow° him and will answer well[4]
The death I gave him. So, again, good night.
I must be cruel only to be kind.
This bad begins and worse remains behind.[5]
One word more, good lady—

Gertrude

What shall I do?

Hamlet

Not this, by no means, that I bid you do:
bloated Let the bloat° King tempt you again to bed,

1 *in craft*

By cunning

2 *dear concernings*

Important matters

3 *Unpeg the basket on the house's top, / Let the birds fly, and, like the famous ape, / To try conclusions in the basket creep / And break your own neck down.*

The precise story to which Hamlet alludes is lost. Hamlet warns his mother not to let his secret out of the basket; if she does so she, like the ape who fatally broke his neck trying to imitate the birds, will come to a bad end.

4 *They must sweep my way / And marshal me to knavery.*

They must prepare my road and lead me into some trap

5 *Hoist with his own petard*

Blown up by his own explosives

6 *And 't shall go hard / But I will delve*

And it will only be because of bad luck if I do not dig

7 *blow them*

I.e., blow them up

8 *When in one line two crafts directly meet*

When two plots meet in the same place (i.e., when, by digging my tunnel so as to intersect theirs, I take them by surprise)

Pinch wanton on your cheek, call you his mouse,
filthy And let him, for a pair of reechy° kisses
stroking Or paddling° in your neck with his damned fingers,
disclose Make you to ravel° all this matter out
That I essentially am not in madness
But mad in craft.[1] 'Twere good you let him know,
only For who that's but° a queen, fair, sober, wise,
toad / tomcat Would from a paddock,° from a bat, a gib,°
Such dear concernings[2] hide? Who would do so?
No, in despite of sense and secrecy,
Unpeg the basket on the house's top,
Let the birds fly, and, like the famous ape,
To try conclusions in the basket creep
And break your own neck down.[3]

Gertrude

Be thou assured, if words be made of breath
And breath of life, I have no life to breathe
What thou hast said to me.

Hamlet

I must to England, you know that?

Gertrude

Alack,
I had forgot. 'Tis so concluded on.

Hamlet

There's letters sealed, and my two schoolfellows,
poisonous snakes Whom I will trust as I will adders° fanged,
They bear the mandate. They must sweep my way
proceed And marshal me to knavery.[4] Let it work,°
bomb maker For 'tis the sport to have the engineer°
Hoist with his own petard.[5] And 't shall go hard
tunnels But I will delve[6] one yard below their mines°
And blow them[7] at the moon. Oh, 'tis most sweet
When in one line two crafts directly meet.[8]

1 *draw toward an end with you*

Conclude my interactions with you (and perhaps also "drag you toward your grave")

2 [They] exit, [**Hamlet** carrying **Polonius** offstage].

Q2 merely marks a single exit, though the stage must be cleared. The Folio adds "Hamlet tugging in Polonius."

This man shall set me packing.
I'll lug the guts into the neighbor room.
Mother, good night. Indeed this counselor
Is now most still, most secret, and most grave
Who was in life a most foolish prating knave.
—Come, sir, to draw toward an end with you.[1]
—Good night, mother.

*[They] exit, [***Hamlet** *carrying* **Polonius** *offstage].*[2]

1 *brainish apprehension*

deranged misconception

2 *It had been so with us, had we been there.*

He would have done the same with me, had I been there (employing the royal first-person plural pronoun).

3 *out of haunt*

In seclusion

Act 4, Scene 1

Enter King [**Claudius**] *and Queen* [**Gertrude**], *with* **Rosencrantz** *and* **Guildenstern**.

Claudius

ificance / deep sighs There's matter° in these sighs; these profound heaves°
You must translate. 'Tis fit we understand them.
Where is your son?

Gertrude

Bestow this place on us a little while.

[**Rosencrantz** *and* **Guildenstern** *exit.*]

Ah, mine own lord, what have I seen tonight!

Claudius

What, Gertrude? How does Hamlet?

Gertrude

Mad as the sea and wind when both contend
uncontrollable Which is the mightier. In his lawless° fit,
Behind the arras hearing something stir,
Whips out his rapier, cries, "A rat, a rat!"
And in this brainish apprehension[1] kills
The unseen good old man.

Claudius

O heavy deed!
It had been so with us, had we been there.[2]
His liberty is full of threats to all—
To you yourself, to us, to everyone.
Alas, how shall this bloody deed be answered?
ttributed / foresight It will be laid° to us, whose providence°
controlled Should have kept short,° restrained, and out of haunt[3]
This mad young man. But so much was our love,
We would not understand what was most fit,
But, like the owner of a foul disease,
being seen To keep it from divulging,° let it feed

1 [...,]

In both Q2 and the folio some word or phrase is seemingly missing here that would provide a referent for *Whose whisper* in line 41, perhaps something like "So venomous slander."

2 *Whose whisper o'er the world's diameter, / As level as the cannon to his blank, / Transports his poisoned shot*

The rumor of which spread over the whole world—as directly as a cannon ball carries its deadly ammunition to its target.

3 *miss our name / And hit the woundless air*

Avoid wounding our reputation and only strike the invulnerable air

vital part Even on the pith° of life. Where is he gone?

Gertrude

To draw apart the body he hath killed,
precious metal O'er whom—his very madness, like some ore°
mine Among a mineral° of metals base,
he Shows itself pure—'a° weeps for what is done.

Claudius

O Gertrude, come away.
The sun no sooner shall the mountains touch
But we will ship him hence, and this vile deed
authority We must, with all our majesty° and skill,
condone Both countenance° and excuse.—Ho, Guildenstern!

Enter **Rosencrantz** *and* **Guildenstern**.

Friends both, go join you with some further aid:
Hamlet in madness hath Polonius slain,
And from his mother's closet hath he dragged him.
Go seek him out, speak fair, and bring the body
Into the chapel. I pray you, haste in this.
[**Rosencrantz** *and* **Guildenstern** *exit*.]
Come, Gertrude. We'll call up our wisest friends
And let them know both what we mean to do
And what's untimely done. [...,] [1]
Whose whisper o'er the world's diameter,
As level as the cannon to his blank,
its Transports his° poisoned shot, [2] may miss our name
And hit the woundless air. [3] Oh, come away!
My soul is full of discord and dismay. *They exit.*

1 *whereto 'tis kin*

A reference to Genesis 3:19, where God tells Adam and Eve "for thou art dust, and to dust shalt thou return."

2 *keep your counsel and not mine own*

I.e., follow your advice and not protect my own interests

3 *demanded of a sponge*

Questioned by a flatterer (derogatory)

4 *apple*

This is what is printed in Q2; the Folio has "Ape," which many editors prefer, sometimes combining it with Q2's reading to give "like an ape an apple." Q1 has "as an Ape doth nuttes."

Act 4, Scene 2

Enter **Hamlet**.

Hamlet

hidden Safely stowed.° But soft, what noise? Who calls on Hamlet? Oh, here they come.

Enter **Rosencrantz**, [**Guildenstern**,] *and others.*

Rosencrantz

What have you done, my lord, with the dead body?

Hamlet

Mixed Compounded° it with dust, whereto 'tis kin.[1]

Rosencrantz

Tell us where 'tis, that we may take it thence
And bear it to the chapel.

Hamlet

Do not believe it.

Rosencrantz

Believe what?

Hamlet

That I can keep your counsel and not mine own.[2] Besides, to be demanded of a sponge![3] What *reply* replication° should be made by the son of a King?

Rosencrantz

Take you me for a sponge, my lord?

Hamlet

favor Ay, sir, that soaks up the King's countenance,° his rewards, his authorities. But such officers do the King best service in the end. He keeps them, like an apple,[4] in the corner of his jaw, first mouthed to be last swallowed.

1 *A knavish speech sleeps in a foolish ear.*

I.e., insulting remarks have no effect on a fool who cannot understand them.

2 *The body is with the King, but the King is not with the body.*

Hamlet's sally of metaphysical wit is a piece of madness, but, as so often, it has method in it. He is playing on the influential political doctrine of the king's two bodies, which distinguishes between the monarch's own, mortal, physical body, and the enduring body of the state that he heads. (Rosencrantz and Guildenstern play on the same idea in flattering Claudius at 3.3.8ff. Hamlet's first *body* may refer to either of these two; the second *body* refers most directly to Polonius's corpse but hints at a possible separation between Claudius and his state, or even his mortal form.

gathered When he needs what you have gleaned,° it is but squeezing you and, sponge, you shall be dry again.

Rosencrantz

I understand you not, my lord.

Hamlet

I am glad of it. A knavish speech sleeps in a foolish ear.[1]

Rosencrantz

My lord, you must tell us where the body is and go with us to the King.

Hamlet

The body is with the King, but the King is not with the body.[2] The King is a thing—

Guildenstern

A thing, my lord?

Hamlet

Of nothing. Bring me to him. *They exit.*

1 and two or three

The imprecision of the stage direction is often taken as evidence that Q2 (the text this edition is based on) was printed from an authorial manuscript rather than from one prepared for performance (which would need to be more exact in its specifications for actors).

2 *Who like not in their judgment, but in their eyes*

Whose affections are guided not by logic, but by appearances

3 *And where 'tis so, th' offender's scourge is weighed, / But never the offense.*

And where this is the case, (the public) condemns the punisher but not the criminal.

4 *bear all smooth and even*

Manage these events so everything seems normal and straight forward

5 *Deliberate pause*

(To be the result of) careful thought

Act 4, Scene 3

Enter King [**Claudius**] *and two or three.* [1]

Claudius

I have sent to seek him and to find the body.
How dangerous is it that this man goes loose!
Yet must not we put the strong law on him:
by / irrational He's loved of° the distracted° multitude,
Who like not in their judgment, but their eyes. [2]
And where 'tis so, th' offender's scourge is weighed,
But never the offense. [3] To bear all smooth and even, [4]
This sudden sending him away must seem
Deliberate pause. [5] Diseases desperate grown
remedy By desperate appliance° are relieved,
Or not at all.

Enter **Rosencrantz**, [**Guildenstern**,] *and all the rest.*

How now, what hath befall'n?

Rosencrantz

Where the dead body is bestowed, my lord,
We cannot get from him.

Claudius

But where is he?

Rosencrantz

Outside (the door) Without,° my lord; guarded, to know your pleasure.

Claudius

Bring him before us.

Rosencrantz

—Ho! Bring in the lord.

Enter [**Hamlet** *with guards*].

1 *convocation of politic worms*

Probably an allusion to the Diet of Worms, a council of Catholic clergy held in 1521, with a parody of its debate about transubstantiation (the transformation of the blood and body of Christ into the wine and wafer of the Communion service). At this council, Martin Luther defended his ideas concerning the reformation of the church, establishing the doctrinal foundations of Protestantism.

2 *Your worm is your only emperor for diet.*

I.e., the worm has the most exclusive diet. (*Your* is used colloquially in a general sense.)

3 *variable service*

Different dishes

4 *go a progress*

Go on a formal, royal journey

5 *th' other place*

I.e., Hell

Claudius

Now, Hamlet, where's Polonius?

Hamlet

At supper.

Claudius

At supper where?

Hamlet

he Not where he eats, but where 'a° is eaten. A certain con-
even now vocation of politic worms[1] are e'en° at him. Your worm
fatten is your only emperor for diet.[2] We fat° all creatures
besides ourselves else° to fat us, and we fat ourselves for maggots. Your
fat king and your lean beggar is but variable service[3]—
two dishes, but to one table. That's the end.

Claudius

Alas, alas!

Hamlet

eaten A man may fish with the worm that hath eat° of a king,
and eat of the fish that hath fed of that worm.

Claudius

What dost thou mean by this?

Hamlet

Nothing but to show you how a king may go a progress[4] through the guts of a beggar.

Claudius

Where is Polonius?

Hamlet

there In Heaven. Send thither° to see. If your messenger find
him not there, seek him i' th' other place[5] yourself. But
if indeed you find him not within this month, you shall
smell nose° him as you go up the stairs into the lobby.

Claudius

[*to attendants*] Go; seek him there!

1 *at help*

Favorable

2 *I see a cherub that sees them.*

***Cherubim* were the second highest rank of angels thought to be particularly watchful of human affairs. Hamlet is suggesting that he can (or Heaven can) perceive Claudius's purposes—better than Claudius imagines.**

3 *man and wife is one flesh*

From the marriage ceremony described in the Book of Common Prayer (echoing Genesis 2:24 and Matthew 19:5–6)

4 *at foot*

Closely

5 *leans on*

Is relevant to

Hamlet

He ’A° will stay till you come.

[*Attendants exit.*]

Claudius

Hamlet, this deed, for thine especial safety—
value Which we do tender° as we dearly grieve
For that which thou hast done—must send thee hence.
Therefore prepare thyself.
ship The bark° is ready and the wind at help,[1]
wait / bound Th’ associates tend,° and everything is bent°
For England.

Hamlet

For England?

Claudius

Ay, Hamlet.

Hamlet

Good.

Claudius

So is it, if thou knew’st our purposes.

Hamlet

I see a cherub that sees them.[2] But come; for England.
Farewell, dear mother.

Claudius

Thy loving father, Hamlet.

Hamlet

My mother. Father and mother is man and wife; man and wife is one flesh:[3] so, my mother.—Come; for England! *He exits.*

Claudius

Follow him at foot.[4] Tempt him with speed aboard.
Delay it not. I’ll have him hence tonight.
Away! For everything is sealed and done
That else leans on[5] th’ affair. Pray you, make haste.

1 *hold'st at aught*

Value at all

2 *As my great power thereof may give thee sense*

As my position should make you realize (the value of my love)

3 *free awe*

Uncompelled respect (since Denmark has no army in England)

4 *coldly set*

Lightly disregard

5 *sovereign process*

Royal command

6 *imports at full*

Explicitly orders

7 *congruing*

Agreeing. The Folio prints "conjuring," probably trying to make sense of an unfamiliar word.

8 *Howe'er my haps*

Whatever my fortunes might be

[*All but* **Claudius**] *exit.*

i.e., King of England And, England,° if my love thou hold'st at aught[1]—
As my great power thereof may give thee sense,[2]
still / scar Since yet° thy cicatrice° looks raw and red
After the Danish sword, and thy free awe[3]
Pays homage to us—thou mayst not coldly set[4]
Our sovereign process,[5] which imports at full,[6]
By letters congruing[7] to that effect,
immediate The present° death of Hamlet. Do it, England,
fever For like the hectic° in my blood he rages,
And thou must cure me. Till I know 'tis done,
Howe'er my haps,[8] my joys will ne'er begin. *He exits.*

1 *the conveyance of*

Permission for

2 *would aught*

Wishes anything

3 *let*

This is an order to the Captain (like *Tell* in line 2)

4 *Go softly on.*

None of the rest of this scene appears in the Folio.

5 *How purposed*

For what purpose

Act 4, Scene 4

Enter **Fortinbras** *with his army [, including the* **Captain**,*] over the stage.*

Fortinbras

Go, Captain; from me greet the Danish King.
permission Tell him that, by his license,° Fortinbras
Craves the conveyance of[1] a promised march
Over his kingdom. You know the rendezvous.
If that his Majesty would aught[2] with us,
presence We shall express our duty in his eye,°
And let[3] him know so.

Captain

I will do 't, my lord.

Fortinbras

carefully Go softly° on.[4]

[*All but* **Captain** *exit.*]

Enter **Hamlet, Rosencrantz**, [**Guildenstern**], *etc.*

Hamlet

troops [*to* **Captain**] Good sir, whose powers° are these?

Captain

They are of Norway, sir.

Hamlet

How purposed,[5] sir, I pray you?

Captain

Against some part of Poland.

Hamlet

Who commands them, sir?

Captain

The nephew to old Norway, Fortinbras.

1 *To pay five ducats, five, I would not farm it*

I.e., I would not rent it for five ducats.

2 *Nor will it yield to Norway or the Pole / A ranker rate should it be sold in fee*

Nor will it provide the King of Norway or the King of Poland a higher amount, even if they were to sell it outright.

3 *Two thousand souls and twenty thousand ducats / Will not debate the question of this straw.*

Two thousand men and twenty thousand ducats will not contest this trifling piece of land (i.e., no one would spend so much for so little).

4 *That inward breaks and shows no cause without / Why the man dies*

That ruptures inside the body without any symptoms on the outside that would explain his death

5 *inform against*

Accuse

6 *Looking before and after*

Contemplating both future and past

Hamlet

central part Goes it against the main° of Poland, sir,
Or for some frontier?

Captain

exaggeration Truly to speak, and with no addition,°
We go to gain a little patch of ground
That hath in it no profit but the name.
To pay five ducats, five, I would not farm it,[1]
Nor will it yield to Norway or the Pole
A ranker rate should it be sold in fee.[2]

Hamlet

Why, then the Polack never will defend it.

Captain

defended by armies Yes; it is already garrisoned.°

Hamlet

Two thousand souls and twenty thousand ducats
Will not debate the question of this straw.[3]
abscess This is th' impostume° of much wealth and peace,
That inward breaks and shows no cause without
Why the man dies.[4] I humbly thank you, sir.

Captain

i.e., be with God by° you, sir.

Rosencrantz

Will 't please you go, my lord?

Hamlet

I'll be with you straight. Go a little before.

[*All but* **Hamlet** *exit.*]

How all occasions do inform against[5] me
And spur my dull revenge. What is a man
profit If his chief good and market° of his time
Be but to sleep and feed? A beast, no more.
understanding Sure he that made us with such large discourse,°
Looking before and after,[6] gave us not

1 *Now, whether it be / Bestial oblivion, or some craven scruple / Of thinking too precisely on th' event*

Now, whether it is an animal-like forgetfulness, or else some cowardly hesitation that comes from too carefully considering the consequences

2 *mass and charge*

Size and cost

3 *Makes mouths at the invisible event*

Makes faces (i.e., laughs in scorn) at the unforeseeable outcome

4 *Rightly to be great / Is not to stir without great argument, / But greatly to find quarrel in a straw / When honor's at the stake.*

I.e., true greatness does not hold back, waiting for an undeniable justification to act; when honor is at stake, one must boldly fashion a compelling reason even out of trifling matters.

5 *Whereon the numbers cannot try the cause*

I.e., which is so small that it cannot hold the armies that will fight for it

i.e., of understanding That capability° and godlike reason
decay To fust° in us unused. Now, whether it be
Bestial oblivion, or some craven scruple
Of thinking too precisely on th' event[1]—
broken into fourths A thought which, quartered,° hath but one part wisdom
And ever three parts coward—I do not know
Why yet I live to say this thing's to do,
Since Sith° I have cause and will and strength and means
obvious To do 't. Examples gross° as earth exhort me:
Witness this army of such mass and charge[2]
young Led by a delicate and tender° prince,
inspired Whose spirit with divine ambition puffed°
Makes mouths at the invisible event,[3]
vulnerable Exposing what is mortal and unsure°
To all that fortune, death, and danger dare,
something worthless Even for an eggshell.° Rightly to be great
Is not to stir without great argument,
But greatly to find quarrel in a straw
When honor's at the stake.[4] How stand I then,
dishonored That have a father killed, a mother stained,°
Provocations Excitements° of my reason and my blood,
And let all sleep, while, to my shame, I see
The imminent death of twenty thousand men,
illusion That for a fantasy and trick° of fame
Go to their graves like beds, fight for a plot
Whereon the numbers cannot try the cause,[5]
container Which is not tomb enough and continent°
To hide the slain? Oh, from this time forth,
My thoughts be bloody or be nothing worth! *He exits.*

1 *will needs be*

Must be

2 *Spurns enviously at straws*

Becomes angry at nothing

3 *in doubt*

Obscurely

4 *unshapèd use*

Incoherence

5 *yawn at*

Are bewildered by. The Folio prints "aim" (guess).

6 *Though nothing sure, yet much unhappily*

Though nothing clear, still much that comes uncomfortably near the truth. Many editors insist that *thought* in line 12 refers not to Ophelia's thought but to the inferences about it drawn by observers, and thus take this phrase to mean "though nothing definitive, still much that could be maliciously construed." Either is possible.

Act 4, Scene 5

Enter **Horatio**, **Gertrude**, *and a* **Gentleman**.

Gertrude

I will not speak with her.

Gentleman

insistent — She is importunate,°

mad — Indeed distract.° Her mood will needs be[1] pitied.

Gertrude

What would she have?

Gentleman

She speaks much of her father, says she hears

plots / stutters — There's tricks° i' th' world, and hems,° and beats her heart,

Spurns enviously at straws,[2] speaks things in doubt[3]

nonsense — That carry but half sense. Her speech is nothing,°

Yet the unshapèd use[4] of it doth move

ke sense of it / wonder — The hearers to collection.° They yawn° at[5] it

rearrange — And botch° the words up fit to their own thoughts,

i.e., Her words — Which,° as her winks and nods and gestures yield them,

intended — Indeed would make one think there might be thought,°

Though nothing sure, yet much unhappily.[6]

Horatio

'Twere good she were spoken with, for she may strew

Dangerous conjectures in ill-breeding minds.

Gertrude

Let her come in. [**Gentleman** *exits*.]

Enter **Ophelia** [*with the* **Gentleman**].

[*aside*] To my sick soul, as sin's true nature is,

trifle / calamity — Each toy° seems prologue to some great amiss.°

1 *So full of artless jealousy is guilt, / It spills itself in fearing to be spilt.*

I.e., guilt is so full of uncontrolled suspicion that it reveals itself in its own fear of being revealed.

2 *cockle hat*

A hat decorated with a *cockle* (scallop) shell was the mark of a pilgrim returning from the shrine of St. James of Compostela in Spain.

So full of artless jealousy is guilt,
It spills itself in fearing to be spilt.[1]

Ophelia

Where is the beauteous Majesty of Denmark?

Gertrude

How now, Ophelia?

Ophelia

[*sings*] How should I your true love know
From another one?
By his cockle hat[2] and staff,
shoes And his sandal shoon.°

Gertrude

means Alas, sweet lady, what imports° this song?

Ophelia

Say you? Nay, pray you, mark.
[*sings*] He is dead and gone, lady;
He is dead and gone,
At his head a grass-green turf,
At his heels a stone.
Oh, ho!

Gertrude

Nay, but, Ophelia—

Ophelia

Pray you, mark.
[*sings*] White his shroud as the mountain snow—

Enter King [**Claudius**].

Gertrude

Alas, look here, my lord.

Ophelia

Adorned [*sings*] Larded° all with sweet flowers,
Which bewept to the ground did not go

1 *God 'ield you*

May God reward (*yield*) you (i.e. thank you for asking)

2 *They say the owl was a baker's daughter.*

An allusion to a folktale in which a baker's daughter only gave Christ a small loaf of bread when he asked for food; he retaliated by turning her into an owl.

3 *Conceit upon her father.*

Imaginings provoked by her father's death.

4 *St. Valentine's day*

Alluding to the traditional belief that the first member of the opposite sex seen on this holiday will become one's *Valentine* (i.e., sweetheart)

5 *By Cock*

I.e., by God; *Cock* was a common euphemistic corruption, but also a pun here on *cock* as "penis."

i.e., tears With true-love showers.°

Claudius

How do you, pretty lady?

Ophelia

Well, God 'ield you![1] They say the owl was a baker's daughter.[2] Lord, we know what we are, but know not what we may be. God be at your table.

Claudius

Conceit upon her father.[3]

Ophelia

Pray, let's have no words of this, but when they ask you what it means, say you this:

[*sings*] Tomorrow is Saint Valentine's day,[4]
early All in the morning betime,°
And I a maid at your window,
To be your Valentine.
put on Then up he rose, and donned° his clothes,
unlatched And dupped° the chamber door.
Let in the maid that out a maid
Never departed more.

Claudius

Pretty Ophelia—

Ophelia

of Indeed, without an oath I'll make an end on° 't:

i.e., Jesus [*sings*] By Gis° and by Saint Charity,
Alack, and fie for shame!
Young men will do 't, if they come to 't;
By Cock,[5] they are to blame.
i.e., had sex with Quoth she, "Before you tumbled° me,
You promised me to wed."
He answers:
have "So would I ha'° done, by yonder sun,
If An° thou hadst not come to my bed."

1 *choose but weep*

I.e., help weeping

2 *single spies*

As solitary soldiers

3 *just remove*

Justifiable removal

4 *we have done but greenly / In hugger-mugger to inter him*

We have acted naïvely in burying him secretly

5 *as much containing*

As important

6 *Feeds on this wonder*

Takes advantage of this confusion (of the people)

7 *himself in clouds*

His own intentions secret

8 *wants not buzzers*

Does not lack rumormongers

9 *Wherein necessity, of matter beggared, / Will nothing stick our person to arraign / In ear and ear*

I.e., and out of their need for gossip, which is deprived of true, scandalous information, the scandalmongers will not hesitate to accuse me to all who will listen

Claudius

How long hath she been thus?

Ophelia

I hope all will be well. We must be patient, but I cannot choose but weep[1] to think they would lay him i' th' cold ground. My brother shall know of it, and so I thank you for your good counsel. Come, my coach! Good night, ladies. Good night, sweet ladies. Good night, good night. [**Ophelia** *exits.*]

Claudius

Follow her close. Give her good watch, I pray you.
[**Horatio** *exits.*]
Oh, this is the poison of deep grief. It springs
All from her father's death, and now behold!
O Gertrude, Gertrude,
When sorrows come, they come not single spies[2]
But in battalions: first, her father slain;
instigator Next, your son gone, and he most violent author°
stirred up Of his own just remove;[3] the people muddied,°
confused Thick° and unwholesome in thoughts and whispers
For good Polonius' death, and we have done but
greenly
In hugger-mugger to inter him;[4] poor Ophelia
Divided from herself and her fair judgment,
., imitations of humans Without the which we are pictures,° or mere beasts;
Last—and as much containing[5] as all these—
Her brother is in secret come from France,
Feeds on this wonder,[6] keeps himself in clouds,[7]
And wants not buzzers[8] to infect his ear
With pestilent speeches of his father's death,
Wherein necessity, of matter beggared,
Will nothing stick our person to arraign
In ear and ear.[9] O my dear Gertrude, this,

1 *murdering-piece*

Small cannon loaded with shrapnel rather than a single large ball

2 *superfluous*

Redundant (in that it kills him many times over)

3 *Switzers*

Swiss mercenaries, employed throughout Europe as royal bodyguards

4 *overpeering of his list*

Rising over its barriers (i.e., flooding the shore)

5 *as the world were now but to begin*

As if the world were only now beginning

6 *The ratifiers and props of every word*

I.e., Which (*Antiquity* and *custom*) are the approvers and upholders of every social convention

7 *counter*

In the wrong direction (a term from hunting with dogs, as in the previous line)

Like to a murdering-piece,[1] in many places
Gives me superfluous[2] death. *A noise within.*

Enter a **Messenger**.

Claudius

Attend. Where is my Switzers?[3] Let them guard the door.
What is the matter?

Messenger

Save yourself, my lord.
The ocean, overpeering of his list,[4]
shores / merciless Eats not the flats° with more impiteous° haste
insurrection Than young Laertes, in a riotous head,°
O'erbears your officers. The rabble call him "Lord"
And—as the world were now but to begin,[5]
Antiquity forgot, custom not known,
The ratifiers and props of every word[6]—
They cry, "Choose we! Laertes shall be king!"
Caps, hands, and tongues applaud it to the clouds:
"Laertes shall be king! Laertes king!"

Gertrude

i.e., follow noisily How cheerfully on the false trail they cry.° *A noise within*
Oh, this is counter,[7] you false Danish dogs!

Enter **Laertes** *with others*.

Claudius

The doors are broke.

Laertes

Where is this King?—Sirs, stand you all without.

1 *give me leave*

I.e., let me be alone with the King.

2 *brands the harlot*

Refers to the idea that prostitutes might be punished with branding (see 3.4.44)

3 *treason can but peep to what it would, / Acts little of his will*

Treason can only glance at what it would like to do, unable to do much to enact its desires. (An ironic statement, coming from a man who successfully committed regicide to become king.)

All

No, let's come in!

Laertes

I pray you, give me leave.[1]

All

We will; we will.

Laertes

Guard I thank you. Keep° the door. [**Laertes**'s *followers exit.*]
—O thou vile King,
Give me my father!

Gertrude

Calmly, good Laertes.

Laertes

That drop of blood that's calm proclaims me bastard,
Cries "Cuckold!" to my father, brands the harlot[2]
Even here between the chaste unsmirchèd brow
Of my true mother.

Claudius

What is the cause, Laertes,
That thy rebellion looks so giant-like?
fear for —Let him go, Gertrude. Do not fear° our person.
surround; protect There's such divinity doth hedge° a king
That treason can but peep to what it would,
its Acts little of his° will.[3]—Tell me, Laertes,
Why thou art thus incensed.—Let him go, Gertrude.
—Speak, man.

Laertes

Where is my father?

Claudius

Dead.

Gertrude

But not by him.

1 *juggled with*

Manipulated; deceived

2 *To Hell, allegiance! Vows, to the blackest devil! / Conscience and grace to the profoundest pit*

Laertes' epithets and outraged, blaspheming self-assertion—*I dare damnation!*—would have marked him to contemporary audiences as a conventional revenge hero, consumed by bloodlust and reckless of the consequences, worldly or eternal. He takes up the role, that is, which Hamlet is so reluctant to play; but that role offers Laertes little defense against the manipulations of Claudius, who persuades him all too easily to adopt poison and subterfuge instead of choosing open revenge.

3 *both the worlds I give to negligence*

I.e., I do not care about the consequences either in this world or in the next

4 *My will, not all the world's.*

I.e., by my will, not all the world's will (will stop me).

5 *dear father*

The Folio prints "dear father's death," which is more direct but also is extrametrical. The King here is perhaps being diplomatic in not saying "death."

6 *swoopstake*

Indiscriminately; an alternate form of *sweepstake*, a situation in which one gambler wins the stakes of all the other players

7 *the kind, life-rendering pelican*

According to traditional folklore, the pelican nourished her young with blood from her own breast.

Claudius

Let him demand his fill.

Laertes

How came he dead? I'll not be juggled with.[1]
To Hell, allegiance! Vows, to the blackest devil!
Conscience and grace to the profoundest pit;[2]
I dare damnation! To this point I stand
That both the worlds I give to negligence.[3]
Let come what comes, only I'll be revenged
perfectly Most throughly° for my father.

Claudius

prevent Who shall stay° you?

Laertes

My will, not all the world's.[4]
manage And for my means, I'll husband° them so well,
They shall go far with little.

Claudius

Good Laertes,
If you desire to know the certainty
Of your dear father,[5] is 't writ in your revenge
take from That, swoopstake,[6] you will draw° both friend and foe,
Winner and loser?

Laertes

None but his enemies.

Claudius

Will you know them then?

Laertes

To his good friends thus wide I'll ope my arms
And, like the kind, life-rendering pelican,[7]
Feed Repast° them with my blood.

Claudius

Why, now you speak
Like a good child and a true gentleman.

1 *Till our scale turn the beam*

I.e., until our side of the scale is so heavy that the balance tilts in our favor. Laertes draws on the traditional metaphor of justice as a set of scales; here, the weight of Ophelia's madness is measured against (and compensated by) the weight of Laertes' revenge.

2 *poor*

The Folio prints "old," perhaps a clearer reference to Polonius; *poor*, however, can be an expression of affection.

3 *barefaced on the bier*

I.e., in an open coffin

4 *move thus*

I.e., be as moving as this

5 *You*

Indicating one of the others onstage

6 *It is the false steward that stole his master's daughter.*

Likely a specific reference to an unidentified ballad or folktale

7 *This nothing's more than matter.*

I.e., Ophelia's nonsense words have more meaning than rational speech.

That I am guiltless of your father's death
sympathetically — And am most sensibly° in grief for it,
plain / appear — It shall as level° to your judgment 'pear°
As day does to your eye. *A noise within.*

Enter **Ophelia**.

Laertes

Let her come in.
How now? What noise is that?
O heat, dry up my brains; tears seven times salt
power — Burn out the sense and virtue° of mine eye!
By Heaven, thy madness shall be paid with weight,
Till our scale turn the beam.[1] O rose of May,
Dear maid, kind sister, sweet Ophelia!
O heavens, is 't possible a young maid's wits
Should be as mortal as a poor[2] man's life?

Ophelia

[*sings*] They bore him barefaced on the bier,[3]
And in his grave rained many a tear.
Fare you well, my dove.

Laertes

urge — Hadst thou thy wits and didst persuade° revenge,
It could not move thus.[4]

Ophelia

You[5] must sing "A-down a-down," and you, "Call him
refrain — a-down-a."—Oh, how the wheel° becomes it! It is the
false steward that stole his master's daughter.[6]

Laertes

This nothing's more than matter.[7]

1 *fennel*

A parsley-like herb, conventionally associated with flattery and deceit

2 *columbines*

Herbaceous plants with variously colored, five-petalled flowers, conventionally associated with ingratitude and infidelity

3 *rue*

A medicinal herb, associated with sorrow and repentance (and sometimes known as *herb of grace*).

4 *with a difference*

I.e., for a different reason (in the terminology of heraldry, *difference* is a small variation in a coat of arms)

5 *daisy*

The flower is associated with springtime and innocent love.

6 *violets*

Violets are also associated with spring, but see 1.3.7 and 5.1.221.

Ophelia

There's rosemary: that's for remembrance. Pray you,
love, remember. And there is pansies: that's for
thoughts.

Laertes

lesson A document° in madness; thoughts and remembrance
connected fitted.°

Ophelia

There's fennel[1] for you, and columbines.[2]—There's
rue[3] for you, and here's some for me. We may call it
on "herb of grace" o'° Sundays.—You may wear your
rue with a difference.[4]—There's a daisy.[5] I would give
you some violets,[6] but they withered all when my
father died. They say 'a made a good end.
[*sings*] For bonny sweet Robin is all my joy—

Laertes

elancholy / suffering Thought° and afflictions, passion,° Hell itself,
omething charming She turns to favor° and to prettiness.

Ophelia

he [*sings*] And will 'a° not come again?
And will 'a not come again?
No, no, he is dead.
Go to thy deathbed;
He never will come again.
His beard was as white as snow,
White-haired / head Flaxen° was his poll.°
He is gone, he is gone,
And we cast away moan.
God ha' mercy on his soul.
i.e., be with And of all Christians' souls, God by° you.

[*She exits*.]

Laertes

Do you see this, O God?

1 *commune with*

Share in, or perhaps merely, "speak with" (i.e., get through to)

2 *Go but apart*

I.e., let's discuss this privately

3 *by direct or by collateral hand*

Directly or indirectly

4 *hatchment*

A tablet placed on a tomb bearing the coat of arms of the deceased

Claudius

Laertes, I must commune with[1] your grief,
what is fitting Or you deny me right.° Go but apart,[2]
whomever among Make choice of whom° your wisest friends you will,
And they shall hear and judge 'twixt you and me.
If by direct or by collateral hand[3]
involved They find us touched,° we will our kingdom give—
Our crown, our life, and all that we call ours—
recompense To you in satisfaction;° but if not,
Be you content to lend your patience to us,
And we shall jointly labor with your soul
satisfaction To give it due content.°

Laertes

Let this be so.
His means of death, his obscure funeral—
memorial No trophy,° sword, nor hatchment[4] o'er his bones,
ceremony No noble rite nor formal ostentation°—
Cry to be heard, as 'twere from Heaven to Earth,
So that That° I must call 't in question.

Claudius

So you shall.
And where th' offense is, let the great axe fall.
I pray you, go with me. *They exit.*

1 *an 't*

If it

2 *let to know*

Informed

3 *compelled valor*

Necessary brave defense

4 *thieves of mercy*

I.e., merciful thieves

Act 4, Scene 6

Enter **Horatio** *and* [*a* **Gentleman**].

Horatio

What are they that would speak with me?

Gentleman

Seafaring men, sir. They say they have letters for you.

Horatio

Let them come in. [**Gentleman** *exits.*]
I do not know from what part of the world I should be greeted, if not from Lord Hamlet.

Enter **Sailors**.

Sailor

God bless you, sir.

Horatio

Let Him bless thee too.

Sailor

He

'A° shall, sir, an 't[1] please Him. There's a letter for you, sir—it came from th' ambassador that was bound for England—if your name be Horatio, as I am let to know[2] it is.

Horatio

read / access · *pirate ship* · *equipment*

[*reads the letter*] "Horatio, When thou shalt have overlooked° this, give these fellows some means° to the King. They have letters for him. Ere we were two days old at sea, a pirate° of very warlike appointment° gave us chase. Finding ourselves too slow of sail, we put on a compelled valor,[3] and in the grapple I boarded them. On the instant, they got clear of our ship, so I alone became their prisoner. They have dealt with me like thieves of mercy,[4] but they knew what

1 *yet they are much too light for the bore of the matter*

The *bore* of a gun refers to the diameter of its barrel; Hamlet's words (though horrible enough to render a man speechless) would still be inadequate to convey the full significance of the matter, just as too-small bullets would be inadequate in a large gun.

2 *He that thou knowest thine, Hamlet*

The polite closing and the signature of the letter Horatio reads.

favor (in return) they did; I am to do a turn° for them. Let the King
come have the letters I have sent, and repair° thou to
escape me with as much speed as thou wouldst fly° death.
speechless I have words to speak in thine ear will make thee dumb,°
yet are they much too light for the bore of the matter.[1]
These good fellows will bring thee where I am.
Rosencrantz and Guildenstern hold their course for
England. Of them I have much to tell thee. Farewell.
He that thou knowest thine, Hamlet."[2]
access Come, I will give you way° for these your letters,
And do 't the speedier that you may direct me
To him from whom you brought them. *They exit.*

1 *my acquittance seal*

Accept my innocence

2 *be it either which*

Whichever it is

3 *the star moves not but in his sphere*

According to Ptolemaic astronomy, the stars and planets traveled around the Earth inside hollow, transparent globes, which were concentrically nesting within one another.

4 *general gender*

Common people

5 *the spring that turneth wood to stone*

Due to rich mineral deposits in the soil, rivers in the English countryside carry high concentrations of limestone; objects placed in the river for long periods of time become covered in residue and eventually petrify.

6 *gyves to graces*

Shackles (i.e., faults) into virtues

7 *Too slightly timbered*

Of too light wood

Act 4, Scene 7

Enter King [**Claudius**] *and* **Laertes**.

Claudius

Now must your conscience my acquittance seal,[1]
And you must put me in your heart for friend,
Sith° [*Since*] you have heard, and with a knowing ear,
That he which hath your noble father slain
Pursued my life.

Laertes

It well appears. But tell me
Why you proceed not against these feats,° [*actions*]
So criminal and so capital° [*deserving execution*] in nature,
As by your safety, greatness, wisdom, all things else,
You mainly° [*very much*] were stirred up.

Claudius

Oh, for two special reasons,
Which may to you perhaps seem much unsinewed,° [*weak*]
But yet to me they're strong. The Queen, his mother,
Lives almost by his looks, and for myself—
My virtue or my plague, be it either which[2]—
She is so conjunct° [*closely joined*] to my life and soul,
That, as the star moves not but in his sphere,[3]
I could not° [*i.e., not live*] but by her. The other motive
Why to a public count° [*indictment*] I might not go
Is the great love the general gender[4] bear him,
Who, dipping all his faults in their affection,
Work like the spring that turneth wood to stone,[5]
Convert his gyves to graces[6]—so that my arrows,
Too slightly timbered[7] for so loud° [*fierce*] a wind,
Would have reverted° [*returned*] to my bow again,
But not where I have aimed them.

1 *may go back again*

May describe what she used to be

2 *Stood challenger on mount of all the age / For her perfections*

I.e., Ophelia's excellence towered over the whole world, challenging anyone to match her perfections

Laertes

And so have I a noble father lost,
circumstances A sister driven into desperate terms,°
Whose worth, if praises may go back again,[1]
Stood challenger on mount of all the age
For her perfections.[2] But my revenge will come.

Claudius

Break not your sleeps for that. You must not think
That we are made of stuff so flat and dull
by That we can let our beard be shook with° danger
sport And think it pastime.° You shortly shall hear more.
I loved your father, and we love ourself,
And that, I hope, will teach you to imagine—

Enter a **Messenger** *with letters.*

Messenger

These to your Majesty, this to the Queen.

Claudius

From Hamlet? Who brought them?

Messenger

Sailors, my lord, they say. I saw them not.
They were given me by Claudio. He received them
Of him that brought them.

Claudius

Laertes, you shall hear them.—Leave us.

[**Messenger** *exits.*]

[*reads*] "High and mighty, You shall know I am set
unarmed naked° on your kingdom. Tomorrow shall I beg leave
to see your kingly eyes, when I shall, first asking you
pardon thereunto, recount the occasion of my sudden
return."

1 *devise me*

Make sense of this for me. It is possible, however, that the Folio's "advise me" is the correct reading.

2 *checking at*

Turning away from (the image is of a falcon suddenly turning away from its prey)

3 *uncharge the practice*

Not see any guilt in the act

What should this mean? Are all the rest come back?
Or is it some abuse,° and no such thing?

Laertes

Know you the hand?

Claudius

'Tis Hamlet's character.° "Naked"?
And in a postscript here, he says "alone."
Can you devise me?[1]

Laertes

I'm lost in it, my lord, but let him come.
It warms the very sickness in my heart
That I live and tell him to his teeth,
"Thus didst thou."

Claudius

If it be so, Laertes—
As how should it be so? How otherwise?—
Will you be ruled by me?

Laertes

Ay, my lord—
So° you will not o'errule me to a peace.

Claudius

To thine own peace. If he be now returned,
As checking at[2] his voyage, and that he means
No more to undertake it, I will work him
To an exploit, now ripe in my device,°
Under the which he shall not choose but fall.
And for his death no wind of blame shall breathe,
But even his mother shall uncharge the practice[3]
And call it accident.

Laertes

My lord, I will be ruled
The rather if you could devise it so

trick

handwriting

As long as

planning

1 *It falls right.*

I.e., that's perfect

2 *sum of parts*

Full list of qualities

3 *unworthiest siege*

Least importance

4 *settled age his sables and his weeds*

Comfortable old age (is suited by) its fur coats and clothes

5 *As had he been encorpsed and demi-natured / With the brave beast*

As if he shared one body and one nature with the noble animal

6 *in forgery of shapes and tricks, / Come short of what he did*

In my imaginative re-creation of his feats, fall short of the actual achievements

7 *Lamord*

The name has never been convincingly identified with any historical figure; perhaps there is some play on the French *la mort* (death).

instrument That I might be the organ.°

Claudius

It falls right.[1]

You have been talked of since your travel much—
And that in Hamlet's hearing—for a quality
Wherein, they say, you shine. Your sum of parts[2]
Did not together pluck such envy from him
As did that one, and that, in my regard,
Of the unworthiest siege.[3]

Laertes

What part is that, my lord?

Claudius

A very ribbon in the cap of youth,
is suited by Yet needful too, for youth no less becomes°
uniform The light and careless livery° that it wears
Than settled age his sables and his weeds,[4]
Signifying Importing° health and graveness. Two months since,
Here was a gentleman of Normandy.
I have seen myself, and served against, the French,
perform skillfully And they can well° on horseback. But this gallant
Had witchcraft in 't. He grew unto his seat,
And to such wondrous doing brought his horse
As had he been encorpsed and demi-natured
surpassed With the brave beast.[5] So far he topped° my thought
That I, in forgery of shapes and tricks,
Come short of what he did.[6]

Laertes

, a man from Normandy A Norman° was 't?

Claudius

A Norman.

Laertes

Upon my life, Lamord![7]

1 *made confession of you*

Told us about you

2 *motion, guard, nor eye*

Practiced moves, defensive ability, nor visual acuity

3 *to play*

I.e., so he could play (fence)

4 *passages of proof*

I.e., experiences that have demonstrated this

5 *snuff*

The part of the wick that is burned and which, if not removed, will prevent the candle from giving light

Claudius

The very same.

Laertes

ornament I know him well. He is the brooch,° indeed,
And gem of all the nation.

Claudius

He made confession of you,[1]
And gave you such a masterly report
fencing For art and exercise in your defense,°
And for your rapier most especial,
That he cried out 'twould be a sight indeed
rs (French, escrimeurs) If one could match you. The 'scrimers° of their nation,
He swore, had neither motion, guard, nor eye[2]
If you opposed them. Sir, this report of his
i.e., embitter Did Hamlet so envenom° with his envy
That he could nothing do but wish and beg
mediate / i.e., fence Your sudden° coming o'er to play[3] with you.
Now, out of this—

Laertes

What out of this, my lord?

Claudius

Laertes, was your father dear to you?
Or are you, like the painting of a sorrow,
A face without a heart?

Laertes

Why ask you this?

Claudius

Not that I think you did not love your father
circumstance But that I know love is begun by time,°
And that I see, in passages of proof,[4]
moderates Time qualifies° the spark and fire of it.
There lives within the very flame of love
A kind of wick or snuff[5] that will abate it,

1 *at a like goodness still*

Always (*still*) at the same level of goodness

2 *a spendthrift sigh / That hurts by easing*

I.e., a sigh that does harm even as it expresses relief (according to a common belief that each sigh expended—hence a *spendthrift*—a drop of blood)

3 *the quick of th' ulcer*

I.e., the central matter

4 *murder sanctuarize*

Offer sanctuary to a murderer

5 *put on those shall*

Incite people who will

6 *in fine*

Finally

7 *pass of practice*

Treacherous sword thrust

8 *mountebank*

Usually this means something like the modern "quack," an itinerant drug salesman selling potions of little or no value, but here Laertes obviously believes in the efficacy of the poison he has bought.

And nothing is at a like goodness still,[1]
excess For goodness growing to a pleurisy°
overabundance Dies in his own too-much.° That we would do,
We should do when we would, for this "would" changes
reductions And hath abatements° and delays as many
As there are tongues, are hands, are accidents.
And then this "should" is like a spendthrift sigh
That hurts by easing.[2] But to the quick of th' ulcer:[3]
Hamlet comes back. What would you undertake
To show yourself in deed your father's son
More than in words?

Laertes

To cut his throat i' th' church.

Claudius

No place, indeed, should murder sanctuarize.[4]
Revenge should have no bounds. But, good Laertes,
If you will Will° you do this, keep close within your chamber.
Hamlet returned shall know you are come home.
We'll put on those shall[5] praise your excellence
And set a double varnish on the fame
The Frenchman gave you, bring you in fine[6] together
careless And wager o'er your heads. He, being remiss,°
noble minded Most generous,° and free from all contriving,
examine Will not peruse° the foils; so that, with ease,
Or with a little shuffling, you may choose
unblunted A sword unbated,° and in a pass of practice[7]
Requite him for your father.

Laertes

I will do 't.
And for that purpose I'll anoint my sword.
ointment I bought an unction° of a mountebank[8]
deadly So mortal° that, but dip a knife in it,

1 *touch my point*

Annoint my sword tip

2 *May fit us to our shape*

(1) suit our plan; (2) prepare us for the parts we are to act

3 *our drift look*

Our scheme become known

4 *back or second*

Backup plan

5 *blast in proof*

Backfire when we use it

6 *willow*

Conventionally associated with mourning and forsaken love

medicine Where it draws blood no cataplasm° so rare,
herbs / healing power Collected from all simples° that have virtue°
Under the moon, can save the thing from death
with it That is but scratched withal.° I'll touch my point[1]
poison / graze With this contagion,° that if I gall° him slightly
It may be death.

Claudius

Let's further think of this,
Weigh what convenience both of time and means
May fit us to our shape.[2] If this should fail,
And that our drift look[3] through our bad performance,
'Twere better not assayed. Therefore this project
Should have a back or second[4] that might hold
If this did blast in proof.[5] Soft, let me see.
skills We'll make a solemn wager on your cunnings.°
exercise I ha 't! When in your motion° you are hot and dry
(As make your bouts more violent to that end)
And that he calls for drink, I'll have proffered him
occasion A chalice for the nonce,° whereon but sipping,
thrust If he by chance escape your venomed stuck,°
Our purpose may hold there. But stay, what noise?

Enter Queen [**Gertrude**].

Gertrude

One woe doth tread upon another's heel,
So fast they follow.—Your sister's drowned, Laertes.

Laertes

Drowned? Oh! Where?

Gertrude

across There is a willow[6] grows askant° the brook
silvery That shows his hoary° leaves in the glassy stream.
Therewith fantastic garlands did she make

1 *long purples*

Purple orchids

2 *That liberal shepherds give a grosser name*

That free-speaking shepherds call by a more obscene name. The dangling outgrowths on some species of the flower have given rise to indecent aliases for *long purples*, including *dog's cullions* (testicles) and *priest's-pintle* (penis).

3 *coronet weeds*

I.e., garlands of twigs and flowers

4 *envious sliver*

Malicious branch

5 *weedy trophies*

I.e., her garlands

6 *incapable of*

Insensible to

7 *When these are gone, / The woman will be out.*

I.e., when my tears are finished, everything womanlike in me will be gone.

buttercups Of crowflowers,° nettles, daisies, and long purples,[1]
That liberal shepherds give a grosser name[2]
chaste But our cold° maids do "dead men's fingers" call them.
hanging There, on the pendant° boughs her coronet weeds[3]
Clambering to hang, an envious sliver[4] broke,
When down her weedy trophies[5] and herself
Fell in the weeping brook. Her clothes spread wide,
And mermaid-like a while they bore her up,
hymns Which time she chanted snatches of old lauds°
As one incapable of[6] her own distress,
adapted Or like a creature native and endued°
i.e., water Unto that element.° But long it could not be
Till that her garments, heavy with their drink,
song Pulled the poor wretch from her melodious lay°
To muddy death.

Laertes

Alas, then she is drowned.

Gertrude

Drowned, drowned.

Laertes

Too much of water hast thou, poor Ophelia,
And therefore I forbid my tears. But yet
natural response It is our trick.° Nature her custom holds;
Let shame say what it will. [*weeps*] When these are gone,
The woman will be out.[7]—Adieu, my lord.
gladly I have a speech o' fire that fain° would blaze,
But that this folly drowns it. *He exits.*

Claudius

Let's follow, Gertrude.
How much I had to do to calm his rage!
Now fear I this will give it start again.
Therefore let's follow *They exit.*

1 Enter two **Clowns**

The two Clowns (a word that could mean *peasants* as well as *jesters*, and also was used to identify the primary comic actors in the troupe) are arguing in a mix of rustic dialect—a good deal lower in social register than the rest of the talk in the play—and mangled legalese, which then as now included a fair amount of Latin. Hamlet, a gifted mimic, picks up some of their language (as in the rough diction of *How the knave jowls it to the ground* at 5.1.69–70) and recognizes the gravedigger's *absolute* (5.1.122), i.e., precise, wit. Compare this talk with the introduction of Osric at 5.2.67ff.

2 *Christian burial*

According to church law, those who die by suicide are to be denied full Christian funeral rites (which include burial in consecrated ground).

3 *salvation*

Probably a mistake for *damnation*

4 *The crowner hath sat on her and finds it Christian burial.*

The coroner has conducted an inquest and decided that it was not a suicide.

5 se offendendo

This is the reading of the Folio (Q2 reads "so offended"). The Folio probably represents the gravedigger's ignorant error for *se defedendo*, which is the Latin term for "self-defense."

6 *wittingly*

Deliberately. The First Clown's argument parodies a well-known lawsuit of 1562, which attempted to determine whether one Sir James Hales could be posthumously punished (by having his property seized) for having committed suicide. As part of their case, the defense separated the act of suicide into three parts: imagination, resolution, and accomplishment.

7 *Argal*

This is the Folio reading, a corruption of the Latin *ergo* (i.e., therefore).

8 *Goodman Delver*

Mister Digger. The prefix *Goodman* was often used politely before identifying a man by his occupation.

9 *willy-nilly*

I.e. whether he likes it or not (literally "will he, nill he," as it is printed in Q2)

Act 5, Scene 1

Enter two **Clowns** [1] [*as gravediggers*].

First Clown

Is she to be buried in Christian burial[2] when she willfully seeks her own salvation?[3]

Second Clown

immediately / *coroner*

I tell thee she is; therefore make her grave straight.° The crowner° hath sat on her and finds it Christian burial.[4]

First Clown

How can that be, unless she drowned herself in her own defense?

Second Clown

Why, 'tis found so.

First Clown

It must be *se offendendo*.[5] It cannot be else. For here lies the point: if I drown myself wittingly,[6] it argues an act, and an act hath three branches—it is to act, to do, to perform. Argal,[7] she drowned herself wittingly.

Second Clown

Nay, but hear you, Goodman Delver[8]—

First Clown

Give me leave. Here lies the water. Good. Here stands the man. Good. If the man go to this water and drown himself, it is, willy-nilly,[9] he goes. Mark you that. But if the water come to him and drown him, he drowns not himself. Argal, he that is not guilty of his own death shortens not his own life.

Second Clown

But is this law?

First Clown

inquest

Ay, marry, is 't. Crowner's 'quest° law.

1 *there thou say'st*

I.e., you said that right

2 *even-Christian*

Fellow Christians

3 *Come, my spade.*

Probably an order to the Second Clown to hand him his shovel.

4 *hold up*

Carry on

5 *bore arms*

A pun: both "was given a coat of arms" (the symbol of a gentleman) and "was created with limbs."

6 *confess thyself*

I.e., "confess thyself and be hanged," a proverbial expression along the lines of "To Hell with you"

7 *Go to.*

I.e., shut up (an expression of impatience or irritation)

8 *does well*

I.e., is an excellent response (and also "provides a good service")

Second Clown

Will you ha' the truth on 't? If this had not been a gentlewoman, she should° (*would*) have been buried out o' Christian burial.

First Clown

Why, there thou say'st,[1] and the more pity that great folk should have countenance° (*permission*) in this world to drown or hang themselves more than their even-Christian.[2] Come, my spade.[3] There is no ancient gentleman but° (*except for*) gardeners, ditchers, and grave-makers. They hold up[4] Adam's profession.

Second Clown

Was he a gentleman?

First Clown

'A was the first that ever bore arms.[5] I'll put another question to thee. If thou answerest me not to the purpose, confess thyself[6]—

Second Clown

Go to.[7]

First Clown

What is he that builds stronger than either the mason, the shipwright, or the carpenter?

Second Clown

The gallows-maker, for that° (*i.e., the gallows*) outlives a thousand tenants.

First Clown

I like thy wit well, in good faith. The gallows does well, but how does it well? It does well[8] to those that do ill. Now thou dost ill to say the gallows is built stronger than the church. Argal, the gallows may do well to thee. To 't again, come.

1 *unyoke*

I.e., end your mental labor (the image is of unhitching a team of oxen after plowing)

2 *Cudgel thy brains*

Proverbial expression, similar to the more modern "rack your brains"

3 *In youth*

The First Clown sings a corrupt version of "The Aged Lover Renounceth Love," a poem by Thomas Lord Vaux that was first published in the highly popular collection commonly known as *Tottel's Miscellany* (1557). The o's and a's in lines 58 and 59 may represent grunts of exertion, as the clown proceeds to dig Ophelia's grave.

4 *Custom hath made it in him a property of easiness.*

Habit has made digging graves a matter of complete comfort.

5 *The hand of little employment hath the daintier sense.*

The hand that is not frequently used (i.e., without calluses) has the sharper sense of touch.

Second Clown

Who builds stronger than a mason, a shipwright, or a carpenter?

First Clown

Ay, tell me that and unyoke.[1]

Second Clown

Marry, now I can tell.

First Clown

To 't.

Second Clown

By the mass Mass,° I cannot tell.

First Clown

Cudgel thy brains[2] no more about it, for your dull ass *improve* will not mend° his pace with beating. And when you are asked this question next, say "A grave-maker." The houses he makes lasts till doomsday. Go, get thee *tankard* in and fetch me a stoup° of liquor. [**Second Clown** *exits.*]

[*sings*] In youth[3] when I did love, did love,
Methought it was very sweet
shorten / advantage To contract°—o—the time, for—a—my behove,°
suitable Oh, methought, there—a—was nothing—a—meet.°

Enter **Hamlet** *and* **Horatio**.

Hamlet

Has this fellow no feeling of his business? 'A sings in grave-making.

Horatio

Custom hath made it in him a property of easiness.[4]

Hamlet

'Tis e'en so. The hand of little employment hath the daintier sense.[5]

1 *Cain's*

Cain was the son of Adam who killed his brother Abel (the world's *first murder*); see 1.2.105 and note.

2 *politician*

Usually used pejoratively, as one who schemes to gain political power

3 *o'erreaches*

Surpasses. The Folio prints "o'er offices" (lords it over by virtue of his current position).

4 *revolution*

I.e., change of fortune

5 *Did these bones cost no more the breeding but to play at loggets with them?*

I.e., was the value of raising these people so little that their bones can now be used as *loggets* (small wooden sticks that are thrown at a stake in the game of the same name)?

6 *For and*

And furthermore

First Clown

[*sings*] But age with his stealing steps
Hath clawed me in his clutch
sent / i.e., the earth And hath shipped° me into the land°
a young man in love As if I had never been such.° [*tosses up a skull*]

Hamlet

That skull had a tongue in it and could sing once. How
slams the knave jowls° it to the ground, as if 'twere Cain's[1]
jawbone, that did the first murder. This might be the
head pate° of a politician,[2] which this ass now o'erreaches,[3]
one that would circumvent God, might it not?

Horatio

It might, my lord.

Hamlet

Or of a courtier, which could say, "Good morrow, sweet
lord; how dost thou, sweet lord?" This might be my
Lord Such-a-one that praised my Lord Such-a-one's
borrow horse when 'a went to beg° it, might it not?

Horatio

Ay, my lord.

Hamlet

without the lower jaw Why, e'en so. And now my Lady Worm's, chapless° and
head knocked about the mazard° with a sexton's spade.
if / skill Here's fine revolution,[4] an° we had the trick° to see 't.
Did these bones cost no more the breeding but to play
at loggets with them?[5] Mine ache to think on 't.

First Clown

[*sings*] A pickax and a spade, a spade,
For and[6] a shrouding sheet,
Oh, a pit of clay for to be made
appropriate For such a guest is meet.° [*tosses up another skull*]

1 *action of battery*

Prosecution for assault

2 *his statutes, his recognizances, his fines, his double vouchers, his recoveries*

A string of legal and financial terms: *statutes* (bonds in which a creditor held a debtor's property in case of default); *recognizances* (bonds that acknowledge a debt); *fines* (a kind of lawsuit to legally transfer ownership of land); *double vouchers* (summonses for two witnesses to verify the land's ownership); *recoveries* (other kinds of lawsuits that legally transferred land)

3 *a pair of indentures*

A legal document written on one large piece of parchment, which was then torn in half irregularly. Each party took one piece; when the document was needed again, the segments could be fit together to prove that they both belonged to the original.

4 *box*

Coffin (and also alludes to the "deed box" used for legal documents)

5 *sheep and calves*

I.e., fools

6 *assurance*

Security (and also punning on the meaning "property title")

7 *sirrah*

A common form of address used for social inferiors

8 *out on 't*

Outside of it

Hamlet

There's another. Why, may not that be the skull of a lawyer? Where be his quiddities° now, his quillities,° his cases, his tenures,° and his tricks? Why does he suffer this mad knave now to knock him about the sconce° with a dirty shovel and will not tell him of his action of battery?[1] Hum! This fellow might be in 's time a great buyer of land, with his statutes, his recognizances, his fines, his double vouchers, his recoveries.[2] To have his fine° pate full of fine° dirt? Will vouchers vouch° him no more of his purchases and doubles than the length and breadth of a pair of indentures?[3] The very conveyances° of his lands will scarcely lie in this box,[4] and must th' inheritor° himself have no more, ha?

tle distinctions / quibbles
property titles
head
refined / fine-grained
guarantee
deeds
owner

Horatio

Not a jot more, my lord.

Hamlet

Is not parchment made of sheepskins?

Horatio

Ay, my lord, and of calfskins too.

Hamlet

They are sheep and calves[5] which seek out assurance[6] in that. I will speak to this fellow.— Whose grave's this, sirrah?[7]

First Clown

Mine, sir. [*sings*] Oh, a pit of clay for to be made—

Hamlet

I think it be thine, indeed, for thou liest in 't.

First Clown

You lie out on 't,[8] sir, and therefore 'tis not yours. For my part, I do not lie in 't, and yet it is mine.

1 *by the card*

Precisely

2 *picked*

Refined; affected; fastidious

3 *galls his kibe*

Irritates his chilblain (heel sore), i.e., follows so closely as to erase all distinction

Hamlet

Thou dost lie in 't, to be in 't and say it is thine. 'Tis for *living* the dead, not for the quick.° Therefore thou liest.

First Clown

lively 'Tis a quick° lie, sir. 'Twill away again from me to you.

Hamlet

What man dost thou dig it for?

First Clown

For no man, sir.

Hamlet

What woman, then?

First Clown

For none, neither.

Hamlet

Who is to be buried in 't?

First Clown

One that was a woman, sir, but, rest her soul, she's dead.

Hamlet

precise —How absolute° the knave is! We must speak by the *ambiguity* card,[1] or equivocation° will undo us. By the Lord, Horatio, this three years I have took a note of it: the age is grown so picked[2] that the toe of the peasant comes so near the heel of the courtier he galls his kibe.[3]—How long hast thou been grave-maker?

First Clown

Of the days i' th' year, I came to 't that day that our last King Hamlet overcame Fortinbras.

Hamlet

How long is that since?

First Clown

Cannot you tell that? Every fool can tell that. It was that very day that young Hamlet was born, he that is mad

1 *Upon what ground?*

Hamlet means "for what reason," but the clown takes the words literally.

2 *thirty years*

This establishes that Hamlet is thirty years old, since the Sexton began his job *that very day that young Hamlet was born* (lines 131–132). Many critics have been troubled by assigning this age to a man who has just returned from the midst of his studies at Wittenberg, and who is so many times described as *young*. Explanations have included an accommodation to the age of the lead actor of Shakespeare's company, Richard Burbage. It may also be that we should simply relax our expectation of strict realism here: Hamlet seems older and wiser in Act Five, but we need not and should not read that back into previous acts.

3 *as we have many pocky corses that will scarce hold the laying in*

Since we have many corpses that are already rotten with syphilis, which can hardly stay intact during their burial

and sent into England.

Hamlet

Ay, marry, why was he sent into England?

First Clown

he Why, because 'a° was mad. 'A shall recover his wits there, or, if 'a do not, 'tis no great matter there.

Hamlet

Why?

First Clown

noticed 'Twill not be seen° in him there. There the men are as mad as he.

Hamlet

How came he mad?

First Clown

Very strangely, they say.

Hamlet

How "strangely"?

First Clown

Faith, e'en with losing his wits.

Hamlet

Upon what ground?[1]

First Clown

Why, here in Denmark. I have been sexton here, man and boy, thirty years.[2]

Hamlet

How long will a man lie i' th' earth ere he rot?

First Clown

Faith, if 'a be not rotten before 'a die—as we have many pocky corpses that will scarce hold the laying in[3]—'a will last you some eight year or nine year. A tanner will last you nine year.

Hamlet

Why he more than another?

1 *lien you*

Lain (*you* here is a largely expletive colloquialism meaning "you see" or "for you")

2 *chapfallen*

"Dejected"; but literally here, "without a lower jaw (*chap*)"

3 *let her paint an inch thick, to this favor she must come*

Even if she were to put an inch of makeup on her face, she will someday come to look like this.

First Clown

Why, sir, his hide is so tanned with his trade that 'a will keep out water a great while, and your water is a sore decayer of your whoreson° dead body. [*picks up a skull*] Here's a skull now. Here's a skull now hath lien you[1] in the earth twenty-three years.

vile

Hamlet

Whose was it?

First Clown

A whoreson mad fellow's it was. Whose do you think it was?

Hamlet

Nay, I know not.

First Clown

A pestilence on him for a mad rogue! 'A poured a flagon of rhenish° on my head once. This same skull, sir, was, sir, Yorick's skull, the King's jester.

Rhine wine

Hamlet

This?

First Clown

E'en that.

Hamlet

Alas, poor Yorick! I knew him, Horatio—a fellow of infinite jest, of most excellent fancy. He hath bore me on his back a thousand times, and now, how abhorred in my imagination it is! My gorge° rises at it. Here hung those lips that I have kissed I know not how oft. Where be your gibes° now—your gambols,° your songs, your flashes of merriment that were wont to set the table on a roar? Not one now to mock your own grinning? Quite chapfallen?[2] Now get you to my lady's table° and tell her, let her paint an inch thick, to this favor she must come.[3] Make her laugh at that.

i.e., vomit

taunts / leaps; dances

dressing table

1 *Alexander*

Alexander the Great, who ruled Greece in the fourth century B.C.

2 *bunghole*

Spout in a cask or barrel. Hamlet contends that even the remains of a great man like Alexander, being mixed with the earth after burial, will eventually resurface in an ignoble new form.

3 *loam*

A mixture of sand, clay, and straw, used as a mortar or plaster

—Prithee, Horatio, tell me one thing.

Horatio

What's that, my lord?

Hamlet

Dost thou think Alexander[1] looked o' this fashion i' th' earth?

Horatio

E'en so.

Hamlet

And smelt so? Pah!

Horatio

E'en so, my lord.

Hamlet

To what base uses we may return, Horatio. Why may not imagination trace the noble dust of Alexander till *he* 'a° find it stopping a bunghole?[2]

Horatio

ingeniously 'Twere to consider too curiously° to consider so.

Hamlet

No, faith, not a jot. But to follow him thither with *moderation* modesty° enough and likelihood to lead it: Alexander died, Alexander was buried, Alexander returneth to dust, the dust is earth, of earth we make loam[3]—and why of that loam, whereto he was converted, might they not stop a beer barrel?

Imperious Caesar, dead and turned to clay,
Might stop a hole to keep the wind away.
Oh, that that earth, which kept the world in awe,
gusts of wind Should patch a wall t' expel the winter's flaw!°

But soft, but soft a while.

Enter King [**Claudius**], *Queen* [**Gertrude**], **Laertes**, [**Lords**, *a* **Priest**,] *and the corpse* [*of* **Ophelia**].

1 *maimèd rites*

Abbreviated ceremony

2 *Couch we awhile and mark.*

Let's conceal ourselves for a bit and observe. The two actors must hide themselves on stage.

3 *warranty*

Official sanction

4 *but that great command o'ersways the order*

Except for the fact that the King's command overrides the Church's practice

5 *the last trumpet*

I.e., the trumpet blast that proclaims the moment of final judgment when both living and dead Christians are transported bodily to Heaven (1 Corinthians 15:52)

6 *Shards*

Broken pieces of pottery (the word, from the Folio, is absent in Q2 but necessary for the meter)

7 *virgin crants*

Garlands of flowers designed for a young woman (*crants* comes from the German *kranz* = crown)

8 *the bringing home / Of bell and burial*

I.e., the bringing of her body to its grave accompanied by the normal funeral rites and ringing bells

9 *a*

The Folio prints "sage" (solemn)

Here comes the King,
The Queen, the courtiers—who is this they follow,
And with such maimèd rites?[1] This doth betoken
The corpse they follow did with desperate hand
Put an end to / rank Fordo° its own life. 'Twas of some estate.°
Couch we awhile and mark.[2]

Laertes

in addition What ceremony else?°

Hamlet

[*aside to* **Horatio**] That is Laertes, a very noble youth;
mark.

Laertes

What ceremony else?

Priest

funeral rites Her obsequies° have been as far enlarged
suspicious As we have warranty.[3] Her death was doubtful,°
And, but that great command o'ersways the order,[4]
She should in ground unsanctified been lodged
Instead of Till the last trumpet.[5] For° charitable prayers,
Shards,[6] flints, and pebbles should be thrown on her,
Yet here she is allowed her virgin crants,[7]
strewn flowers Her maiden strewments,° and the bringing home
Of bell and burial.[8]

Laertes

Must there no more be done?

Priest

No more be done.
We should profane the service of the dead
To sing a[9] requiem and such rest to her
As to peace-parted souls.

Laertes

Lay her i' th' earth,
And from her fair and unpolluted flesh

1 *double*

Folio prints "treble"

2 *ingenious sense*

Sharp intelligence

3 *Pelion*

According to Greek mythology, the giants once tried to invade Mount Olympus (home of the gods) by placing Mount Ossa on top of Mount Pelion.

4 *wandering stars*

I.e., the planets

May violets spring! I tell thee, churlish priest,
A ministering angel shall my sister be
i.e., in Hell When thou liest howling.°

Hamlet

[*aside*] What? The fair Ophelia?

Gertrude

Sweets to the sweet. Farewell!
I hoped thou shouldst have been my Hamlet's wife;
I thought thy bride-bed to have decked, sweet maid,
And not have strewed thy grave.

Laertes

Oh, treble woe
Fall ten times double[1] on that cursèd head,
Whose wicked deed thy most ingenious sense[2]
Deprived thee of! Hold off the earth awhile
Till I have caught her once more in mine arms.
[*leaps into the grave*]
living Now pile your dust upon the quick° and dead,
Till of this flat a mountain you have made
lofty T' o'ertop old Pelion[3] or the skyish° head
Of blue Olympus.

Hamlet

[*coming forward*] What is he whose grief
passioned expression Bears such an emphasis,° whose phrase of sorrow
Conjures the wandering stars[4] and makes them stand
awestruck Like wonder-wounded° hearers? This is I,
Hamlet the Dane. [*They fight.*]

Laertes

The devil take thy soul!

Hamlet

Thou pray'st not well.
I prithee, take thy fingers from my throat,
hot tempered For, though I am not splenative° and rash,

1 *Pluck them asunder!*

Pull them apart!

2 *wag*

Blink (Hamlet vows to fight as long as he has any strength at all to continue.)

Yet have I in me something dangerous,
Which let thy wisdom fear. Hold off thy hand!

Claudius

Pluck them asunder![1]

Gertrude

Hamlet, Hamlet!

All

Gentlemen—

Horatio

Good my lord, be quiet.

Hamlet

Why, I will fight with him upon this theme
Until my eyelids will no longer wag.[2]

Gertrude

O my son, what theme?

Hamlet

I loved Ophelia. Forty thousand brothers
Could not with all their quantity of love
Make up my sum. What wilt thou do for her?

Claudius

Oh, he is mad, Laertes.

Gertrude

have patience with For love of God, forbear° him.

Hamlet

By God's wounds 'Swounds,° show me what thou'lt do.
Will you Woul't° weep? Woul't fight? Woul't fast? Woul't tear
thyself?
vinegar Woul't drink up eisel,° eat a crocodile?
I'll do 't. Dost come here to whine,
defy To outface° me with leaping in her grave?
alive Be buried quick° with her—and so will I.
chatter And if thou prate° of mountains, let them throw
Millions of acres on us, till our ground,

1 *till our ground, / Singeing his pate against the burning zone, / Make Ossa like a wart!*

Till the mound of earth piled on top of us, burning its peak as it nears the sun, makes Mount Ossa look like a wart by comparison!

2 *Anon, as patient as the female dove / When that her golden couplets are disclosed, / His silence will sit drooping.*

Soon he will sit in exhausted silence, as quiet as the female dove who has just hatched her yellow chicks.

3 *Let Hercules himself do what he may, / The cat will mew, and dog will have his day.*

I.e., let Hercules (a Greek hero renowned for his supernatural strength) do whatever he can, nature will take its usual course, and my time will come.

4 *present push*

Immediate trial

5 *living monument*

Lasting memorial, perhaps with an added implication for Laertes that the impending death of Hamlet will be a monument to Ophelia's death

Singeing his pate against the burning zone,
if / speak excessively Make Ossa like a wart! [1] Nay, an° thou'lt mouth,°
I'll rant as well as thou.

Gertrude

absolute This is mere° madness.
And this awhile the fit will work on him.
Anon, as patient as the female dove
When that her golden couplets are disclosed,
His silence will sit drooping. [2]

Hamlet

[*to* **Laertes**] Hear you, sir.
What is the reason that you use me thus?
I loved you ever. But it is no matter.
Let Hercules himself do what he may,
The cat will mew, and dog will have his day. [3] *He exits.*

Claudius

I pray thee, good Horatio, wait upon him.

Horatio *exits.*

confidence [*to* **Laertes**] Strengthen your patience° in our last night's speech.
We'll put the matter to the present push. [4]
—Good Gertrude, set some watch over your son.
—This grave shall have a living monument. [5]
An hour of quiet thereby shall we see.
Till then in patience our proceeding be. *They exit.*

1 *our ends*

The outcomes of our action

2 *sea-gown*

Sailor's coat

3 *them*

I.e., Rosencrantz and Guildenstern

4 *in fine*

Finally

5 *such bugs and goblins in my life*

Such imaginary dangers that would befall should I remain alive

6 *no leisure bated*

With no delay allowed

Act 5, Scene 2

Enter **Hamlet** *and* **Horatio**.

Hamlet

i.e., other matter So much for this, sir; now shall you see the other.°
You do remember all the circumstance?

Horatio

Remember it, my lord?

Hamlet

Sir, in my heart there was a kind of fighting
That would not let me sleep. Methought I lay
mutineers / shackles Worse than the mutines° in the bilboes.° Rashly—
acknowledge And praised be rashness for it—let us know°
impulsive action Our indiscretion° sometime serves us well
grow weak When our deep plots do pall,° and that should learn us
There's a divinity that shapes our ends,[1]
crudely shape Rough-hew° them how we will.

Horatio

That is most certain.

Hamlet

Up from my cabin,
wrapped loosely My sea-gown[2] scarfed° about me, in the dark
Groped I to find out them,[3] had my desire,
Stole Fingered° their packet, and in fine[4] withdrew
To mine own room again, making so bold
—My fears forgetting manners—to unfold
Their grand commission, where I found, Horatio,
A royal knavery, an exact command,
Adorned / different Larded° with many several° sorts of reasons
Importing Denmark's health, and England's too,
With—ho!—such bugs and goblins in my life[5]
reading That, on the supervise°—no leisure bated,[6]
wait for / sharpening No, not to stay° the grinding° of the axe—

1 *Or I could make a prologue to my brains, / They had begun the play*

I.e., before I could give it much thought, my brains had come up with a plan of action (literally, "Before I could deliver the opening prologue, my brains had begun to perform the play")

2 *baseness*

Beneath me. Nobles had secretaries and scribes to write their letters and documents, and the ability to write in a professional manner was viewed as a vocational skill.

3 *that learning*

I.e., the ability to write in an elegant and legible script

4 *yeoman's service*

Valuable service. *Yeoman* here has its oldest sense of an attendant in a royal household.

5 *tributary*

A country paying money (tribute) to a nation that had conquered it or to one that agreed to defend it. See 3.1.168–169.

6 *wheaten garland*

Traditional symbol of peace

7 *stand a comma 'tween their amities*

I.e., act as a link between their separate friendships

8 *"as"es*

Clauses that begin with *as*

9 *of great charge*

(1) having great importance; (2) heavily loaded (with a play on "*as*" as asses)

10 *shriving time*

Opportunity to make confession

My head should be struck off.

Horatio

Is 't possible?

Hamlet

Here's the commission. Read it at more leisure.
But wilt thou hear now how I did proceed?

Horatio

I beseech you.

Hamlet

surrounded Being thus benetted° round with villains—
Before Or° I could make a prologue to my brains,
They had begun the play[1]—I sat me down,
clearly Devised a new commission, wrote it fair.°
politicians I once did hold it, as our statists° do,
A baseness[2] to write fair, and labored much
How to forget that learning,[3] but, sir, now
It did me yeoman's service.[4] Wilt thou know
essence Th' effect° of what I wrote?

Horatio

Ay, good my lord.

Hamlet

request An earnest conjuration° from the King,
As England was his faithful tributary,[5]
As love between them like the palm might flourish,
always As peace should still° her wheaten garland[6] wear
And stand a comma 'tween their amities,[7]
And many such like "as"es[8] of great charge,[9]
That, on the view and knowing of these contents,
Without debatement further, more or less,
He should those bearers put to sudden death,
Not shriving time[10] allowed.

Horatio

How was this sealed?

1 *signet*

Small seal (usually part of a ring) for making an impression in wax to authenticate a document

2 *to this was sequent*

Followed this

3 *'Tis dangerous when the baser nature comes / Between the pass and fell incensèd points / Of mighty opposites.*

It is dangerous when inferior beings come between the deadly thrusts of the swords of powerful adversaries.

4 *stand me now upon*

Become my duty

5 *perfect conscience*

Perfectly in accord with the dictates of a good conscience. The Folio text has 14 additional lines at this point; see Appendix page 395.

6 Enter [**Osric**], a courtier

Osric is first identified by name in line 170. He is a courtier—a court hanger-on—more obsequious and fawning than Rosencrantz and Guildenstern, and his stilted diction makes sport for Hamlet and Horatio. He has been born to great land (5.2.71–74) but little wit, and he abuses the high language (*the continent of what part a gentleman would see*, 5.2.94–95) that Hamlet so deftly parodies in 5.2.96–103. His principal role seems to be to cast in high relief the rich, flexible, vivid speech of Hamlet, who is fresh from his conversation with the gravedigger and who has cultivated an idiom of his own that mixes high and low.

7 *water-fly*

A small, bright-colored bug (hence, an insignificant, if gaudily dressed, person)

Hamlet

in control; directing Why, even in that was Heaven ordinant.°
I had my father's signet[1] in my purse,
image Which was the model° of that Danish seal.
document Folded the writ° up in the form of th' other,
Signed / (of the seal) Subscribed° it, gave 't th' impression,° placed it safely,
exchange The changeling° never known. Now, the next day
Was our sea fight, and what to this was sequent[2]
Thou knowest already.

Horatio

i.e., to their deaths So Guildenstern and Rosencrantz go to 't.°

Hamlet

destruction They are not near my conscience. Their defeat°
meddling Does by their own insinuation° grow.
'Tis dangerous when the baser nature comes
cruel Between the pass and fell° incensèd points
Of mighty opposites.[3]

Horatio

Why, what a king is this!

Hamlet

Does it not, think thee, stand me now upon[4]—
He that hath killed my King and whored my mother,
Popped in between th' election and my hopes,
fishhook Thrown out his angle° for my proper life,
deceit And with such cozenage°—is 't not perfect conscience?[5]

*Enter [**Osric**,] a courtier.*[6]

Osric

Your lordship is right welcome back to Denmark.

Hamlet

I humbly thank you, sir. [*to* **Horatio**] Dost know this water-fly?[7]

1 *Let a beast be lord of beasts and his crib shall stand at the king's mess.*

If an animal owned great amounts of property, his trough (*crib*) would find a place near the king's table (*mess*).

2 *chough*

A crow or jackdaw, both scavenging birds that shrilly communicate with the flock (here applied to Osric as a man who thrives by gossiping)

3 *Your bonnet to his right use*

I.e., put your hat on

4 *remember—*

Remember your courtesy (i.e., put your hat back on), as Hamlet presumably gestures to complete the thought.

Horatio

[*to* **Hamlet**] No, my good lord.

Hamlet

blessed [*to* **Horatio**] Thy state is the more gracious,° for 'tis a vice to know him. He hath much land, and fertile. Let a beast be lord of beasts and his crib shall stand at the king's mess.[1] 'Tis a chough,[2] but, as I say, spacious in the possession
i.e., land of dirt.°

Osric

Sweet lord, if your Lordship were at leisure, I should impart a thing to you from his Majesty.

Hamlet

attentiveness I will receive it, sir, with all diligence° of spirit. Your
its bonnet to his° right use:[3] 'tis for the head.

Osric

I thank your Lordship. It is very hot.

Hamlet

No, believe me, 'tis very cold. The wind is northerly.

Osric

moderately It is indifferent° cold, my lord, indeed.

Hamlet

But yet methinks it is very sultry and hot for my
constitution complexion.°

Osric

Exceedingly, my lord. It is very sultry, as 'twere—I cannot tell how. My lord, his Majesty bade me signify to you that 'a has laid a great wager on your head. Sir, this is the matter—

Hamlet

I beseech you, remember—[4]

Osric

Nay, good my lord, for my ease, in good faith. Sir, here is newly come to court Laertes, believe me, an

1 *soft society and great showing*

Easy companionability and impressive appearance

2 *card or calendar of gentry*

Model of proper gentlemanly behavior. *Card* is a term for a sailor's chart or map; *calendar* is an account book or directory.

3 *in him the continent of what part a gentleman would see*

In Laertes every attribute one gentleman would like to see in another

4 *perdition in you*

Diminution in your telling

5 *to divide him inventorially would dazzle th' arithmetic of memory, and yet but yaw neither, in respect of his quick sail*

The task of listing his attributes one by one would confound the ability of memory to recall everything, but even a detailed description would only mark an erratic course when compared with his speedy sailing (i.e., his true accomplishments).

6 *But, in the verity of extolment, I take him to be a soul of great article, and his infusion of such dearth and rareness as, to make true diction of him, his semblable is his mirror, and, who else would trace him, his umbrage, nothing more.*

But, in truthful praise, I take him to be a person of excellent qualities, and his inborn essence is of such a preciousness and rareness, to speak truly of him, that the only thing that can be said to resemble him is his own reflection in the mirror; and anyone who would attempt to imitate him, merely his shadow.

7 *rawer breath*

I.e., words that are inadequate (to do justice to him)

8 *Is 't not possible to understand in another tongue? You will do 't, sir, really.*

Wouldn't this be more intelligible in a foreign language? You are almost at that point already.

stinguishing qualities absolute gentleman, full of most excellent differences,° of very soft society and great showing.[1] Indeed, to speak sellingly of him, he is the card or calendar of gentry,[2] for you shall find in him the continent of what part a gentleman would see.[3]

Hamlet

description Sir, his definement° suffers no perdition in you,[4] though I know to divide him inventorially would dazzle th' arithmetic of memory, and yet but yaw neither, in respect of his quick sail.[5] But, in the verity of extolment, I take him to be a soul of great article, and his infusion of such dearth and rareness as, to make true diction of him, his semblable is his mirror, and, who else would trace him, his umbrage, nothing more.[6]

Osric

Your Lordship speaks most infallibly of him.

Hamlet

relevance The concernancy,° sir? Why do we wrap the gentleman in our more rawer breath?[7]

Osric

Sir?

Horatio

[*to* **Hamlet**] Is 't not possible to understand in another tongue? You will do 't, sir, really.[8]

Hamlet

mention What imports the nomination° of this gentleman?

Osric

Of Laertes?

Horatio

[*to* **Hamlet**] His purse is empty already. All 's golden words are spent.

Hamlet

[*to* **Osric**] Of him, sir.

1 *lest I should compare with him in excellence*

Lest I seem to claim that I am as excellent as he

2 *but to know a man well were to know himself*

I.e., in order to truly know another man's excellence, one must be capable of it himself.

3 *Three of the carriages, in faith, are very dear to fancy, very responsive to the hilts, most delicate carriages, and of very liberal conceit.*

Three of the straps, in truth, are very fancifully designed and in perfect keeping with the hilts; they are most skillfully wrought and of a very ingenious design. (See lines 141–142 and gloss.)

4 *I knew you must be edified by the margin ere you had done.*

I knew that you were going to need the help of an explanatory note (such as the glosses found in the margin of a difficult text) before you were finished.

Osric

I know you are not ignorant—

Hamlet

commend

I would you did, sir. Yet in faith, if you did, it would not much approve° me. Well, sir?

Osric

You are not ignorant of what excellence Laertes is—

Hamlet

I dare not confess that lest I should compare with him in excellence,[1] but to know a man well were to know himself.[2]

Osric

reputation
merit / unequaled

I mean, sir, for his weapon. But in the imputation° laid on him by them, in his meed° he's unfellowed.°

Hamlet

What's his weapon?

Osric

Rapier and dagger.

Hamlet

That's two of his weapons, but well.

Osric

staked
accessories
sword belt / straps

The King, sir, hath wagered with him six Barbary horses, against the which he has impawned,° as I take it, six French rapiers and poniards with their assigns°—as girdle,° hangers,° and so. Three of the carriages, in faith, are very dear to fancy, very responsive to the hilts, most delicate carriages, and of very liberal conceit.[3]

Hamlet

What call you the "carriages"?

Horatio

[*to* **Hamlet**] I knew you must be edified by the margin ere you had done.[4]

1 *The phrase would be more germane to the matter if we could carry a cannon by our sides.*

The term *carriages* would make more sense if we were carrying *cannon by our sides* (instead of swords).

2 *He hath laid on twelve for nine*

This has never been convincingly explained. Perhaps it is that, following on the King's bet that in twelve bouts Laertes will not win by more than three, Laertes himself (*He*) wagers that he will win nine of the twelve instead of the eight that would win the King's bet.

3 *vouchsafe the answer*

Accept the challenge (but Hamlet responds as if he meant "reply")

4 *the odd hits*

I.e., whatever hits I happen to achieve

5 *Shall I deliver you so?*

Shall I take this back as your response?

Osric

straps

The carriages, sir, are the hangers.°

Hamlet

relevant / accessories / generously termed

The phrase would be more germane° to the matter if we could carry a cannon by our sides.[1] I would it might be "hangers" till then. But on: six Barbary horses against six French swords, their assigns,° and three liberal-conceited° carriages—that's the French bet against the Danish. Why is this all "impawned," as you call it?

Osric

wagered / bouts / i.e., Laertes

The King, sir, hath laid,° sir, that in a dozen passes° between yourself and him,° he shall not exceed you three hits. He hath laid on twelve for nine,[2] and it would come to immediate trial if your Lordship would vouchsafe the answer.[3]

Hamlet

How if I answer "No"?

Osric

I mean, my lord, the opposition of your person in trial.

Hamlet

exercising / if

Sir, I will walk here in the hall. If it please his Majesty, it is the breathing° time of day with me. Let the foils be brought, the gentleman willing, and the King hold his purpose. I will win for him an° I can. If not, I will gain nothing but my shame and the odd hits.[4]

Osric

Shall I deliver you so?[5]

Hamlet

verbal elaboration

To this effect, sir, after what flourish° your nature will.

Osric

submit

I commend° my duty to your Lordship. *[He exits.]*

Hamlet

praise

Yours. He does well to commend° it himself.

1 *The lapwing runs away with the shell on his head.*

A proverbial expression for naïve foolishness; the chicks of the lapwing were believed to run around with their eggshells still on their heads (and a further joke about Osric's hat).

2 *'A did so, sir, with his dug before 'a sucked it.*

He behaved in this way with his mother's breast before he nursed.

3 *tune of the time*

I.e., fashionable jargon

4 *yeasty collection*

frothy mixture

5 *carries them through and through the most profane and winnowed opinions*

Allows them to bluff their way in any company, no matter how vulgar or refined

6 *do but blow them to their trial, the bubbles cut out*

If you test them by blowing on them, the bubbles burst.

7 *If his fitness speaks*

I.e., if it satisfies Laertes' convenience

8 *use some gentle entertainment*

Behave courteously

purpose There are no tongues else for 's turn.°

Horatio

This lapwing runs away with the shell on his head.[1]

Hamlet

'A did so, sir, with his dug before 'a sucked it.[2] Thus has he—and many more of the same breed that *worthless* I know the drossy° age dotes on—only got the tune of the time[3] and, out of an habit of encounter, a kind of yeasty collection[4] which carries them through and through the most profane and winnowed opinions;[5] and do but blow them to their trial, the bubbles are out.[6]

Enter a **Lord**.

Lord

My lord, his Majesty commended him to you by young Osric, who brings back to him that you attend him in *fence* the hall. He sends to know if your pleasure hold to play° *if* with Laertes, or that° you will take longer time.

Hamlet

I am constant to my purposes; they follow the King's pleasure. If his fitness speaks,[7] mine is ready, now or whensoever, provided I be so able as now.

Lord

The King and Queen and all are coming down.

Hamlet

In happy time.

Lord

The Queen desires you to use some gentle entertainment[8] to Laertes before you fall to play. [*He exits.*]

Hamlet

She well instructs me.

1 *since no man of aught he leaves knows, what is 't to leave betimes?*

Since no man can have any certain knowledge about the world he will leave behind, what difference does it make if he dies early (*betimes*).

2 the state

The nobles

Horatio

You will lose, my lord.

Hamlet

I do not think so. Since he went into France, I have been in continual practice. I shall win at the odds. Thou wouldst not think how ill all's here about my heart—but it is no matter.

Horatio

Nay, good my lord—

Hamlet

misgiving It is but foolery, but it is such a kind of gaingiving° as would perhaps trouble a woman.

Horatio

If your mind dislike anything, obey it. I will forestall *coming* their repair° hither and say you are not fit.

Hamlet

divination Not a whit. We defy augury.° There is special providence in the fall of a sparrow. If it be now, 'tis not to come. If it be not to come, it will be now. If it be not now, yet it will come. The readiness is all; since no man of aught he leaves knows, what is 't to leave betimes?[1] Let be.

*[Enter servants with] a table prepared; trumpets, drums, and officers with cushions, foils, daggers; King [***Claudius***], Queen [***Gertrude***], and all the state,[2] and* **Laertes***.*

Claudius

i.e., Laertes' Come, Hamlet, come and take this° hand from me.

Hamlet

[*to* **Laertes**] Give me your pardon, sir. I've done you wrong.
royal company But pardon 't, as you are a gentleman. This presence°
knows,
And you must needs have heard, how I am punished

1 *Let my disclaiming from a purposed evil*

Let my denial of intended harm

2 *in nature*

I.e., as far as filial emotions

3 *I have a voice and precedent of peace / To keep my name ungored*

I have judgment and some previous example of a similar reconcilliation that will preserve my reputation

4 *foil*

The setting of a jewel; the background against which something shines (though punning on the meaning "rapier")

With a sore distraction. What I have done,
motion / disapproval That might your nature,° honor, and exception°
Roughly awake, I here proclaim was madness.
Was 't Hamlet wronged Laertes? Never Hamlet.
If Hamlet from himself be ta'en away,
And when he's not himself does wrong Laertes,
Then Hamlet does it not. Hamlet denies it.
Who does it, then? His madness. If 't be so,
side; party Hamlet is of the faction° that is wronged;
His madness is poor Hamlet's enemy.
Let my disclaiming from a purposed evil[1]
Free me so far in your most generous thoughts
As to imagine That° I have shot my arrow o'er the house
And hurt my brother.

Laertes

I am satisfied in nature,[2]
Whose motive in this case should stir me most
To my revenge. But in my terms of honor
desire I stand aloof, and will° no reconcilement
Till by some elder masters of known honor
I have a voice and precedent of peace
To keep my name ungored.[3] But all that time
I do receive your offered love like love
And will not wrong it.

Hamlet

I embrace it freely,
freely And will this brother's wager frankly° play.
—Give us the foils.

Laertes

Come, one for me.

Hamlet

I'll be your foil,[4] Laertes. In mine ignorance
Your skill shall, like a star i' th' darkest night,

1 *odds*

I.e., set the odds to reflect that fact (of Laertes' superiority); see lines 144–146 and note.

2 *have all a length*

Are all the same length

3 *Or quit in answer of the third exchange*

Repay the previous hits of Laertes by winning the third round

4 *better breath*

Superior energy

Sparkle Stick° fiery off indeed.

Laertes

You mock me, sir.

Hamlet

No, by this hand.

Claudius

Give them the foils, young Osric.—Cousin Hamlet,
You know the wager?

Hamlet

Very well, my lord.
Your Grace has laid the odds o' th' weaker side.

Claudius

I do not fear it. I have seen you both.
But since he is better we have therefore odds.[1]

Laertes

This is too heavy. Let me see another.

Hamlet

pleases This likes° me well. These foils have all a length?[2]

Osric

Ay, my good lord.

Claudius

tankards Set me the stoups° of wine upon that table.
If Hamlet give the first or second hit
Or quit in answer of the third exchange,[3]
Let all the battlements their ordnance fire.
The King shall drink to Hamlet's better breath,[4]
pearl And in the cup an union° shall he throw
Richer than that which four successive kings
In Denmark's crown have worn. Give me the cups,
kettledrum And let the kettle° to the trumpet speak,
outside The trumpet to the cannoneer without,°
The cannons to the heavens, the heavens to Earth,

1 *a piece goes off*

A cannon is fired.

Now the King drinks to Hamlet. Come, begin.

Trumpets the while.

—And you, the judges, bear a wary eye.

Hamlet

Come on, sir.

Laertes

Come, my lord.

[**Hamlet** *and* **Laertes** *fence.*]

Hamlet

One!

Laertes

No!

Hamlet

—Judgment?

Osric

definite A hit, a very palpable° hit.

Laertes

Well, again.

Claudius

Stop Stay;° give me drink.—Hamlet, this pearl is thine.
Here's to thy health.

Drums, trumpets, and shot. Florish, [and] a piece goes off. [1]

Give him the cup.

Hamlet

I'll play this bout first. Set it by a while.
[*to* **Laertes**] Come. [*They fence.*] Another hit. What say you?

Laertes

I do confess 't.

Claudius

Our son shall win.

Gertrude

sweaty He's fat° and scant of breath.

1 *make a wanton of me*

Toy with me; treat me like a child

handkerchief —Here, Hamlet, take my napkin;° rub thy brows.

toasts; drinks [*taking the poisoned cup*] The Queen carouses° to thy fortune, Hamlet.

Hamlet

Good madam.

Claudius

Gertrude, do not drink.

Gertrude

I will, my lord. I pray you, pardon me.

Claudius

[*aside*] It is the poisoned cup. It is too late.

Hamlet

I dare not drink yet, madam. By and by.

Gertrude

Come; let me wipe thy face.

Laertes

[*to* **Claudius**] My lord, I'll hit him now.

Claudius

[*aside*] I do not think 't.

Laertes

[*aside*] And yet it is almost against my conscience.

Hamlet

Come for the third, Laertes. You do but dally.
thrust I pray you, pass° with your best violence.
I am sure you make a wanton of me.[1]

Laertes

Say you so? Come on.

[**Hamlet** *and* **Laertes** *fence.*]

Osric

Nothing, neither way.

Laertes

I will thrust [*to* **Hamlet**] Have° at you now!

[**Laertes** *wounds* **Hamlet**.
In scuffling, they change rapiers.
Hamlet *wounds* **Laertes**.]

Claudius

Part them! They are incensed.

Hamlet

[*to* **Laertes**] Nay, come again. [**Queen** *swoons.*]

Osric

Look to the Queen there, ho!

Horatio

They bleed on both sides.—How is it, my lord?

Osric

How is 't, Laertes?

Laertes

trap Why, as a woodcock to mine own springe,° Osric.
I am justly killed with mine own treachery.

Hamlet

How does the Queen?

Claudius

She swoons to see them bleed.

Gertrude

No, no, the drink, the drink!—O my dear Hamlet!
The drink, the drink! I am poisoned. [*She dies.*]

Hamlet

O villainy! Ho, let the door be locked.
Treachery! Seek it out. [**Osric** *exits.*]

Laertes

It is here, Hamlet. Thou art slain.
No med'cine in the world can do thee good.
In thee there is not half an hour's life.
The treacherous instrument is in thy hand,
Sharp; not protected Unbated° and envenomed. The foul practice

1 *union*

I.e., the pearl (see lines 241 and 256) that identifies the poisoned cup or is itself the source of the poison, but also here the marital *union* of Claudius and Gertrude.

2 *come not upon thee*

I.e., are not to be blamed on you

3 *fell sergeant*

Cruel arresting officer

Hath turned itself on me. Lo, here I lie,
Never to rise again. Thy mother's poisoned;
I can no more. The King, the King's to blame.

Hamlet

The point envenomed too?—Then, venom, to thy work.

[**Hamlet** *stabs* **Claudius**.]

All

Treason! Treason!

Claudius

Oh, yet defend me, friends; I am but hurt.

Hamlet

Here, thou incestuous, damnèd Dane,
Drink of this potion. Is the union[1] here?
Follow my mother.

[**Claudius** *dies*.]

Laertes

He is justly served.
prepared It is a poison tempered° by himself.
Exchange forgiveness with me, noble Hamlet.
Mine and my father's death come not upon thee,[2]
Nor thine on me. [**Laertes** *dies*.]

Hamlet

Heaven make thee free of it. I follow thee.—
I am dead, Horatio.—Wretched Queen, adieu!
—You that look pale and tremble at this chance,
onlookers That are but mutes° or audience to this act,
Had I but time (as this fell sergeant,[3] death,
Is strict in his arrest), oh, I could tell you—
But let it be.—Horatio, I am dead.
accurately Thou livest. Report me and my cause aright°
uninformed To the unsatisfied.°

Horatio

Never believe it.

1 *antique Roman*

The ancient Romans believed that to commit suicide was more honorable than to live a dishonored life, as opposed to the Christian view discussed by the Clowns in 5.1.1–24.

2 *what a wounded name, / Things standing thus unknown, shall I leave behind me*

What a dishonored name, if the truth of what has happened goes unreported, shall live on after me

3 *Absent thee from felicity for awhile*

I.e., postpone your death

4 *warlike volley*

Military salute

5 *o'ercrows*

Triumphs over (a metaphor taken from cockfighting)

6 *the election lights / On Fortinbras*

I.e., Fortinbras will be chosen King (*lights* = alights)

7 *So tell him, with th' occurents, more and less, / Which have solicited—*

This you should tell Fortinbras, along with all that has occurred of both major and minor importance that has moved—(Hamlet is unable to finish the sentence that would justify his actions)

I am more an antique Roman[1] than a Dane.
Here's yet some liquor left.

Hamlet

As thou'rt a man,
Give me the cup. Let go! By Heaven, I'll ha 't.
O God, Horatio, what a wounded name,
Things standing thus unknown, shall I leave behind me![2]
If thou didst ever hold me in thy heart,
Absent thee from felicity awhile[3]
And in this harsh world draw thy breath in pain
To tell my story.

A march afar off [and shots fired.]

What warlike noise is this?

Enter **Osric**.

Osric

Young Fortinbras, with conquest come from Poland,
To th' ambassadors of England gives
This warlike volley.[4]

Hamlet

Oh, I die, Horatio.
The potent poison quite o'ercrows[5] my spirit.
I cannot live to hear the news from England,
But I do prophesy the election lights
vote On Fortinbras.[6] He has my dying voice.°
occurrences So tell him, with th' occurrents,° more and less,
Which have solicited[7]—The rest is silence.

[**Hamlet** *dies.*]

Horatio

Now cracks a noble heart.—Good night, sweet Prince,
And flights of angels sing thee to thy rest!
—Why does the drum come hither?

1 *This quarry cries on havoc.*

This pile of slaughtered bodies (like the pile of *quarry*, or game, at the end of a hunt) announces that there has been a massacre.

2 *accidental judgments, casual slaughters*

Retribution brought about by accident, killings that happened by chance

3 *put on by cunning*

Carefully plotted

4 *for no cause*

The Folio prints "forced cause" (foul means, or perhaps, compelled actions), a very different sense of what drives tragedy.

Enter **Fortinbras** *[and his officers], with the* **Ambassadors**.

Fortinbras

Where is this sight?

Horatio

What is it you would see?
anything If aught° of woe or wonder, cease your search.

Fortinbras

This quarry cries on havoc.[1] O proud death,
being prepared What feast is toward° in thine eternal cell
That thou so many princes at a shot
So bloodily hast struck?

Ambassador

The sight is dismal,
And our affairs from England come too late.
The ears are senseless that should give us hearing
i.e., Claudius To tell him° his commandment is fulfilled,
That Rosencrantz and Guildenstern are dead.
Where should we have our thanks?

Horatio

i.e., the King's Not from his° mouth,
Had it th' ability of life to thank you.
He never gave commandment for their death.
immediately / matter But since so jump° upon this bloody question,°
You from the Polack wars, and you from England,
Are here arrived, give order that these bodies
platform High on a stage° be placèd to the view,
And let me speak to th' yet-unknowing world
How these things came about. So shall you hear
Of carnal, bloody, and unnatural acts,
Of accidental judgments, casual slaughters,[2]
Of deaths put on by cunning[3] and for no cause,[4]
And, in this upshot, purposes mistook

1 *rights of memory*

Traditional rights

2 *whose voice will draw no more*

Who will draw no more breaths (i.e., Hamlet). The Folio prints "draw on more," which would mean that Hamlet's words will attract additional support for Fortinbras.

3 *put on*

Tested; given opportunity

4 *shows much amiss*

Is greatly out of place

5 They exit.

Q2 only specifies the exit; the Folio gives a fuller direction: "Exeunt marching: after the which, a Peale of Ordenance are shot off."

Fallen on th' inventors' heads. All this can I
report Truly deliver.°

Fortinbras

Let us haste to hear it,
And call the noblest to the audience.
For me, with sorrow I embrace my fortune.
I have some rights of memory[1] in this kingdom,
advantageous situation Which now to claim my vantage° doth invite me.

Horatio

Of that I shall have also cause to speak,
And from his mouth whose voice will draw no more.[2]
But let this same be presently performed,
Even while men's minds are wild, lest more mischance
On top of On° plots and errors happen.

Fortinbras

Let four captains
Bear Hamlet like a soldier to the stage,
For he was likely, had he been put on,[3]
(from life to death) To have proved most royal; and for his passage,°
The soldiers' music and the rites of war
Speak loudly for him.
Take up the bodies. Such a sight as this
i.e., battlefield Becomes the field,° but here shows much amiss.[4]
Go. Bid the soldiers shoot. *They exit.*[5]

1 *the very substance of the ambitious*

The materials on which ambitious people feed their ambition

Appendix: *Hamlet* Folio-only Readings

In the Folio, the following text appears after 2.2.234:

Hamlet

Let me question more in particular. What have you, my good friends, deserved at the hands of Fortune that she sends you to prison hither?

Guildenstern

Prison, my lord?

Hamlet

Denmark's a prison.

Rosencrantz

Then is the world one.

Hamlet

large / enclosures

cells

A goodly° one, in which there are many confines,° wards,° and dungeons, Denmark being one o' th' worst.

Rosencrantz

We think not so, my lord.

Hamlet

Why, then, 'tis none to you, for there is nothing either good or bad but thinking makes it so. To me it is a prison.

Rosencrantz

Why, then, your ambition makes it one. 'Tis too narrow for your mind.

Hamlet

O God, I could be bounded in a nutshell and count myself a king of infinite space, were it not that I have bad dreams.

Guildenstern

Which dreams indeed are ambition, for the very substance of the ambitious[1] is merely the shadow of a dream.

1 *Then are our beggars bodies, and our monarchs and outstretched heroes the beggars' shadows.*

I.e., if ambitious men are only shadows, then beggars, who have no ambition, are the only ones who have substantial bodies, and thus monarchs and bigger-than-life heroes, who do have ambition, must be the shadows of the beggars' bodies.

2 *No such matter.*

Definitely not.

3 *most dreadfully attended*

Very badly waited upon; also, accompanied by frightening things (i.e., his father's ghost)

Hamlet

A dream itself is but a shadow.

Rosencrantz

Truly, and I hold ambition of so airy and light a quality that it is but a shadow's shadow.

Hamlet

Then are our beggars bodies, and our monarchs and outstretched heroes the beggars' shadows.[1] Shall we to th' court? For, by my fay,° I cannot reason.°

faith / argue logically

Rosencrantz, Guildenstern

We'll wait upon you.

Hamlet

No such matter.[2] I will not sort° you with the rest of my servants, for, to speak to you like an honest man, I am most dreadfully attended.[3]

place; classify

1 *keeps in the wonted pace*

Continues as usual

2 *there is, sir, an aerie of children, little eyases that cry out on the top of question and are most tyrannically clapped for 't*

I.e., there is, sir, a nest of children, small, unfledged hawks that speak shrilly to drown out any real dialogue and are most outrageously applauded for it. In 1600, a troupe of boy actors began performing at Blackfriars, a private indoor theater, providing competition for the larger,open-air amphitheaters such as the Globe.

3 *so berattled the common stages . . . that many wearing rapiers are afraid of goose quills*

I.e., the satiric writing of the children's companies has so discredited the public theaters that many fashionable gentlemen will no longer visit them.

4 *Will they pursue the quality no longer than they can sing?*

I.e., will they continue to work as actors only until their voices change?

5 *Will they not say afterwards, if they should grow themselves to common players (as it is most like if their means are no better), their writers do them wrong to make them exclaim against their own succession?*

Will they not later say, if they should end up being actors in the adult theaters (as is most likely, if they have no better opportunities for making money), that their writers do them wrong by making them speak deprecatingly of their future profession?

6 *There was, for awhile, no money bid for argument unless the poet and the player went to cuffs in the question.*

I.e., for a while, no one would pay any money for the rights to a new play unless it contained a debate between the dramatists (who wrote for the boys' company) and the actors (from the public theaters).

7 *much throwing about of brains*

I.e., a great battle of wits

8 *carry it away*

Take the victory

9 *Hercules and his load too*

According to classical myth, one of Hercules' twelve labors was to hold the world on his shoulders for a day, a task usually performed by the Titan Atlas. The image of Hercules holding the Earth was an emblem of Shakespeare's Globe Theatre, suggesting that the immediate reference of this exchange was the competition between Shakespeare's company, the King's Men, in residence at the Globe, and the increasingly popular children's companies.

In the Folio, the following appears after 2.2.302:

Hamlet

How comes it? Do they grow rusty?

Rosencrantz

Nay, their endeavor keeps in the wonted pace,[1] but there is, sir, an aerie of children, little eyases that cry out on the top of question and are most tyrannically clapped for 't.[2] These are now the fashion, and so berattled the common stages—so they call them—that many wearing rapiers are afraid of goose quills[3] and dare scarce come thither.

Hamlet

supported / profession

What? Are they children? Who maintains 'em? How are they escoted?° Will they pursue the quality° no longer than they can sing?[4] Will they not say afterwards, if they should grow themselves to common players (as it is most like if their means are no better), their writers do them wrong to make them exclaim against their own succession?[5]

Rosencrantz

populace / incite

Faith, there has been much to-do on both sides, and the nation° holds it no sin to tar° them to controversy. There was, for awhile, no money bid for argument unless the poet and the player went to cuffs in the question.[6]

Hamlet

Is 't possible?

Guildenstern

Oh, there has been much throwing about of brains.[7]

Hamlet

Do the boys carry it away?[8]

Rosencrantz

Ay, that they do, my lord. Hercules and his load too.[9]

1 *a man's lifes no more than to say "one"*

I.e., a man's life lasts no longer than the time it takes to pronounce the word *one*

2 *count his favors*

Recognize his favorable qualities

In the Folio, the following appears after 5.2.66:

Hamlet

repay To quit° him with this arm? And is 't not to be damned
spreading cancer To let this canker° of our nature come
Into In° further evil?

Horatio

It must be shortly known to him from England
result What is the issue° of the business there.

Hamlet

It will be short. The interim's mine.
And a man's life's no more than to say "one."[1]
But I am very sorry, good Horatio,
That to Laertes I forgot myself,
reflection For by the image° of my cause I see
The portraiture of his. I'll count his favors.[2]
ostentation But sure the bravery° of his grief did put me
Into a tow'ring passion.

Horatio

Peace.—Who comes here?

The Tragedie of

HAMLET

Prince of Denmarke.

Enter Barnardo, and Francisco, two Centinels.

Bar. VVHoſe there?
Fran. Nay anſwere me. Stand and vnfolde your ſelfe.
Bar. Long liue the King,
Fran. *Barnardo.*
Bar. Hee.
Fran. You come moſt carefully vpon your houre,
Bar. Tis now ſtrooke twelfe, get thee to bed *Franciſco,*
Fran. For this reliefe much thanks, tis bitter cold,
And I am ſick at hart.
Bar. Haue you had quiet guard?
Fran. Not a mouſe ſtirring.
Bar. Well, good night:
If you doe meete *Horatio* and *Marcellus,*
The riualls of my watch, bid them make haſt.

Enter Horatio, and Marcellus.

Fran. I thinke I heare them, ſtand ho, who is there?
Hora. Friends to this ground.
Mar. And Leedgemen to the Dane,
Fran. Giue you good night.
Mar. O, farwell honeſt ſouldiers, who hath relieu'd you?
Fran. *Barnardo* hath my place; giue you good night. *Exit Fran.*

B. *Mar.*

A reproduction of the first page of *Hamlet* in the Second Quarto (1604).

Editing *Hamlet*

by David Scott Kastan

Although *Hamlet* is arguably the best known play in the English language, oddly the *Hamlet* that is usually read and performed is rarely the play that Shakespeare actually wrote. Almost always, the *Hamlet* we read or see is a conflated text, combining materials from the three earliest printed versions of the play (Q1, a quarto published in 1603; Q2, a quarto first published late in 1604; and the text in the 1623 Folio), and in fact combining them differently, so that, in addition, no two conflated editions are exactly the same. This edition, however, is an edition of Q2, the so called Second Quarto, which represents, I believe, the most authoritative form of the play that Shakespeare wrote before it was reshaped in the playhouse.

Q2, published by James Roberts and Nicholas Ling, claims on its title page to be printed "according to the true and perfect Coppie," and indeed it does seem to be printed from Shakespeare's manuscript or a scribal copy of it. It contains about 230 lines that do not appear in the Folio version (though the Folio has about eighty lines that do not appear in Q2, many of which are printed here in an appendix). The Folio *Hamlet*, like all of the thirty-six plays in the volume that claim to be printed "according to the True Originall Copies," has its own claim to authority, though the Folio text seems further from Shakespeare's original intentions (or, put differently, closer to the play in the playhouse, which is, of course, itself of considerable, if different, interest).

Further complicating the picture of the "text" of *Hamlet* is the existence of the enigmatic First Quarto (1603), a far shorter version than either of the other two (some 2,200 lines instead of the 3,800 of Q2), which was apparently reconstructed by a number of actors who had appeared in the play. Though the first version to reach print, it is almost certainly not the first version written. It seems in fact to be an abridgement, possibly for a touring company, of the text of the Folio, though it differs widely in some aspects of the plot, in the names of some characters (the counselor, for example, called Polonius in Q2 and F, is here known as Corambis), and familiar speeches are often missing, misplaced, or garbled. It is a version once derided as a "bad quarto," but its qualities, if they make it unreliable as a text of the play, are enormously revealing about acting traditions in Shakespeare's time, perhaps even recording some of the play's original staging.

Still, if we are to recover the play that Shakespeare wrote, the practice of conflation must be abandoned. Although each of three versions holds a genuine interest for readers and scholars, combining them results in a play that could never have been seen or read in Shakespeare's lifetime. The edition here is an edition of Q2, though Q2 cannot be merely reprinted. There are omissions, duplications, and deficiencies in Q2 that must be repaired either with readings from the Folio or from later edited editions, never, of course, with absolute certainty that these represent what Shakespeare wrote but, on the basis of what we know about Shakespeare's habits of composition and the process of textual transmission, with as much confidence as is possible that these are correct readings. The textual notes below record the substantive changes in this edition from the readings of Q2.

In general, the editorial work of this present edition is conservative, a matter of modernizing spelling and punctuation, normalizing capitalization, removing superfluous italics, regularizing the names of characters, and rationalizing entrances and exits. A comparison of the edited text of 1.1.1–18 with the facsimile page of Q2 (on p. 396) reveals some of the issues in this modernization. The speech prefixes are expanded and normalized for clarity, so that "*Bar.*" and "*Fran.*" become Barnardo and Francisco. Spelling, capitalization, and italicization in this edition regularly follow modern practices rather than the habits of the Quarto's printers. As neither spelling nor punctuation in Shakespeare's time had yet been standardized, words were spelled in various ways that indicated their proximate pronunciation; and punctuation, which then was largely a rhythmical pointer rather than predominantly designed, as it is now, to clarify logical relations, was necessarily far more idiosyncratic than today. In any case, as compositors were under no obligation to follow either the spelling or punctuation of their copy, the spelling and punctuation of the Q2 text would not necessarily reflect Shakespeare's own preferences. For most readers, then, there is little advantage in an edition that reproduces the spelling and punctuation of the Q2. It does not accurately represent Shakespeare's writing habits, and it makes reading difficult, in a way Shakespeare could never have anticipated or desired.

Therefore, "anfwere" in the second line unproblematically becomes "answer," and "felfe" at the end of the line becomes the familiar "self." The verb "vnfolde" similarly becomes "unfold," though it is interesting to notice how early modern practice differs from our own. They use a "v" at the beginning of a word where we would use a "u" (also in line six of the facsimile in "vpon") but in line ten the word "Haue" is our "Have," here using a "u" where we use a "v." This edition eliminates the capitalization (and regularizes the spelling) of "Leedgmen" (liegemen) in line seventeen of the facsimile. The italics used for proper names are removed. Punctuation is changed to modern practice: the commas at the end of some lines that we would treat as full sentences are replaced with periods, as after "houre" in line six of the facsimile. Though the extensive use of commas in line endings on this first page of text in the facsimile of Q2 is anomalous, in general Elizabethan punctuation tended to be used to indicate the length of the desired pause (look at the comma after "them" in the facsimile's line fifteen), rather than define a precise grammatical relation as it would in modern practice. In this edition, punctuation is adopted that accords with modern grammatical practices. All of the changes made to the early printed text are undertaken with the aim to clarify rather than alter Shakespeare's intentions. Thus, Francisco and Barnardo's exchange (1.1.6–9 in this edition) reads in Q2:

Fran. You come moft carefully vpon your houre,
Bar. Tis now ftrooke twelfe, get thee to bed *Francisco,*
Fran. For this reliefe much thanks, tis bitter cold,
And I am fick at hart.

Modernized this reads:

Francisco
You come most carefully upon your hour.
Barnardo
'Tis now struck twelve. Get thee to bed, Francisco.
Francisco
For this relief much thanks. 'Tis bitter cold,
And I am sick at heart.

No doubt there is some loss in this modernization. Clarity and consistency are admittedly gained at the expense of expressive detail, but normalizing spelling, capitalization, and punctuation allows the text to be read with far greater ease than the original, and essentially as it was intended to be understood. We lose the archaic feel of the text in exchange for clarity of meaning. Old spellings are consistently modernized in this edition, but old *forms* of words (e.g., "hath" in the second line up from the bottom of the facsimile page) are retained. If, inevitably, in such modernization we lose the historical feel of the text Shakespeare's contemporaries read, it is important to remember that Shakespeare's contemporaries would not have thought the playbook in any sense archaic or quaint, as these details inevitably make it for a reader today. The text would have seemed to them as modern as the edition you are now reading does to you. Modern readers, however, cannot help but be distracted by the different conventions they encounter on the page of the earliest texts. While it is indeed of interest to see how orthography and typography have changed over time, these changes are not primary concerns for most readers of this edition. What little, then, is lost in a careful modernization of the text is more than made up for by the removal of the artificial obstacle of unfamiliar spelling forms and punctuation habits, which Shakespeare never could have intended as interpretive difficulties for his readers.

Textual Notes

The following list records all substantive departures in this edition from the 1604/1605 Second Quarto of the play. It does not record modernizations of spelling, normalization in the use of capitals, corrections of obvious typographical errors, adjustments of lineation, minor rewording and repositioning of stage directions, or regularizations of speech prefixes. The adopted reading in this edition is given first in boldface and followed by the original, rejected reading of the Second Quarto (Q2), or noted as being absent from the Quarto text. Editorial stage directions are not collated but are enclosed within brackets in the text. Latin stage directions are translated (e.g., *They all exit* for "Exeunt omnes"). There are no act and scene divisions marked in Q2, and this edition follows the traditional divisions that derive from eighteenth-century editions. In the list below, Q2corr. refers to the corrected state of Q2; Q2uncorr. refers to the uncorrected state.

1.1.17 soldier [F] souldiers; **1.1.46 harrows** [F] horrowes; **1.1.65 Polacks** pollax; **1.1.96 designed** desseigne; **1.1.123 feared** feare; **1.2.58 He hath** [F] Hath; **1.2.83 denote** [F] devote; **1.2.132 self-slaughter** [F] seale slaughter; **1.2.133 weary** [F] wary; **1.2.178 see** [F] Not in **Q2; 1.2.217 its** it; **1.2.226, 227, 228 SP Marcellus, Barnardo** All; **1.2.239 tonight** [**to Night F**] to nigh; **1.2.254 foul** [F] fonde; **1.3.3 is** [F] in; **1.3.12 bulk** [F] bulkes; **1.3.48 like** [F] Not in Q2; **1.3.73 Are** [F] Or; **1.3.74 be** [F] boy; **1.3.75 loan** [**lone F**] loue; **1.3.76 th'** Not in Q2; **1.3.82 invites** [F] inuests; **1.3.108 Running** Wrong; **1.3.114 springes** [F] springs; **1.3.124 tether** [F] tider; **1.3.130 beguile** [F] beguide; **1.3.132 moment's** moment; **1.4.17 revel** reueale; **1.4.36 evil** eale; **1.4.82 artery** arture; **1.4.87 imagination** [F] imagion; **1.5.19 on** an; **1.5.43 wit** wits; **1.5.47 a** [F] Not in Q2; **1.5.55 lust** [F] but; **1.5.56 sate** [F] sort; **1.5.65 wi' th'** with; **1.5.77 unaneled** [F] vnanueld; **1.5.79 With all** [F] Withall; **1.5.118 bird** [F] and; **1.5.183 With all** [F] Withall; **2.1.28 no** [F] Not in Q2; **2.1.57 o'ertook** [F] or tooke; **2.1.109 quoted** [F] coted; **2.2.90 since** [F] Not in Q2; **2.2.134 winking** [F] working; **2.2.140 his** [F] her; **2.2.145 watch** wath; **2.2.146 a** [F] Not in Q2; **2.2.164** SD **Enter Hamlet** [**reading a book**]. Q2 *Enter Hamlet*. F *Enter Hamlet reading on a Booke*; **2.2.206 sanity** [F] sanctity; **2.2.209 more** [F] not more; **2.2.219 excellent** [F] extent; **2.2.222 over** [F] ever; **2.2.222 cap** [F] lap; **2.2.236 even** [F] euer; **2.2.267 What a** [F] What; **2.2.286 blank** [F] black; **2.2.307 lest my** [F] let me; **2.2.356 By 'r** [F] by; **2.2.361 French falconers** [F] friendly Fankners; **2.2.374 affectation** [F] affection; **2.2.404 Then senseless Ilium** [F] Not in Q2; **2.2.411 And** [F] Not in Q2; **2.2.425 fellies** follies; **2.2.444 husband's** [F] husband; **2.2.468 dozen** [F] dozen lines; **2.2.472 till** [F] tell; **2.2.475 Goodbye** God by; **2.2.509 father** not in Q2 or F; **2.2.514 brains** [Q2corr] braues [Q2 uncorr]; **2.2.525 devil . . . devil** [F] deale . . . deale; **3.1.27 on to** [F] into; **3.1.45 loneliness** [F] lowlines; **3.1.82 cowards of us all** [F] cowards; **3.1.84 sicklied** [F] sickled; **3.1.117 inoculate** [F] euocutat; **3.1.120 to** [F] Not in Q2; **3.1.143 lisp** [F] list; **3.1.144 wantonness your** [F] wantonnes; **3.1.187 unwatched**

[F] vnmacht; **3.2.1 pronounced** [F] pronoun'd; **3.2.9–10 tatters** [F] totters; **3.2.61 Sh' hath** S'hath; **3.2.119 devil** deule; **3.2.122 by 'r** ber; **3.2.127 miching *malhecho***; [**Miching Malicho F**] munching *Mallico*; **3.2.129–130 keep counsel** [F] keepe; **3.2.143 orbèd** [F] orb'd the; **3.2.157 love** [F] Lord; **3.2.178 like** [F] the; **3.2.187 joys** [F] ioy; **3.2.187 grieves** [F] griefes; **3.2.229 wince** [Q1] winch; **3.2.243 infected** [F] inuected; **3.2.292 start** [F] stare; **3.2.300–301 my business** [F] business; **3.2.339 thumb** [F] the vmber; **3.2.347–348 the top of** [F] Not in Q2; **3.2.352 fret me** fret me not; **3.2.374 daggers** [F] dagger; **3.3.6 near us** neer's; **3.3.18 summit** somnet; **3.3.19 huge** [F] hough; **3.3.22 ruin** [F] raine; **3.3.23 with** [F] Not in Q2; **3.3.50 pardoned** [F] pardon; **3.3.75 revenged** [F] reuendge; **3.4.5 warrant** [F] wait; **3.4.19 inmost** [F] most; **3.4.52 That . . . index** *Ham.* That . . . index; **3.4.52 loud** low'd; **3.4.59 Heaven-kissing** [F] heaue, a kissing; **3.4.97 tithe** [F] kyth; **3.4.143 I**[F] Not in Q2; **3.4.158 live** [F] leaue; **3.4.165 Refrain** [F] to refrain; **3.4.169 house** Not in Q2; **3.4.186 ravel** [F] rouell; **4.1.35 dragged** [F] dreg'd; **4.1.40** [. . . ,] Not in Q2; **4.2.4 Compounded** [F] Compound; **4.5.51 clothes** [F] close; **4.5.71–72 Good...Good...Good...good** [F] God...god...god...god; **4.5.105 They** [F] the; **4.5.194 see** [F] Not in Q2; **4.5.207 trophy,** [F] trophe; **4.6.8 an 't** [**and't F**] and; **4.6.25 bore** [F] bord; **4.6.29 He** [F] So;**4.6.30 give** [F] Not in Q2; **4.7.14 conjunct** concliue [F has coniunctiue]; **4.7.22 loud a wind** [F] loued Arm'd; **4.7.60 checking** [F] the King; **4.7.86 my** [F] me; **4.7.98 'scrimers** Scrimures; **4.7.123 in deed** indeede; **4.7.136 pass** pace;**4.7.138 that** [F] Not in Q2; **4.7.156 proffered** prefard; **4.7.168 cold** [F] cull-cold; **4.7.187 o'** a; **5.1.1, 3 SP First Clown, Second Clown** Regularizing *Clowne* and *Other*, as throughout the scene; **5.1.9 *se offendendo*** [F] so offended; **5.1.12 Argal** [F] or all; **5.1.55 stoup** [F] soope; **5.1.64 daintier** [F] dintier; **5.1.81 mazard** [F] massene; **5.1.108 Oh** [F] or; **5.1.198 winter's** [F] waters; **5.1.203 its** it; **5.1.212 Shards** [F] Not in Q2; **5.1.242 splenative and rash** [F] spleenatiue rash; **5.2.5 Methought** [F] my thought; **5.2.6 bilboes** [F] bilbo; **5.2.9 pall** [**F, Q2 uncorr.**]; fall [Q2 corr]; **5.2.43 "as" es** as sir [Assis F]; **5.2.52 Subscribed [F]** Subscribe; **5.2.68 humbly [F]** humble; **5.2.82 sultry . . . for [F]** sully . . . or; **5.2.91 gentleman** gentlemen; **5.2.93 sellingly [Q2uncorr.]** fellingly [Q2corr.]; **5.2. 97 dazzle** dozy [Q2uncorr.] dazzie [Q2corr.]; **5.2.98 yaw [Q2uncorr.]** raw [Q2corr.]; **5.2.109 do 't [doo 't Q2corr.]** to 't [Q2uncorr.]; **5.2.122 his** this; **5.2. 130 hangers [F]** hanger; **5.2.137 carriages [F]** carriage; **5.2.139 might be [F]** be might [Q2corr.] be [Q2uncorr.]; **5.2.143 this all "impawned," as** this all you [Q2], this impon'd as [F]; **5.2.159 He does well** doo's well [Q2], he does [F]; **5.2. 166 yeasty [yesty F]** histy; **5.2.167 winnowed [F]** trennowed; **5.2.187 gaingiving [F]** gamgiuing; **5.2.192 now [F]** Not in Q2; **5.2.194 will [F]** well; **5.2.219 keep [F]** Not in Q2; **5.2.241 union [F]** Vnice [Q2uncorr.], Onixe [Q2corr.]; **5.2.246 heavens to** heaven to; **5.2.293 thy [F]** my; **5.2.301 Here [F]** Heare; **5.2. 302 union [F]** Onixe; **5.2. 355 th' [F]** Not in Q2; **5.2.375 rites [F]** right

Hamlet on the Early Stage

by Jeff Dolven

There seem to have been several Hamlets before Hamlet. The Prince made his first appearance (as "Amleth") in the twelfth-century *Historiae Danicae* of Saxo Grammaticus, which appeared in print in 1514; a Frenchman, François de Belleforest, retold the story in his *Histoires Tragiques* of 1570. Shakespeare may well have read Belleforest, but he also knew a play now lost to us, one Thomas Nashe made fun of in 1589 when he blasted the revenge tragedies of his day for their "whole Hamlets, I should say handfuls of tragical speeches." The *Ur-Hamlet*, as scholars call this lost play, must have had its share of blood and shouting. Shakespeare's pensive, dilatory, spasmodically violent transformation of these materials came about a decade later, when the fashion for stories of revenge in London's public theaters was on the wane. The First Quarto was printed in 1603, the second in 1604, and the best guess of most scholars puts the original performance at around 1600.

The act of imagination by which the reader envisions Hamlet's "words, words, words" (2.2.188) on the stage is as important as listening to the words themselves. Modern directors take spectacular liberties with the play, and the performance history that follows will give a sample of these experiments. But it is valuable to ask what that first performance would have looked like—what particular resources

Fig 1. In the large London playhouses, the balcony above the stage could be used for staging, seating, or to house musicians.

Fig 2. English Renaissance drama made minimal use of sets or backdrops. In the absence of a set, the stage pillars could be incorporated into the action, standing in for trees and other architectural elements.

Fig 3. The discovery space, located in the middle of the backstage wall, could be used as a third entrance as well as a location for scenes requiring special staging, such as in a tomb or bedchamber.

Fig 4. A trapdoor led to the area below the stage, known as "Hell" (as contrasted with the painted ceiling, known as "Heaven" or the "heavens"). Ghosts or other supernatural figures could descend through the trap, and it could also serve as a grave.

and constraints were in place when the play was written. It debuted at a theater called the Globe, to which Shakespeare's company, the Lord Chamberlain's Men, had moved in 1599. (Is Hamlet half aware of this when he vows at 1.5.96–97 to remember the Ghost's command "whiles memory holds a seat / In this distracted globe"?) The place was roughly circular in construction—a twenty-sided polygon, like a small, modern-day stadium—and consisted of three stories of galleries, all facing inward onto a yard that was about seventy-five feet in diameter. The stage, a wooden platform, projected out into the yard; plays were put on by daylight, in the afternoon, but the stage faced north and the actors worked in shadow. Beneath that platform was a cellar known as "Hell," which could be accessed by a trapdoor. Behind it, and curtained off from the audience, there was a three-story tiring-house from which the actors made their entrances and exits via two main doors, stage left and right. The tiring-house featured a balcony and, above that, a windowed space.

Hamlet makes ingenious use of the Globe's resources—none more so than the trapdoor, sometimes called the gravetrap. It is through that door, theater historians suspect, that the Ghost made his entrance and exit in Act One, scene four, rising up from below the stage and then descending again to roam the cellar, crying "wears" while Hamlet scrambled blindly after him on the boards above. That this space was known as "Hell" both specifies the Ghost's torment and inducts us into the play's self-consciousness about its own theatricality, the self-consciousness of Hamlet's "distracted globe." The same trapdoor likely served in Act Five, scene one to bury Ophelia, and if Hamlet is understood to leap down into the grave to contend with the mourning Laertes, he is entering the very hole from which the Ghost emerged four acts before—a stage coincidence that gives us much to meditate about in a play so preoccupied with the proper attitude to death.

The play-within-a-play affords another opportunity for imagining the opportunities of the original staging. For example, one might picture the curtains of the tiring-house as a backdrop for *The Murder of Gonzago*, with the players coming and going between their folds while Gertrude, Claudius, and the rest of the audience watch from either side of the stage. The play would thus face the real audience more or less the same way it faces Hamlet. One might also, however, draw back those curtains to reveal what was sometimes called the back stage, and seat the King and Queen there while the action plays out in front of them, leaving the other characters off to the side—an arrangement that would emphasize how Hamlet has put Claudius himself front and center, in order to test his so-far masterful performance as King in view of all the court. In the next act, those same curtains could serve as Polonius's fatal hiding place, as perhaps they had earlier concealed the old counselor and his King while they eavesdropped on Hamlet in Act Three. This continual reuse of the same spaces was a necessary feature of Elizabethan theaters, where the companies might perform several different plays in a week and props and sets were therefore minimal. In *Hamlet*, one can imagine this economy might conspire with the imprisoning claustrophobia of Elsinore.

Such thought experiments will help the reader grasp just how resourcefully theatrical the play is. But *Hamlet* is not only ingeniously adapted to its medium: it is also, as we have begun to see, strangely aware of it. Some aspects of this awareness are quite particular to its historical situation. There is, for example, the back-and-forth in the Folio version of the play between Hamlet and Rosencrantz about the "little eyases" (see p. 309, 2.2.305) who hold the stage in the city. Scholars agree that this is a reference to troupes of boy players who were all the rage in London in 1600 and 1601, and whose success threatened the livelihood of the Lord Chamberlain's Men and other companies (which were, we must always remember, made up solely of men, with teenaged boys typically taking the women's parts). We learn from this exchange that Hamlet has a keen interest in theatrical gossip, which, like his scholarship, is not altogether becoming to a young prince. Unlike his scholarship, however, this interest in theater brings him subtly closer to his audience, to the bakers, sailors, and tradesmen who paid a penny each to stand in the yard, or two for a seat in the galleries—a closeness essential to the complicated, unstable balance Shakespeare strikes between his protagonist's aloofness and his common touch.

Other of Hamlet's reflections on theater seem to reach to perdurable fundamentals of the art. When he commissions the players to mount *The Murder of Gonzago* and adds a few lines of his own, he comes close to the very combination of playwright, actor, and impresario that defined the career of Shakespeare himself. From this vantage he gives his famous advice about acting: "Suit the action to the word, the word to the action, with this special observance: that you o'erstep not the modesty of nature. For anything so o'erdone is from the purpose of playing, whose end, both at the first and now, was and is to hold, as 'twere, the mirror up to nature" (3.2.17–22). It is safe to say that acting in the period was more stylized than it is now: we may have a specimen of it in Ophelia's description of Hamlet leaving her chamber, holding her by the wrist "with his other hand thus o'er his brow" (2.1.86) in a conventional gesture of grief. In general Hamlet seems to hate this sort of thing, as Nashe hated those "*Hamlets,* I should say handfuls of tragical speeches." It is tempting to think of him therefore as a proselytizer for theatrical realism, another dimension of his peculiar modernity. But this would not be quite right: for what Hamlet is concerned with is better described as accuracy, a representation of our virtues and vices true enough that we cannot help but see ourselves reflected back. This is an older (though still potent) idea of theater as a moral instrument, a spectacle to provoke our reformation. Hamlet is not wholly a citizen of the popular, commercial theaters where he starred.

One could call all this self-consciousness "metatheatricality," where the prefix *meta*, meaning "above," describes the play's seeming ability to look down on itself as a play. This detachment, much more than any apparent agenda of realism, seems to define *Hamlet*'s modernity. And yet, as we have seen, such reflexiveness is closely bound to the particular conventions and circumstances of performance in the period. If we disallow ourselves the frisson of calling *Hamlet* modern, what do we have left—why is this metatheatrical bent (which one might expect to alienate us from the play, rather than to draw us in) still so compelling? Why would it have been compelling to an audience in 1600? Perhaps it has something to do with the sense that Hamlet is half aware that he is in the same room with us, and like the audience in the Globe we feel closer to him for sharing that space. It tempers, without dispelling, his aristocratic and scholarly remoteness. But his uncanny freedom may be just as important. If Hamlet can ask the grandest, most unconditioned of questions, "To be, or not to be?", still he may learn more over time by a gradual working out of the rules of a game that seemed, at the outset, so badly stacked against him. Those rules are the rules of the theater, its structures and its customs, and in five acts he figures out how to play them to his advantage. What would it be like to have such knowledge ourselves, to know the distracted globe in which we all sit for what it is, from the outside? Hamlet lets on that this just might be possible, and when he does, at once inside and outside his play, he possesses in its fullest measure the devastating double charisma of the actor.

Significant Performances

by Jeff Dolven

1600 In the first performances, Richard Burbage, the most famous actor of the day, likely played Hamlet; an anonymous elegy written for him in 1619 says, "Oft I have seen him leap into the grave . . . That there, I would have sworn, he meant to die."

1607–1608 Records from Captain William Keeling's ship, the *Dragon*, describe a performance on board while it was anchored off the coast of Sierra Leone: an early indication of how well the play would travel.

1661 Thomas Betterton begins his run as the great Hamlet of the Restoration, the revival of the London theaters after their long closure during the Civil War and Interregnum (1642–1660). His manner was formal and aristocratic; he continued playing the role into the next century.

1742 David Garrick joins the Theatre Royal, Drury Lane, where he played the role until he retired in 1776. His Hamlet was much praised as "natural," and his terror at the Ghost's appearance particularly moved audiences (indeed, Samuel Johnson feared that his mighty "start" would terrify the Ghost himself). Garrick, also a playwright, adapted the text, speeding up the ending but also restoring passages of doubt and deliberation that had fallen out of performance.

1783 John Philip Kemble debuts as Hamlet, also at Drury Lane; his performance is a high-water mark of Shakespearian classicism, restrained and aristocratic. The *Gazetteer and Daily News* reported that "His tones are beautifully modulated . . . and he so accurately possesses and conveys the meaning of the poet that it is a feast to hear him."

1814 Edmund Kean, the Romantic Hamlet, whose "nature" was rougher and stormier than Garrick's, takes on the role at Drury Lane. The poet Samuel Taylor Coleridge wrote that "seeing him act was like reading Shakespeare by flashes of lightning."

1864 Edwin Booth begins a run of one hundred performances as Hamlet in New York City, offering the audience a Prince of strong intelligence, fine sensibilities, and fragile will. Kean had leapt into Ophelia's grave; Booth did not.

1874 Henry Irving's was a melodramatic, Victorian Hamlet, and his performances at London's Lyceum Theatre (where he was actor-manager) had exceptional popular appeal: he made the play's caviar accessible to the general masses and was celebrated for the moral seriousness of his productions. He was the first English actor to be knighted, in 1895.

1922 Arthur Hopkins's production at the Sam H. Harris Theater in New York, with John Barrymore as Hamlet. The shifting scenery used in most older productions was replaced by a single, stark set dominated by a central staircase, the stamp of the modernist avant-garde. Barrymore in black doublet and hose was a meditative melancholic, who paused even before stabbing Polonius.

1925 Barry Jackson and H. K. Ayliff's production at the Kingsway Theatre in London put Hamlet in modern dress, with spats, cigarettes, and motor cars. Hamlet himself (played by Colin Keith-Jackson) was more caustic, disenchanted, and moodily violent, and reviewers remarked that the production's relative neglect of the poetry diminished his centrality and allowed other characters to emerge more sharply.

1930 John Gielgud takes the role at London's Old Vic in a production by Harcourt Williams, offering another antiromantic Prince: he later described trying to "find the violent and ugly colors in the part." He played the role countless times in subsequent years, dominating productions even as a "director's theater"—the dominance of the director's vision over the actor's—came to be the twentieth-century norm.

1948 Barry Jackson's Victorian setting of the play at Stratford-upon-Avon, with Paul Scofield and Robert Helpmann alternating nights as Hamlet—another experiment in loosening the grip of the central character on his play.

1948 Lawrence Olivier's landmark film, the tragedy "of a man who could not make up his mind." The production took up the Oedipal interpretation forwarded by Freud and by psychoanalytic critics, infusing the closet scene with the Prince's misdirected passion for his mother.

1964 The Soviet director Grigori Kozintsev's film, with Hamlet imprisoned by a decadent and oppressive state. Many of his soliloquies are spoken in voiceover: Kozintsev wrote that Hamlet is a thinker, and "There is nothing more dangerous" to totalitarianism.

1965 Director Peter Hall's counter cultural *Hamlet* for the '60s at Stratford-upon-Avon, with the Prince as an angry student played by David Wagner: the program explained that "the play will be about the disillusionment which produces an apathy of the will so deep that commitment to politics, to religion or to life is impossible."

1980 The year of two major English productions. John Barton's at Stratford-upon-Avon, with Michael Pennington as a scholar-prince, offered a cerebral exploration of the play's metatheatricality. Richard Eyre's at London's Royal Court, with Jonathan Pryce, was much more politicized, presenting Elsinore as a capital of state surveillance, with listeners behind every door.

Also the year of Derek Jacobi's television production for the BBC, with an antic, often histrionic Hamlet. The production attracted particular praise for Patrick Stewart and Claire Bloom's portrayal of a deep and intimate relationship between Claudius and Gertrude.

1990 A film by the director Franco Zeffirelli, also known for his opera productions. His *Hamlet* is long on spectacle, starring Mel Gibson as the Prince who musters considerable heroic vigor, even cruelty. Helena Bonham-Carter was widely praised for her portrayal of Ophelia.

2000 A film *Hamlet* for the surveillance age, directed by Michael Almereyda with Ethan Hawke as the Prince. Ophelia wears a wire while Polonius listens in; Hamlet's "To be, or not to be?" soliloquy is spoken in the "Action" aisle of a video rental store.

Inspired by *Hamlet*

Since it was first published in 1603, *Hamlet* has become not only Shakespeare's most famous play but also one of the most influential works in all of Western literature. Shakespeare was not the first person to dream up the tale—by the twelfth century, Saxo Grammaticus had already published a lengthy account of the legendary conflict between the Danish Prince Amleth, his mother Gerutha, and his unscrupulous uncle Horwendil—but it is Shakespeare's version that has captured and held the imagination of readers and audience members. Over the years, countless artists and thinkers have drawn inspiration from *Hamlet*, rejecting the Prince's dying claim that "The rest is silence" by continuing to speak about this most famous of plays.

Relocating *Hamlet*

One of the most common methods of adapting Shakespeare's plays involves setting the original plots in new contexts. The *Hamlet* story in particular has proven to be extremely flexible, finding new life in such diverse places as the Old West (1972's spaghetti Western *Johnny Hamlet*), the crime-ridden slums of 1920s Buenos Aires (Tulio Stella and Alberto Félix Alberto's 1999 play *A Hamlet of the Suburbs*), and an anthropomorphized, cartoon version of the animal kingdom (Disney's 1994 blockbuster *The Lion King*).

One discernable trend among *Hamlet* adaptations mirrors a parallel trend in the play's performance history, in which productions—in an attempt to find a suitably cut-throat modern parallel for the Danish monarchy—choose to set the play in the contemporary corporate world. Following a similar impulse, several *Hamlet* spin-offs have used Shakespeare's narrative to hold a "mirror up" (3.2.21) to modern big business.

In Akira Kurosawa's *The Bad Sleep Well* (1960), Kurosawa's frequent leading actor Toshiro Mifune plays Koichi Nishi, a young executive who marries his boss's disabled daughter in an apparent bid to advance within the corporation. Nishi's true motivation for marrying the girl, however, is to get close to her corrupt father, the man who once manipulated Nishi's father into committing suicide. But as Nishi exacts his revenge on his father-in-law, he begins to fall in love with the woman he married, leading to increasing complications when her father becomes aware of Nishi's machinations. Shot in cool, mod black-and-white, *The Bad Sleep Well* is one of several Shakespeare-based Kurosawa films, which also include *Ran* (*King Lear*) and *Throne of Blood* (*Macbeth*).

Finnish director Aki Kaurismaki set his adaptation in the corporate world as well, but to comic effect: in *Hamlet Goes Business* (1987), a young man and his uncle battle for control of Finland's leading rubber duck manufacturer. Kaurismaki's deadpan satire, in turn, had a deep influence on Michael Almereyda's 2000 *Hamlet* film, which stars Ethan Hawke as the moody scion of the massive Denmark Corporation. In 1999's noirish B-movie *Let the Devil Wear Black*, a young, aimless Los Angeles man takes over the family business—a thriving adult entertainment empire—while harboring suspicions that his mother and uncle, now lovers, are secretly responsible for his beloved father's sudden and untimely death.

Backstage at *Hamlet*

Appropriately enough for a play so deeply concerned with issues of performance, pretense, and the theater, several adaptations focus on actors involved in productions of *Hamlet*, drawing connections between the fictional actors' lives and the lives of Shakespeare's characters.

Michael Innes's classic 1937 mystery novel *Hamlet, Revenge!*—one of a series of books featuring Sir John Appleby, a debonair gentleman turned Scotland Yard detective—takes place in a grand country estate, where several members of the British aristocracy have gathered to put on a production of *Hamlet*. The atmosphere of lavish gentility turns chilling, however, when the Lord Chancellor is mysteriously murdered just at the moment he is slotted to die onstage as Polonius. The plot of *Hamlet, Revenge!* is richly allusive of Shakespeare's play, reflecting Innes's experience as an Oxford don (under his real name, J. I. M. Stewart) and the author of critical works such as *Character and Motive in Shakespeare* (1949).

Ernst Lubitsch's darkly comic 1942 film *To Be or Not to Be* takes place in Nazi-occupied Poland, where a troupe of actors led by the arrogant Josef Tura (Jack Benny) are performing a government-mandated production of *Hamlet*. Unbeknownst to Tura, his wife and leading lady Maria (Carole Lombard) is having an affair with a dashing young pilot, and whenever Tura begins the titular soliloquy, Maria and the pilot take the opportunity afforded by her husband's engagement to rendezvous backstage. Maria's relationship with the pilot eventually gets the entire troupe involved in the resistance movement, requiring them to draw on their theatrical experience in order to masquerade as Nazis and infiltrate the enemy. Lubitsch's film, now considered one of his finest, was roundly criticized upon its release, as the United States was still deeply engaged in World War II and many audience members were unwilling to watch what they felt was a callous, casual lampoon of the atrocities of Nazism. A remake in 1983 by Mel Brooks, starring

Brooks, Anne Bancroft, and Charles Durning (who received an Oscar nomination), was a great commercial success.

An early episode of the *Star Trek* television series entitled "The Conscience of the King" (1966) features a Shakespearean actor named Anton Karidian, whom the swashbuckling spaceship captain James T. Kirk believes is actually Kodos the Executioner, an infamous war criminal who mysteriously disappeared before being put on trial. In an attempt to ascertain whether they are in fact the same man, Kirk has Karidian's troupe perform *Hamlet* and then tries to determine whether or not Karidian's voice is the voice of Kodos (who happened to be responsible for the death of many of Kirk's family members). *Star Trek* is just one of many television shows that has featured performances of *Hamlet*. In a more comic vein, characters on *The Three Stooges*, *Gilligan's Island*, and *Sesame Street*'s "Monsterpiece Theater" have all taken turns producing Shakespeare's play.

In Czech playwright Pavel Kohout's *Poor Murderer* (1977), a young actor in turn-of-the-century Russia appears to go mad while playing Hamlet, killing the actor playing Polonius. The question of performance versus reality becomes even more heavily layered when, upon being committed to a mental institution, the young actor is allowed to stage a version of the events leading up to the murder. Like *Hamlet*'s own play-within-a-play *The Mousetrap*, in which Hamlet attempts to expose his uncle's guilt, this performance serves as a kind of makeshift legal tribunal, wherein the young actor attempts to prove his own innocence.

In 1995, writer and director Kenneth Branagh released *A Midwinter's Tale* (a.k.a. *In the Bleak Midwinter*), a modest black-and-white comedy about an out-of-work London actor named Joe Harper. When his sister's church is threatened with foreclosure, Joe decides that he will simultaneously raise money for the community and revitalize his career by directing and starring in a production of *Hamlet*. With no budget and only three weeks to prepare, Joe gathers a motley crew of performers (including a myopic, accident-prone ingénue in the role of Ophelia and a campy gay man as Gertrude) and takes them to the little provincial village of Hope, where the rehearsal process is as predictably disastrous as the results are heartwarming. While Branagh's lavish, large-scale (and uncut) film version of *Hamlet* (1996) uncritically emphasizes the play's outsized nature and reputation, *A Midwinter's Tale* gently mocks those who are too pious in their appreciation of Shakespeare's play.

In Carole Corbeil's 1997 novel *In the Wings*, the lives of three characters involved in a Canadian production of *Hamlet*—a forty-something actress, cast as Gertrude; her younger lover, cast as Hamlet; and a theater critic—become entwined in increasingly complicated ways. Though not strictly an autobiographical novel, *In the Wings* draws on many events from Corbeil's life, including the death of her mother and her experience as a leading drama critic for various Canadian newspapers. The production in the novel is inspired by a 1983 staging of *Hamlet* by the well-known Toronto company Passe Muraille, in which Corbeil's future husband, Layne Coleman, played the Prince. When *In the Wings* was adapted for the stage in 2002 (two years after Corbeil's own death), the production was directed by Coleman and featured several actors from the original Passe Muraille *Hamlet*.

In a cross cultural twist on the formula, Tsutumi Harue's comic play *Kanedehon Hamuretto* ("Kanadehon Hamlet," 1992) takes place in 1897 Japan, as a group of Kabuki actors attempting to stage the first Japanese production of *Hamlet* discover surprising parallels between Shakespeare's play and *Kanedehon Chushingura*, a classic Kabuki revenge tragedy. In both plays, an eccentric hero feigns madness in order to deflect suspicion from friends and enemies alike, and in *Chushingura* a court official, Ono Kudayu, is stabbed to death while eavesdropping on the hero from the shadows, just like Shakespeare's Polonius. In her essay "What's *Hamlet* to Japan?" Professor Kaori Ashizu explains how, while *Hamlet* was a relatively unknown entity in turn-of-the-century Japan, by the early 1990s the play had become very familiar to Japanese audiences. Harue's challenge—like that of her English-speaking peers—lay in making an overly familiar text yield new, fresh surprises.

Hamlet and Parody

Hamlet has had a long history of comic adaptations, from John Poole's 1812 *Hamlet Travestie*—a three-act burlesque that ends with Hamlet yelling, "Going, going, gone!"—to a 2002 sketch on *The Simpsons* called "Do the Bard, Man," in which wiseacre Bart must revenge the death of his beer-guzzling father, Homer. As one of the most famous works of Western literature, *Hamlet* is ripe for parody (or at least what *Hamlet* has become): not only is it widely familiar, its high-toned reputation as an artistic "masterpiece" invites subversively minded comedians.

Comic "translations" of the play constitute one category of *Hamlet* parodies. In each of these translations, the humor arises from the surprising and seemingly inappropriate juxtaposition of high and low culture. Shel Silverstein's poem "*Hamlet* as Told on the Street" (published in *Playboy* in 1998), for example, retells the play in slangy, raunchy contemporary language. When Francisco and Bernardo first see Old Hamlet's ghost on the ramparts, they say, "'Hey, Mr. Ghost, are you our dear departed king?' / But the ghost don't say one motherfuckin' thing. / He goes, 'Wooo-wooo-wooo.' They say, "Hey, we better split, / And go tell Hamlet about this shit." Richard Curtis's short play "The Skinhead Hamlet" (1984) recasts the characters as foul-mouthed skinheads (early 60s precursors to the British punk scene, not to be confused with the American neo-Nazi movement). In this highly abbreviated version, which runs a giddy ten minutes or so, Laertes challenges Hamlet to the duel with a curt, "Oi, wanker: let's get on with it." To which Hamlet replies, "Delighted, fuckface." In the Klingon Institute's 2000 edition of *The Klingon Hamlet: The Tragedy of Khamlet, Son of the Emperor of Qo'nos*, the Shakespearean text is published side by side with a version of the play rendered in Klingon, the fictional alien language featured on the television show *Star Trek*. The conceit of this parody is that the English *Hamlet* actually represents a debased version of a Klingon classic by "Wil'yam Shex'pir."

Thirteen years after publishing *Rosencrantz and Guildenstern Are Dead*, the most famous of his *Hamlet* adaptations, Tom Stoppard revisited the text with a one-act comedy called "Dogg's Hamlet" (1979). Originally written to be performed on a double-decker London bus, the play is set in a world whose inhabitants speak a language, Dogg, which consists of English words haphazardly ascribed with new meanings. Under the guidance of their principal, three schoolchildren put on a dramatically abridged English-language production of *Hamlet* (often excerpted and performed on its own as "The Fifteen Minute *Hamlet*"), which none of the participants can understand. The play is inspired in part by the absurd exchanges between Hamlet and Polonius in 2.2, in which Hamlet evades and deflects the older man's attempts to make sense of his "Words, words, words."

The 1983 Canadian cult classic *Strange Brew* represents a very loose adaptation of *Hamlet*. In the film, the bumbling, beer-loving McKenzie brothers—two popular characters from the sketch comedy show *SCTV*, played by Rick Moranis and Dave Thomas—take jobs at the Elsinore Brewery, where they become embroiled in a goofy plot involving the brewery's heiress, Pam(let), her scheming mother Gertrude, and her inept uncle-cum-stepfather Claude. The McKenzie brothers are roughly analogous to *Hamlet*'s Rosencrantz and Guildenstern, though it's somewhat more difficult to discern a parallel character for the campy "diabolical genius," Brewmeister Smith, played by Max von Sydow.

Paul Rudnick was inspired to write his 1988 comedy *I Hate Hamlet* when he bought an apartment formerly occupied by the famous Shakespearean actor John Barrymore. In the play, a young television star from L.A. named Andrew Rally buys an apartment in New

York, where he is slated to play Hamlet in Central Park. After learning that the apartment was formerly owned by John Barrymore, his girlfriend, agent, and real estate broker convince him to hold a séance to conjure Barrymore's ghost, who sticks around to serve as Andrew's mentor but then wreaks havoc by seducing his virginal girlfriend. In the end, Andrew bombs as Hamlet, but he realizes that the theater is his true calling and decides to abandon television, a decision heartily supported by Barrymore's ghost.

Hamlet Character Studies

Though every adaptation of *Hamlet* necessarily emphasizes certain elements of the play over others, some adaptations choose to focus very specifically on one or more characters' experiences. The most famous example of this kind of adaptation is Tom Stoppard's 1966 play *Rosencrantz and Guildenstern Are Dead*. Stoppard's absurdist, darkly comic play inverts Shakespeare's: in this world, the peripheral and unremarkable Rosencrantz and Guildenstern become the main characters, while Prince Hamlet is relegated to a series of walk-on appearances. As in Shakespeare's play, Rosencrantz and Guildenstern have been called upon by the King to help discover what's troubling their childhood friend, Hamlet, but it is their anxious presence at court that is the center of Stoppard's dark comedy. As the events of *Hamlet* occur offstage, the two men while away the time playing philosophical games and occasionally watching performances by a troupe of players (the same actors who, in *Hamlet*, will perform *The Mousetrap* for the Danish court). Throughout the play, both Rosencrantz and Guildenstern—who continually get mistaken for one another by the other characters and then, eventually, by Rosencrantz and Guildenstern themselves—are unable to figure out why exactly they have been called to this place, or what they're supposed to do now that they're here. Though their actions and destinies are predetermined by the events of Shakespeare's *Hamlet*, Rosencrantz and Guildenstern continue to grapple with feelings of anxiety, doubt, and incomprehension. In its deep concerns with fate, free will, and self-knowledge, *Rosencrantz and Guildenstern Are Dead* is often classified as an existentialist play, inviting frequent comparisons to Samuel Beckett's *Waiting for Godot*.

In *Fortinbras* (1991), Lee Blessing takes on an arguably even more marginal character. The titular Norwegian prince appears only a few times in *Hamlet*, most notably when he storms the castle of Elsinore and discovers the bloody remains of the Danish royal family. In Blessing's farcical play, which serves as a sequel to *Hamlet*, Fortinbras tries to spin the events that occurred just before his assumption of the throne, in an attempt to make his takeover more palatable to the populace. Declaring Horatio's (true) account as ludicrous, Fortinbras suggests blaming the entire tragedy on a Polish spy. While Fortinbras tries to put the country back together—and design a joint Norwegian-Danish nation, potentially called "Normark"—the characters from *Hamlet* start coming back from the dead, infiltrating Elsinore in ghostly forms. Written after the first Gulf War, *Fortinbras* is a slapstick lampoon as well as a sharp piece of political satire.

Gertrude takes center stage in Margaret Atwood's "Gertrude Talks Back" (first printed in the 1992 collection *Good Bones*), a short comic piece conceived as a monologue delivered in response to Hamlet's accusatory assault in Act Three, scene four: the closet scene. Rather than the frightened, traumatized figure we meet in Shakespeare's version, Atwood reimagines Gertrude as a cool, archly diabolical woman who takes the opportunity to set her son straight on several issues: namely, that it was she who killed his father, not Claudius, and that she'd always hated the name "Hamlet" and had originally wanted to call him "George." John Updike's novel *Gertrude and Claudius* (2000) focuses on the events leading up to Shakespeare's play. Gertrude (here called "Geruthe," after the character in the ancient Scandinavian source legend) is the well-meaning and long-suffering wife of a powerful king, Horwendil. The intelligent Queen eventually falls in love with her husband's brother, Feng, and the two embark on an illicit but passionate affair. Both are distraught over their actions, and Feng ends up killing Horwendil not as a political move, but out of desperation upon his brother's discovery of their relationship. The final scene of the novel is the opening scene of *Hamlet*, in which Claudius—confident that his troubles have ended, and assured that he will now be free to love Geruthe openly—addresses the people of Denmark, including his newly returned stepson.

Hamlet's other female character, Ophelia, also has a rich legacy of artistic inspiration. She has held a particularly strong attraction for painters, not only for her physical beauty but also for the dramatic intensity of her mad scenes (Act Four, scene five) and drowning scene (Act Four, scene seven)—the latter of which, as it is only described in the play, allows painters to take expansive imaginative liberties in their own renditions. Victorian and Romantic painters were particularly drawn to her, often depicting her wearing virginal white with flowers in her hair.

Perhaps the most famous of Ophelia paintings is John Everett Millais's 1852 *Ophelia*, which depicts the young woman floating in a river thick with weeds and flowers, her mouth slightly open. Though Ophelia is beautiful in the painting, the heavy density of the vegetation surrounding her—each plant of which carries a specific symbolic meaning—threatens to overwhelm her. Other well-known examples include Arthur Hughes' 1852 *Ophelia* (in which a sickly, consumptive Ophelia wears a thorny-looking crown of straw and peers vacantly into the river), Eugène Delacroix's 1853 *The Death of Ophelia* (a strongly sensual painting, with Ophelia in translucent clothing and a trance-like expression on her face), John W. Waterhouse's 1889 *Ophelia* (which depicts a beautiful, womanly Ophelia sitting calmly by the river with flowers in her hair), and Henrietta Rae's 1890 *Ophelia* (in which the mad, white-gowned Ophelia shares her flowers with a cowering Gertrude and Claudius). During this period, Ophelia was also well represented in literary arts. French poets in particular were drawn to her—Victor Hugo (1802–1885), Alfred de Musset (1810–1857), Stéphane Mallarmé (1842–1898), Arthur Rimbaud (1854–1891), and Jules Laforgue (1860–1887) all wrote poems or poem cycles dedicated to Ophelia.

About the same time that painters like Millais and Hughes were creating their portraits of Ophelia, an early female Shakespeare scholar, Mary Cowden Clarke, was creating her own kind of portrait. In the three volumes of *The Girlhood of Shakespeare's Heroines* (1850–1852), Clarke presents fictional back stories for several of Shakespeare's female characters. In "Ophelia, the Rose of Elsinore," the infant Ophelia is left in the care of her nursemaid while her parents go to court in Paris. In her new home, Ophelia becomes devoted to her foster sister, Jutha, and is both terrified and fascinated by her idiot foster brother, Ulf, who shows a brutish and unhealthy interest in the young girl. During her time in the nursemaid's home, Ophelia watches as Jutha falls ill and dies after being wooed (and perhaps impregnated) by a handsome young man named Eric—a scenario Ophelia will see repeated many years later when, back in the Danish court, her friend Thyra hangs herself after being abandoned by the same Eric. At the end of the story (which marks the point where Shakespeare's play takes over the narrative), Ophelia's beloved mother Aoudra dies. By providing Ophelia with a rich, complex personal history, Clarke offers compelling reasons for Ophelia's curious behavior in Shakespeare's *Hamlet*. Alhough "Ophelia, the Rose of Elsinore" was written many years before Sigmund Freud published his treatises on psychoanalysis, Ophelia's repressed memories, symbolic dreams, and childhood sexual traumas seem to anticipate Freud's theories.

Hamlet on the Couch

Hamlet has become such a central text in Western literature that its influence can often be felt in surprising places, far beyond the expected realms of art, literature, and drama. Sigmund Freud, for example, used Shakespeare's play to help shape his theories of psychoanalysis—a system for diagnosing, interpreting, and treating various types of mental illnesses. Freud argued that the human mind is divided into two separate spheres: the conscious and the unconscious. Individuals interact with the public world using their conscious mind, but their actions, personality, and behavior are always driven by unconscious fears and desires. In almost all cases, the unconscious remains hidden from the individual himself.

The work of literature most often associated with Freud's theories is the ancient Greek tragedy *Oedipus Rex*, by Sophocles, which provided Freud with the paradigm and name for a crucial stage in personality development. In Sophocles' play, the character of Oedipus, abandoned as a child, unknowingly kills his father and marries his mother upon reaching adulthood. Freud claimed that, as children, most people experience what he termed the Oedipus complex: a strong desire for the opposite-sex parent, paired with a fear of and aversion to the same-sex parent, who is seen as both a threat and a rival for the other parent's affections. To Freud, *Oedipus Rex* represents a victory of the unconscious mind—which incestuously desires the mother at the fatal expense of the father—over the civilized, conscious mind, which represses those impulses it deems shameful and unnatural.

Hamlet, however, loomed almost as large in Freud's imagination, coming to seem to the psychoanalyst a crucial revision of the Oedipus myth. In Freud's account, Hamlet suffers from an Oedipus complex, which he is prevented from acting upon—unlike Oedipus—because modern civilization has taught people to repress and deny those feelings. In *The Interpretation of Dreams* (1900), Freud traces Hamlet's notorious hesitation to this unconscious, incestuous fixation:

> Hamlet is able to do anything but take vengeance upon the man who did away with his father and has taken his father's place with his mother—the man who shows him in realization the

> repressed desires of his own childhood. The loathing that should have driven him to revenge is thus replaced by self-reproach, by conscientious scruples, which tell him that he himself is no better than the murderer whom he is required to punish. I have here translated into consciousness what had to remain unconscious in the mind of the hero; if anyone wishes to call Hamlet an hysterical subject I cannot but admit that this is the deduction to be drawn from my interpretation.

With this interpretation, Freud deftly manages at once to accomplish two things: he validates his own theories by linking them with one of the world's greatest works of literature (thereby lending his hypotheses a measure of cultural authority as well as a conceptual framework), and he also purports to definitively answer the long-standing problem of interpreting Hamlet's notorious delay. *Hamlet* shapes psychoanalysis, just as psychoanalysis seems to solve *Hamlet*. Psychoanalysis and literary analysis have had a fruitful partnership ever since. Psychoanalysts such as Ernest Jones and Jacques Lacan have produced significant works of Shakespearean scholarship (Jones's serving as the inspiration for Laurence Olivier's famous film version of *Hamlet* in 1948), and a sizeable contingent of literary critics has adopted Freud's theories to analyze a wide range of texts, characters, authors, and the process of creation itself.

For Further Reading
by Jeff Dolven

Adelman, Janet. *Suffocating Mothers: Fantasies of Maternal Origin in Shakespeare's Plays, "Hamlet" to the "Tempest."* New York: Routledge, 1992. The most powerful psychoanalytic reading of the play, with comprehensive footnotes to criticism in that tradition.

Bate, Jonathan, ed. *The Romantics on Shakespeare.* London: Penguin, 1992. Assembles the best writing about the plays by Coleridge, Hazlitt, and other poets and critics of the early nineteenth century.

Braden, Gordon. *Renaissance Tragedy and the Senecan Tradition: Anger's Privilege.* New Haven: Yale University Press, 1985. Only the last pages treat Hamlet directly, but Braden's treatment of Renaissance Stoicism elaborates a theme central to the play.

Bradley, A. C. *Shakespearean Tragedy: Lectures on "Hamlet," "Othello," "King Lear," "Macbeth."* A classic study, first published in 1904, with a chapter on Hamlet the melancholic.

Bloom, Harold, ed. *William Shakespeare's "Hamlet."* Modern Critical Interpretations. New York: Chelsea House, 1986. A useful collection of essays with an emphasis on Hamlet as a character; the introduction offers a glimpse of ideas Bloom elaborated later in *Shakespeare: The Invention of the Human*.

Cavell, Stanley. *Disowning Knowledge in Six Plays of Shakespeare*. Cambridge: Cambridge University Press, 1987. A philosophical account of the plays, with a chapter on *Hamlet* and a brilliant essay on *King Lear* that sheds light on all of Shakespeare's work.

Dawson, Anthony B. *Hamlet. Shakespeare in Performance.* New York: Manchester University Press, 1995. A very useful short history of productions of the play (to which the list in this edition is indebted).

Eliot, T. S. "Hamlet and His Problems." *Selected Essays*. New York: Harcourt, Brace, 1950. 121–126. A classic essay, first published in 1920, on the irresolvability of interpretive problems in the play.

Empson, William. *Essays on Shakespeare*. David. B. Pirie, ed. Cambridge: Cambridge University Press, 1986. The essay on *Hamlet* ingeniously reimagines Shakespeare's transformation of the conventional revenge tragedy plot.

Greenblatt, Stephen. *Hamlet in Purgatory*. Princeton: Princeton University Press, 2001. Puts the play in the context of sixteenth-century debates about the existence of purgatory, a problem that links the Ghost to England's irregular transition from a Catholic to a Protestant nation.

Gross, Kenneth. *Shakespeare's Noise*. Chicago: University of Chicago Press, 2001. Includes a chapter on rumor and slander in Elsinore.

Mushat Frye, Roland. *The Renaissance "Hamlet": Issues and Responses in 1600*. Princeton: Princeton University Press, 1984. A study of the play in the moment of its composition and first production, especially in relation to contemporary politics.

Johnson, Samuel. *Samuel Johnson on Shakespeare*. New York: Penguin, 1989. An anthology of the eighteenth-century essayist's commentary on the plays.

Kastan, David Scott, ed. *A Companion to Shakespeare*. Oxford: Blackwell, 1999. A useful collection of essays on the historical background of the plays.

Kastan, David Scott, ed. *Critical Essays on Shakespeare's Hamlet*. New York: G. K. Hall, 1995. An anthology of critical essays representative of recent approaches.

Kerrigan, William. *Hamlet's Perfection*. Baltimore: Johns Hopkins University Press, 1994. A short book particularly interesting for its arguments about Hamlet's relation to death.

Mack, Maynard. "The World of *Hamlet*." *Everybody's Shakespeare*. Lincoln: University of Nebraska Press, 1993. A classic essay.

Showalter, Elaine. "Representing Ophelia: Women, Madness, and the Responsibilities of Feminist Criticism." Patricia Parker and Geoffrey Hartman, eds. *Shakespeare and the Question of Theory*. New York: Methuen, 1985. 77–94. An influential feminist approach to the play, focusing on the history of critics' attempts to explain the madness of Opehlia.

Welsh, Alexander. *Hamlet in Modern Guises*. Princeton: Princeton University Press, 2001. A study of the problem of Hamlet's modernity and his literary influence, particularly on the novel.

Wilson Knight, G. *The Wheel of Fire: Interpretations of Shakespearean Tragedy, with Three New Essays*. London: Methuen, 1968. Includes two classic essays on the play, "The Embassy of Death: An Essay on *Hamlet*" and "*Hamlet Reconsidered*."